IN THE SHELTER OF THE MOST HIGH

DANIEL DUANE

authorHOUSE®

AuthorHouse™ UK
1663 Liberty Drive
Bloomington, IN 47403 USA
www.authorhouse.co.uk
Phone: 0800.197.4150

Scripture taken from the Holy Bible, The Jerusalem Bible copyright © 1966, 1967 and 1968 by Darton, Longman & Todd Ltd and Doubleday and Co. Inc.

Published by AuthorHouse 08/28/2018

Library of Congress Control Number: 2018909028

ISBN: 978-1-5462-9135-0 (sc)
ISBN: 978-1-5462-9136-7 (hc)
ISBN: 978-1-5462-9137-4 (e)

Print information available on the last page.

CONTENTS

FOREWORD

I endured much agonising and serious deliberation before I penned these memoirs. I'm conscious of the domino effect and collateral hurt that will arise from their publication, but the Church Tribunal, because of its intransigence in neglecting the evidence I presented, has given me no other choice, and consequently, old wounds will fester again. The tribunal failed to explain the huge chasm between the zero evidence of the state director of public prosecutions (DPP) and the Church reaching its own moral certitude, or the going from the unanimous innocent verdict of the jury (within the hour) to the Church's own moral certitude of my guilt. Indeed, the trial may never have gone to the jury had the DPP included all the claimants' statements in the book of evidence. These were strewn with discrepancies, with multiple ages given for different agencies, and yet these were in the book of evidence for the tribunal. All investigators are well advised to follow the evidence and ignore histrionics and theatrics, but such advice was practised in the civil trials, although those histrionics and theatrics seem to have been considered as evidence, under the guise of credibility, in the Church Tribunal.

I have served the church to which we all belong in the diocese of Cloyne, and the people I served are entitled to know the complete story surrounding my removal from public ministry and the events that ensued. This book recounts these events.

I dedicate this book to my immediate and extended family, alive and deceased; to my friends; to my fellow priests and the other people who stood by me in my trials; to Mgr Maurice Dooley; to Conor O Flynn; and to the late Fr Paidraig Keogh.

ACKNOWLEDGEMENTS

Scripture quotations are taken from the 1963 English translation of the New Jerusalem Bible and the Revised Standard Version of the New Testament, HarperCollins UK.

I thank Dr Patrick Randall, MA (clinical psychology), PsyD, for his assessment of the risk assessment and Dr Patricia Casey for her advice and help.

I acknowledge Mgr Maurice Dooley, my advocate and legal advisor in canon law; Kieran McCarthy and Co., my defence lawyers in the civil trials; and Robert Dore and Co., my present lawyer.

Joe Cuddigan,Joseph S Cuddigan & Co., Solicitors, Cork for his legal advice.

Finally, thank you to AuthorHouse and their staff for their exceptional support and expertise in the production of this book.

CHAPTER 1

August 1956. It was noon, and I was reclining against the great oak in the lawn—the same oak that I'd once used as a goalpost for practising my hurling. Only then, it had a twin, which was hewn away a couple years previously due to old age. Together they were the ideal goalposts.

I'd just received my leaving certificate results in the post, and now it was time to face the truth. Whilst opening the envelope, with mixed emotions of fear and excitement about where my future lay, I quickly scanned the page. I saw 'Honours', and in disbelief, I looked again. Yes, there was no doubt! I needed honours to pursue my choices, and now it was decision time.

The initial euphoria of achievement began to wane as decision time loomed. My three preferable choices were medicine, veterinary, and the priesthood. Again, I put the priesthood last, as it had terrorised and tormented me over the past two years of 'Will I, or won't I?' Its demands were directly contrary to my dream of becoming a doctor, which would be a fulfilling vocation and bring a rewarding lifestyle, and more importantly, I could have a wife and family. I loved the fair sex, and the hormones in my youthful body were impatient for fulfilment. I would be denied this dream if I chose the priesthood, plus there would be all that confinement in an enclosed campus and the intense study. I kept thinking that I was not an academic. I was an outdoors fan. I loved sport, hurling, shooting, fishing, and romancing. I was ready for the good life. But another part of me was dictating otherwise. I was healthy and strong and, more importantly, grounded in robust Catholic values. One of them was to give rather than to take. 'To give or to take?' That was the question. The devil's advocate within me was asking, 'What have I to give? You are not a genius or a holy boy. You don't have a very good voice for preaching. You are a country boy, a farmer's son. In equine terms, you'll fall at the first fence in the towns and cities of this world!' I was listening to what he was saying and justifying it with reality checks. Was he making sense?

All this mental turmoil had been wrecking my equilibrium for at least two years, and now it was time to decide. It would not be sorted out in ten minutes beneath my beloved goalpost but would run for many more years. Later, I learned that the one essential quality of a well-rounded individual is the ability to make decisions. However, I would make an exception for the vocation to the priesthood. It was not immediate or permanent. It vacillated with time and tide, including seven years in a seminary. The strength of one's faith was the main variable in the decision process.

Personal faith in God won out for the present. I recalled the song of the young prince in *The Student Prince*. 'I'll walk with God from this day on. … He'll understand. He'll take my hand.' He was echoing God's promise to Jeremiah. 'Ah, Lord. Look. I do not know how to speak. I am a child!'

'I'm putting my words into your mind,' the Lord replied.

I would give it a go. I'd ring St Colman's and tell the president to book me a place in Maynooth. The die was cast for now. Next, I would inform my family.

My mother was calm when I told her, but I knew she was inwardly holding back her emotion. My father replied, 'You are the best son I ever reared.' He had five sons. I didn't take it too seriously, as he used the same expression with all of us when he was short of a fag (cigarette). He never got too emotional, but I knew he must have been. After all, he had two brothers who were priests and was proud of them. My siblings responded in humorous fashion. 'Be careful with your language. There's a priest in the house.' But they knew damn well that I could more than match their tongues. Generally, they were very supportive, as a priest in the family was socially acceptable in the late 1950s and 1960s in Ireland. They kept me grounded with the usual workload like milking the cows and helping out on the farm. There was no wrapping in cotton wool for the fledgling clerical student.

I was born on 16 March 1938, the seventh child and fifth son to Michael and Elizabeth Duane of Ballyshera, Doneraile, County Cork, Ireland. They called me Daniel Joseph. When I was about 6months, a photo of the family was taken a few yards from my beloved oak. It was my first photograph. Fifteen years later, I was photographed on the butt of the hewn twin oak. There were ten oaks in the lawn (i.e. the field in front of the house), but these twin oaks were constantly recurring in my youth, and later my beloved oak, the surviving twin, saw happy and sad events, the highs and lows, even death.

I have mental flashes of my early childhood at 2years of age when my sister Lil was born. I remember seeing my mother in bed and feeling the wonder of where this baby had come from all of a sudden. I can also recall the time before I started school and my siblings were coming home with other pupils. I remember my first day in school and soiling the blue knickers which I hated and then the drama of going home; it gave me an excuse not to wear the knickers anymore. I have a vague recollection of a mishap in a huge vat of milk from which I was rescued by Nell Turner, the maid working for us. That experience had an after-effect which still persists: my fear of deep water. Even though I learned to swim, I could never go out of my depth. You can imagine how embarrassed I was in Crosshaven after rescuing from the sea a 3-year-old girl who was trapped by the rising tide. Her mother had fallen asleep and lost track of her little daughter, and when I arrived with the little girl, she realised the danger her daughter had been in. She was extremely grateful for the rescue and was under the illusion that I had risked my life in the process. She wanted my name and hinted at a citation for an award. I quickly excused myself and scampered away. The water was up to the little girl's waist—and just above my knees! I laughed at the irony of it all. If only the poor mother had known my dread of deep water!

I was a country boy—and still am a country man—close to the earth, which I love so dearly. My father was a late vocation to the land. He was sent to St Colman's College to study for greater things. He was recalled home after a year to help my grandfather. His three brothers would later go to St Colman's; two would end up as priests, and one would become a doctor. My father would have loved to be a vet; the bookcase was full of veterinary books and volumes about animal husbandry. He was an avid reader of all books, but anything to do with veterinary was his first choice.

We had two farms totalling three hundred acres. Ballyshera was our home. It was an eighteenth-century Georgian building with an extension at the back surrounded by mature beech trees and had a cobbled yard with extensive outhouses. It also had a haggard with hay barns, a kitchen garden, and a half-acre walled orchard with mature apple and pear trees, all compliments of the landed gentry of former days.

The accumulation of land began with my great-grandfather Michael Duane. He was renting lands and houses in Ballintlea, as ownership was forbidden under the English rule in Ireland in the early nineteenth century. When it became legal to own land, he bought bits and pieces of what he was renting, eventually ending up with a house and 158 acres, including a 20-acre orchard. He grew flax and, probably, tomatoes as there are remnants of glasshouses in the present ruins. Also there is a relic of a doghouse. The legend we were told is that as a young man, my great-grandfather was caught hunting on the Limerick mountains with a whippet, which was forbidden to him as a tenant; only the landed gentry could own such dogs. He was summoned to attend Kilfinane Assizes to be tried and sentenced. The case would be decided on proof of ownership of the dog, so he was legally advised to conceal the dog. The story goes that he hid the dog in the kennel beneath the house, and when the bailiff arrived to confiscate the dog, it was nowhere to be found. A significant trial took place in Kilfinane with much publicity. My great-grandfather was represented by a legal eagle from Cork City, and in order to get to Kilfinane, he commuted by train to Killavullen and thence to the trial by horse and trap. Michael Duane was found not guilty (non–habeas corpus—no dog!). As a result of the trial, it became no longer illegal for tenants (nonlandowners) to own whippets. A guilty verdict would have resulted in a gaol sentence.

The original house Michael Duane lived in was about one hundred metres from the present ruin. The present ruin was then occupied by the Curtains, who were agents for the Coote estate. The Duanes and the Curtains were very friendly. When the Curtains decided to sell, Michael Duane bought the house and farm, which was well developed with its huge orchard and glasshouses. He commuted weekly to the Butter Market in Cork with butter, buttered eggs for the ships, poultry, apples, and flax. He had two sons, Michael and Thomas, and two daughters, Elizabeth and Margaret.

Thomas, my grandfather, began purchasing land and property as Michael was due to inherit Ballintlea. In 1867, Ballyshera estate came on the market with a price tag of £380 sterling. It was a fine place, and at a reasonable price, probably because the deceased owner had taken his own life there, and his estranged wife and family were at loggerheads with regard to inheritance rights. Michael Duane bought Ballyshera for Thomas, who didn't live there until 1883, when he married my grandmother, Margaret O Regan, who brought a dowry of £650 sterling with her (€3,000,000 in present-day currency). Why so much? Where did it go? Unfortunately, Michael (Junior) died, and the two farms were passed to Thomas. The custom at the time was that the dowry brought in by the incoming bride was given to the next single sister of the groom as the dowry for her marriage, and Elizabeth was the only spinster left, so she received the £650 sterling. Her other sister, Margaret, had married earlier and had taken her dowry before my grandfather Thomas was married. Her dowry must have been much less, and this caused friction. A dowry was calculated by the acreage and the price of land at the time. I believe the matter was eventually settled, and Margaret did receive some of Elizabeth's dowry. The latter, having never married, lived the good life before she died in her nineties, penniless, in my uncle's parish house in Milford. He paid her funeral expenses.

She'd come to Ballyshera when I was young and showed glimpses of her glorious past while staying with us. The whole family always dined in the kitchen with both male and female staff, but such was not the case for 'old aunt', as she was known; she dined on her own in the pantry. She would have a duck egg, brown bread, and cocoa for her breakfast. She did visit the kitchen every now and then, and on one of these occasions my father asked loudly from his chair of office, 'Who cut their finger?', a euphemism he used for breaking wind, and at this, poor Aunt went around with a bandage looking for who had cut their finger, to our hilarious amusement. She was in her late eighties and was suffering from dementia, or in our language, doting. Children can be cruel, and we were no different; we would knock on her bedroom window downstairs and wait for the answer. 'Who is it?' she would ask. We would answer, 'Miss Creagh of Oldcourt.' 'Oh, do please come in, Miss Creagh.' We, in our childish ignorance, thought it was funny. Miss Creagh lived in a big house at Oldcourt, Doneraile, and was one of Aunt's friends in the good days. I discovered a note delivered by hand which arrived at Ballyshera in 1928 asking Miss Duane to accompany her in her chauffeur-driven car to Cork. She was highly regarded and trusted by her peers, which is illustrated in a letter from William Heaphy, who wrote to her from St Patrick's College, Maynooth, in 1887, informing her of his ordination date and asking her to communicate the news to his family. There is also a reference to her dowry being shared with her sister in Ballinoe.

Michael Duane died in 1883, and his wife, Ellen, died the following year, but not before my father was born in Ballintlea (and not in Ballyshera), as was customary for the eldest or firstborn. After his birth, the midwife went 200 metres across the river to the Morrissey household and delivered Michael Morrissey, later describing her night's work as delivering two babies, one dark and sallow, and the other fair and foxy. The two boy's lives were to be connected together for the following 75 years; they went to school together, and after leaving school, Mike Morrissey came to live and work in Ballyshera until his death in 1973. We all accepted him as one of the family. He is fondly remembered to this day. He was an intelligent man, a marvellous storyteller with a tremendous memory. His job was to take care of the tillage, ploughing, harrowing, sewing, and reaping. He never milked a cow but was usually first up in the morning; he'd light the fire and have his breakfast, and then be off and out with the horses at eight o'clock. We rarely saw or heard my father and Mike argue; it was an amazing relationship. It seemed that Mike was the farm manager and would pre-empt my father's options of which fields to plough and where to plant. What fascinated us was his ability to tell the time even though he never had a watch; it was as if he had a sundial in his head. He was short in stature, fair, and foxy, but sprightly and seemingly a good goalkeeper in hurling. He and two female staff resided with us, and one other worker and his wife and family had accommodation in a house on the farm. The others were usually local, but they would all be fed and found in our kitchen. The kitchen table was a long, heavy contraption but could only seat 12 or 14 maximum, so the remainder would have to find some shelf or lobby and stand. At a full sitting there could be 16 or 17 mouths to be satisfied. And one thing was for sure: it was disastrous to be late! The main ingredients for dinner would be a huge pot of potatoes, a big pot of vegetables, and a goodly chunk of meat with plenty of milk to wash them down. Soup could be a starter, and tapioca or stewed apples were followed by the ever popular pot of tea.

Those were happy times. We weren't very rich (according to my father), but we always had enough to eat. The house and yard were buzzing with activity, the sound of horses' hooves, the bellowing of the cattle, the cackling of geese, the shrill call of the gander, the quacking of ducks, the chorus of turkeys, the craking of hens, the barking of dogs, and the voices of people. I loved all the excitement, and the family working for us had boys and girls my own age, which added to the recreation. We would go down to the stream at the end of the farm and catch little collies and hags and hoard them in jam jars. On one of these safaris, while fishing beneath the bridge, we could hear the sound of trotting horse hooves above us. Curious to see what was happening, we ventured up onto the road to be confronted with the sight of two black horses in shining harness, with tall black plumes above their heads shimmering in the wind, drawing a hearse with a man in black suit and tall black hat perched on top. We were petrified, stuck to the limestone parapet while the hearse passed, momentarily frozen in time, a terrifying experience, but as soon as we recovered, we scooted under the bridge and moved upstream undercover through the fields until we reached home. We explained our story to my mother, who thought it was very funny, to our astonishment. We were told stories of the headless coach and other ghost stories relating to black horses and coaches, and we were convinced this was it. The only hearse we knew about was Dixie Shea's, and it was a motor vehicle. Mother calmed the whole situation by explaining that an old woman from Ballyorgan had stipulated in her will that her coffin be transported to Aglish Cemetery (our local cemetery) in a horse-drawn hearse. Mystery solved! On another occasion, when fishing barefooted with forks, Tommy, a friend of ours, mistook his own toe for a fish and stuck himself, causing consternation and ending another safari prematurely.

Summertime was full of excitement: making the hay, having dinner in the open field, the smell of horses and hay in the air, and the helping out with making wains (cocks of hay). Making a sugan (a binding of twisted hay used as a rope) was simple and a fun thing to do. The harvest would follow the hay, with the reaper and binder leading the way, tossing out the sheaves for the pursuing *meitheal* (Gaelic word for crowd) to stook. We were taught to make stooks and to stack four or more sheaves with the ears of grain on top, and then two sheaves were bound with a little straw from each around the upright four with the butts facing upwards so that the grain was protected from the rain. They looked like an igloo or wigwam from a distance. A field of stooks was a beautiful sight in the summer. After two weeks or so the stooks would be gathered and drawn into the haggard and made into a rick, which also involved a bit of artistry; the butts of the sheaves were placed outwards with the grain always in the inside, with the sides of the rick narrowing as they rose, so that the rain could not lodge but drain off, the rick eventually reaching a peak, which would be covered with straw. It was important in rick making to rake the sheaves or straw downwards for natural draining.

The threshing would follow in October and November. In Ballyshera it usually took two or three days to complete the threshing because of the compulsory tillage programme during the war and for a good while afterwards; the more land one had, the more tillage one had to produce. My father opted for grain, including oats, barley, and wheat. The threshing was a great social event as well as a working event; the meitheal moved to twelve or twenty farms, and it comprised the labour personnel of all the households in the area, allowing some to stay at home to milk the cows. The threshing usually started at 10 a.m., stopped at 1 p.m. for dinner, and resumed until 6 p.m. Dinner and supper were supplied by the host farmer, and then a social night of music and song would follow. Kegs of porter were tapped and distributed to all. I liked the tapping of the kegs; Dinny Heaphy, our neighbour, was the tapper, and he and I were friends. It would take a while before the stout would flow freely, and that waiting part was what I liked. The taste of the froth and early liquid was much nicer than the later drink. Dinny would slip me a glass when nobody was looking.

One night Paddy, a friend, and I borrowed my sisters' dresses and dressed up as girls to fool the older men. We had a little success with the more inebriated. Ned Synan would be first to sing; he regarded himself as another John McCormack, and when he'd reach the high notes, the house would erupt: 'Encore! Encore!' On the days of the threshing I would run all the way home from school to get the most out of the action. We had a cairn dog, Pudsy, and I would urge him on in pursuit of the fleeing rats; at the end of the day there could be a dozen dead rats laid out for all to see. Pudsy's reputation spread far and wide as a 'ratter', until one day he sullied his name by laying out a few cats as well, which didn't fare well with the owner. He was grounded from travelling, which is why he was excited by our threshing days. On some Saturdays I'd take him on safari looking for rats; he would scent every burrow, and if he decided to root, then I was sure there was a rat there. Sometimes I would use a bucket of water to flush out the rat, or I'd dig it out with a spade. Pudsy was always ready to pounce. You probably realise by now that I didn't like rats!

When my father and mother went on holiday to Lisdoonvarna every summer, I and my siblings would have a ball. On one of these occasions we formed a band with no musical instruments, just buckets and cans and anything that would make noise. There were kids from three families with us, so a gang of about twenty started to beat the drums and march around the yard. Harmless enough, you might think, as did we, until the following day when the neighbours had to spend hours sorting out their cows and cattle. They had no idea what had disturbed them, whereas all of us had a very good idea! On another occasion we organised a giant see-saw, and again, a huge crowd attended; the see-saw was an old common cart with two shafts on either side, each of which was straddled with five of us. We went up and down slowly at first until we got the balance right, and then the tempo increased, until suddenly the ones on the opposite side were dislodged when the see-saw hit the ground, except for my sister, Mary. And because of the imbalance of ten against one, she was catapulted into the air and fell head first on a huge rock. I will never forget that experience. Her head had a huge gash, and the blood was all over her face. My brother Jim had some training in first aid and calmly took over. She spent the night in hospital. The following day after school, as I ran home, I was hoping she was still alive. Afterwards it wasn't what happened that scared me but what might have happened!

On another occasion, much later, when I was 16, the older siblings organised a party for their friends, and they had a girlfriend for me—a blind date. I didn't object to the party, but the blind date was an insult; they had their chosen friends, but I was supposed to—sorry, was compelled to—take their choice. No thank you! I got the gun and headed for the pond at the end of the farm with my trusty dog Jack. Now I wasn't allowed to shoot at that age, but there was precious little they could do to stop me. Jack went into the pond, and sure enough a wild mallard duck got up, and to my own amazement I shot the duck. Homeward bound with my first wild duck, I was in ecstasy, and all the objections to the blind date had disappeared. I joined the party, relayed the good news, and finally met my blind date. She was very nice, and I apologised for being late, but I never told her that the wild duck had taken precedence.

All these events were ways of creating our own simple recreation in the pretelevision era. Country life was quiet except for visitors and callers, who would be the subject of more mischief. Because of the compulsory tillage order, we had surplus grain for sale, and at the sound of a strange horse or lorry, my brother Ger would take up his sniper's position in the dairy straight across from the closed yard gate, concealing himself with the pellet gun (air gun) at the ready, aimed at the hatch through which the door could only be opened from the outside. And when the hand appeared, he would pull the trigger. If it was a hit, the hand would be retrieved abruptly with an audible expletive, and that was the cue for us to retreat through the back door of the dairy and nonchalantly amble around to the kitchen. The distance between the dairy and the yard door was about fifty yards, and a pellet starts to lose altitude after twenty yards, so the remaining thirty yards had to be calculated. He had it measured to a T. The effect of a pellet at that distance would be only a slight pinch, leaving no evidence. There were never any complaints, except one person told my father that he thought he got an electric shock from the bolt. My father never suspected anything, but it was a warning shot to stop.

Dan O'Brien, father of the legendary Vincent O'Brien, was one of those who called for oats for his racehorses. He was a third cousin and good friend of my father; nevertheless, they would be haggling and bargaining for ages before a deal was reached. He was lucky, because this was before the sniping began. Ger was a good marksman with the pellet gun and later with the rifle and shotgun. Bill Quinlan was one of the workmen. I don't know if he could be called brave or foolish, because he would hold a safety match between his fingers with the red top extending outwards, while Ger stood fifteen feet away with the pellet gun and could light the match with a pellet, maybe not every time, but one in three attempts. Then they got braver or more foolish, and Ger would quench a lighted cigarette in Bill's mouth from the same distance.

Poor Tim Riordan, our postman, became a victim because of his indiscretion. He snitched information to the teacher that got Ger into trouble. Retribution was executed on a Saturday morning at our lawn gate (200 yards from the house). Ger ambushed him with the help of Tommy, his friend; they had a trial run first by testing his hearing (Tim was very deaf). Ger stood well back so that the pellets would only pinch and not leave marks, and as Tim closed the gate, Ger ambushed him and shot in the ankles with a few pellets. Tim did a little river dance as a result but had no idea what happened. This episode had repercussions. Tim used to wear a long black oilskin, and one fine morning after that incident, he was carrying the oilskin under his arm. My father noticed the holes made by the pellets, and Ger was court-martialled and warned not to be firing pellets at Tim's oilskins under his arms or else the gun would be confiscated. Of course the gun would have been confiscated if my father had known that Tim was wearing the oilskins when the holes occurred.

Much later, as a teenager, I would help Ger to win the prize as best shot at Shanballymore Carnival. The pellet gun range usually had three guns, and these guns were never very accurate, as the sights were possibly damaged by constant use or abuse. My task was to sample all three and discover the best, or determine which one was 'genuine'. It was expensive, but Ger sponsored the venture, and it was fun. The idea was to aim at the bullseye and see where the first pellet struck. If it was left and low or high, I adjusted my aim accordingly with the second pellet, and if it was near the bullseye, I would know where to aim until I got the bullseye. That gun would then be earmarked for the maestro. You got four pellets, and the score to aim at was 39 or 38. The bullseye was 10 points, and all the rings around it ranged from 9 to the 1 at the outside. Ger would regularly score 39. This arrangement went on for a year or two, until one night (by fluke) I scored 40—4 bullseyes—while testing the guns. That didn't go down too well, and the arrangement was strained, but still we supported each other. I didn't beat him very often, but he kept looking over his shoulder.

Ger got a Remington .22 rifle with telescopic sights, and I used the same system as with the pellet guns to zero the sights. We had to mount the sights firmly and then make a target in bullseye fashion, firing alternately and adjusting until we got it right. The final test was a cigarette box, Carroll's Number 1. Ger could put a bullet through each letter from 100 yards. There was no excuse for any of us for missing the target after that. All the early experience with the pellet gun came to fruition.

Guns were part and parcel of our family. There were shotguns and the rifle. My father was a passionate gunman and, according to accounts, an excellent marksman. He was the first in the area to purchase a hammerless gun. One of the workmen usually carried the bag, and he was fascinated with this novelty. One day the workman got the gun and loaded it with two cartridges. He had the safety off. He then put the barrels to his chest and challenged the others to pull the trigger to demonstrate the weapon's safety. Just then, my father appeared on the scene. To put it mildly, the workman got a telling-off, and the Safety Act was read: 'Never point a gun, loaded or empty, at anyone; never load a gun in the house; always keep a gun broken, that is opened; and never trust the safety catch.' We all knew the rules.

I was too young to have seen my father in his prime, but those who did testify to his prowess. He suffered from an arthritic hip which hindered him from long walks, and he used a stick. Nevertheless, I coaxed him to go shooting one day on the excuse that Ger was complaining about the quality of the cartridges, saying that they weren't strong enough to knock pheasants, and adding that the pointer (gun dog) was rushing (not pointing) birds. As we entered a field of turnips, my father handed me the stick. The dog, sure enough, rushed a bird at sixty yards. Nevertheless, my father shot the pheasant dead. I could hear him cursing the dog and mumbling that there was nothing wrong with those cartridges. The dog flushed another pheasant, and again my father shot it. I was ordered to collect the pheasants and tie the dog, the 'mad whore'. Mission accomplished. On our way back we had to climb a fence, and as my father was on his knees with one hand on the fence, a rabbit ran out the field. With one hand, my father put the gun to his shoulder and shot the rabbit. I know I was young, and I know that everything seems big when we are small, but I can still visualise my father on the fence. And although I couldn't see the rabbit being shot, the dead rabbit was proof. Ger wasn't too pleased with the outcome—there was nothing wrong with the cartridges, and it was time to get himself another dog. That was my father's last shot.

It wasn't long after the war, and cars were allowed back, so we got a car, a Hillman Minx ZF 981. My parents had a car before the war, a big yellow Fiat with timber spokes, which was dumped in the haggard. My father had driven that car, and naturally he wanted to drive the new one. Uncle Francy, my mother's brother, was the instructor, and I was the passenger. Everything went well for the drive down the road and back, but as my father was turning in the lawn gate, Uncle Francy asked him to stop. In pressing the brake, my father caught the accelerator as well and crashed into the pier. He used to wear big wide boots, which didn't help. There was a big dent in the front bumper, and I was commissioned to go up to the house under cover and go into in the adjoining field to fetch the sledgehammer and then bring it back down by the same route. Uncle Francy, and indeed all his family, were brilliant mechanics, and in minutes he sorted the bumper. I got a half-crown, a lot of money, to keep my mouth shut. Uncle Francy drove up to the house, and nobody suspected anything. I kept my mouth shut, but my father never drove again. This might explain the tremendous trust between me and my father.

We all called him boss. I called him bosseen, not realising the endearment that implied. My relationship with my father grew as time passed. When he died, I was shattered. There was another watershed occurred when one Sunday I was listening to a match on the radio and smoking a cigarette in the kitchen, and a call came from upstairs. I wasn't supposed to be smoking, at least my parents didn't know, but the match was so exciting that I went into the hall with the cigarette in my hand to answer my father on the landing above. He asked me for a fag, and I was both in shock and in denial for a good while until he interjected, 'What's that in your hand?' I obliged and gave him a cigarette. From then on it was no longer a secret, even though my mother didn't know until I went to Maynooth. Later, it was ironic that I ceased smoking said fags on the eve of her death.

The Boss

As aforementioned, my siblings and I always referred to our father as the boss. He referred to himself as Mike. As I said already, he was a quiet, shy man, well read, humorous, charming, and a tremendous judge of man and beast. He had no time for gossip or calumny and would evade character assassination at all times. He had a style of his own when asked to comment on people, always avoiding direct slander. 'What sort of a man was so-and-so?' If he could not supply a positive comment for the man in question, he would say that his wife was a lovely woman. If he had nothing good to say about someone, then he would say nothing. If we wanted to know the family history of some unfortunate local felon in trouble, he would answer: 'Don't ask me, child. Only the canon knows that.' If some unfortunate young woman got into trouble (i.e. got pregnant), my mother would blame the young woman, but my father would interject: 'It takes two to tango, woman.' We kids learned to read between the lines, but most of our father's comments found a permanent home in us. I rarely heard my siblings slander or gossip. He had one great piece of advice: you make your own bed and sleep on it. Later, as my older siblings were in relationships, he changed it to this: 'You make your own bed and sleep on it; if things go wrong, don't come back to me and blame me for not warning you.' Neither he nor Mother ever interfered in any of their relationships. He was a peace commissioner for oaths, and he took his honorary tasks seriously.

My personal relationship with my father was very close, as I've said. He was in his sixties when I was born. My earliest memories of him go back to when I was 5or 6 years of age. I remember sitting on his lap after he came home from hospital in 1943 or 1944; he had a serious operation for ulcers and had most his stomach removed. Mother told us that he was so ill that it was reported that he died, but he survived and had to observe a strict regimen to survive. He loved *drisheen*, a native Cork dish, and so did we. Every August it would be customary to try out the new potatoes, and he'd take a pike and bucket to dig a few stalks and bring home their produce. Mother would boil the potatoes, mash them with butter and salt, and present them for tasting; they were organic, and they had a special flavour which the present-day potatoes don't have.

As Father got older and I grew bigger, our relationship got stronger. He was never overbearing or threatening, and I had a profound respect and love for him; it was mutual. In my younger days he gave me a sheep—a Hail Mary, an old sheep with few teeth and bad hooves, so that she would kneel on her front legs to eat. Nevertheless, she was my sheep to feed and look after. He had given Pat a calf (with the scour), and it died within days, but Pat was happy to have owned an animal rather than to have it put down. Presenting an aged animal to the child was a custom which Ger held sacred, and which he passed on to his son, Michael. It grieves me now when I reflect on the treatment I received from church authorities after the Church Tribunal: I didn't receive the respect my father had shown for mere animals. The biggest culprits were the abandoning shepherds and not the ravaging wolves.

We weren't spoiled with money, because the boss had O'Leary's deafness, pretending not to hear a request for money by replying, 'Honey? I don't keep bees, child.' A second request would be successful, albeit reduced in value.

The only time I saw my father tipsy was after my uncle Andy's wedding, and he gave me a half-crown. I was hoping there would be more weddings! The next best thing to a wedding was to be in Paul Mannix's pub on Sundays after Mass; Lil and I would accompany Dad and his great friend Dinny O Conor for a few drinks—two half ones of Paddy whiskey—and we would be treated to Smarties and Rolos by Paul, a huge genial man with a sense of humour to match. A commercial traveller called on him during the war and noticed a side of bacon in the shop and asked Paul for a few pounds; Paul said, 'No. There's a war on.' The man appealed for a few rashers, and again Paul refused. At that, the stranger said in no uncertain terms that Paul should stuff the bacon up his. And before the man could finish speaking, Paul interjected: 'Impossible! There's a pot of jam there already this morning.'

Paul had a three-in-one shop: a bar, a grocery, and a bakery. He had a reputation for having good greyhounds, and he entered a very good bitch, just in pup, in the Laurels in Cork, but the race was postponed for two months due to a strike by the staff. By that time the bitch was due to whelp, but anyhow, Paul decided to run her. She broke well and gained a good few lengths on the field, but then she suddenly lay down and had her pups. However, afterwards she got up and still won the race. Not only that, but also one of the pups came second. These types of tall stories were Paul's trademark, but to us he was a kind, generous man.

After two drinks, the boss was good for a shilling. When I went to St Colman's, things changed. For one, the boss was more liberal with pocket money. On one Easter holiday he gave me 100 bullets for the Remington .22 to control the rats that were rooting the spring grain in two fields. I applied myself to the task in hand and noticed that the rats were camouflaged against the earth and not easily detected, but they were also short-sighted and wouldn't see me until I was close, and then they would run into the burrow. But they would always stop at the mouth of the burrow to have one last look, and it was their last look, because by then they would be in my sights. I used most of the bullets and missed very few rats.

There was a heavy crop of corn in the summer, and that earned me some plaudits from the boss. I drove him to Cork for gold injections for his arthritic hip, but it wasn't a success. He spent the last two years of his life in bed. I was in Maynooth, and during the summer holidays, I would give Mother a break and look after him for two weeks. I spent a lot of time chatting with him. He had a whistle to call for help if he needed anything. And I could practise my hurling in the lawn. As a youngster I curiously watched him shaving himself with a cut-throat razor and was fascinated with the routine of sharpening it with the strop and then lathering his face with soap. Then came the skilled handling of the razor, shaving without cutting himself. It is sad now with that fond memory to think of shaving his face for him with modern safety blade and ready foam. He learned knitting and sewing in the national school and was adept with his hands. He was a skilled barber and cut our hair, and indeed the neighbours' as well. He trained Tom to take over from him and continue the practice.

I recall the time the bull kicked my father and smashed the beautiful gold watch in his pocket and injured his ribs. I would one day wear that gold watch and chain with that painful memory. I slept in the room by night, and I was happy if I could hear snoring or breathing, but silence was terrifying. In November 1958, Dr Michael Harty, my dean in Maynooth, called to my room and informed me of my father's deteriorating health. He very kindly drove me to the train for Cork, which arrived early in Mallow, and from there I sped to Ballyshera. The lawn gate was closed. When I opened it, it made its wonted peculiar noise. All the family and neighbours were by my father's bedside. He was unconscious and breathing heavily, but he reacted to the noise of the lawn gate and rallied. When I arrived by his bed, he was still alive. I held his hand. He died within a few minutes. I could hear Mother saying 'He's gone.' I was just numb. It had all happened so quickly. Going down the stairs, I burst out in tears, inconsolable. I felt so proud and privileged to shoulder his coffin with my siblings. In life great heroes were shouldered home by their peers as a mark of great respect, and now in his death I was shouldering my hero to his final resting place.

It took me a long time to recover from my bereavement because my father and I had been so close and because his death was the first I'd experienced. I remember my first visit to the cemetery; the sight of the sunken grave confirmed the dreadful finality. If when he was alive we would ask him about some distant future event, he used to say, 'When I'm over there'— pointing at Aglish, our cemetery— 'and growing daises, it will happen.' The daisies had already begun to grow. That Christmas was a lonely one. As Tennyson wrote, 'But oh, for the touch of a vanish'd hand and the sound of a voice that is still.' I couldn't talk about my father for years without feeling very emotional. He died almost sixty years ago, and I still feel a little pain.

I was very close to my mother too, and even though she was given the all-clear to come home from hospital one day after an illness, she died suddenly at 2 a.m. I awoke suddenly at that very moment and felt unable to go back to sleep, uneasy and shifting from one side to the other. When the phone rang, I knew there was something wrong. I shared the house I was staying in with another priest who took some time to awaken, so I answered the phone; the nurse announced that she was calling from the hospital. Straightaway I said, 'You have bad news for me.' She thought I had already been told by some other source, but I assured her that it was my pathological sense which told me, which is why I was awake and restless. This pathological communication exists with close family ties and is very obvious to detect between identical twins. They say opposites attract. My mother was attracted to horses, and whether on horseback or in trap, was fearless as a rider. She was also fearless as a passenger in the car, which she needed to be when I was behind the wheel. I never heard her complaining during my driving career.

She and my father had a very good relationship. He was the boss, but she had him wrapped around her little finger and had no trouble getting what she wanted. When she would lose the rag and give out to him or to us, he would woo her back to calmness with the old charm: 'My God, she is a cross woman but a good woman! Where would we be without her?' He addressed my mother as 'woman' sometimes, and I used the same term. He had great respect for women and tipped his hat to every woman.

Mother made the major decisions in her children's education, and Father tagged on. This was a peculiar duty of the mother in North Cork and South Limerick society, almost a matriarchal society. If there were parent–teacher meetings in those days, I couldn't imagine my father going. Even though he was very well read, it wasn't his job. He surprised me one day when he spoke in Greek, possibly a remnant of his year in St Colman's.

My mother was born in Avonmore, South Cregg, Fermoy, in her family home perched high above the banks of the River Blackwater. (*Cregg* is 'a large rock cliff' in Gaelic, and *Avonmore* means 'big river'.) Her maiden name was Shinnick. Her father had a merchant seed store in Fermoy, 150 acres along the Blackwater River, a threshing machine, a steam engine, and sawmills. She too must have brought a substantial dowry to Ballyshera in 1923, but she never spoke about it. She had five siblings, Andy, Francy, Eddie, Jonjo, and Eileen. Eddie, Jonjo, and Eileen died as teenagers within three years of one another. Two of them contracted the great flu in 1918, and one died of sepsis. They lived in the parish of Ballyhooly, and the family grave is just outside the church door. Mother's family used to visit the graveside every Sunday after Mass to weep and pray. The local curate changed that routine.

Mother and her brother Francy followed the local foxhound hunt on horseback. She loved horses and dogs, and she wasn't disappointed when she came to Ballyshera. I spent many happy holidays in Cregg with Uncle Andy and Uncle Francy. There were old discarded motor cars in which I could sit and imagine driving. I was fascinated with cars and machinery, a piece of DNA I inherited from the Shinnicks, who were mechanical aces. My great-uncles Fr Ned and Fr Joe Shinnick were the first priests in the diocese to have motorbikes and then cars. Fr Joe lived in my present abode in 1928. There were no garages or service stations back then, so they serviced their own cars. My cousin Noel and his son John continue the tradition in Cregg; John assembled a car from scratch for fun, and he and Noel take their vintage tractors apart and reassemble them as recreation.

Fr Joe was a character with a wicked sense of humour. Having chanced on a stranded American tourist whose car had broken down, he offered his help. He noticed two horses looking at them from behind a fence across from them and, guessing that the dust from the Irish road had caused the motorist's plugs to malfunction, said to the tourist, 'Did you hear what one of those horses said?' The man replied, 'No.' Fr Joe said, 'Try the plugs.' And at that, he cleaned the plugs and the car started, leaving the tourist grateful but baffled. Fr Joe told the man to take the car for further inspection to a garage owned by a friend of his in the next town. When the tourist arrived, he laughingly narrated the episode about the horse and Fr Joe, but the garage man remained serious and asked, 'What colour was the horse?' 'White,' the tourist replied. The garage man remained serious and said, 'You're lucky. The black one knows nothing about cars.'

Fr Joe repeated the same ruse on Bishop Robert Browne, whose car refused to start after a thundershower in Fermoy. The locals sent for Fr Joe, who was visiting his relatives in the town, and he duly obliged. By this time a crowd of onlookers had assembled, including the town clown, who was friendly with Fr Joe. Fr Joe asked the town clown in earshot of the bishop and surrounding gallery what the problem could be, and the clown just pointed at the engine. While general laughter was distracting the crowd, Fr Joe dried the two plugs and invited the clown to shake his handkerchief over the engine. Then he asked the chauffeur to start the car. It started. Fr Joe waved goodbye, knowing that the crowd knew that he had pulled one over on the bishop.

Uncle Andy married Elizabeth Cagney of Springfort, Charleville, and she became our auntie Lizzie who died only recently at the ripe age of 101. As a student, I spent many happy holidays with them in Cregg. Uncle Andy was a brilliant angler and taught me the basics of angling. On August evenings I would take my gun and rod down to the island and wait for the 'night rise'. When that finished, it would be duck time. Auntie Lizzie was a great hostess; nobody would lose weight in her house. Her father was a first cousin of the famous Archbishop Mannix of Melbourne. I still keep in touch with all my cousins from Fermoy (Mary, Noel, Dan, John, and Andy) and their spouses and families.

Uncle Francy married Helen Walsh from Ballindangan, and they lived in Strawhall near Fermoy, where I spent every third Sunday when I was a pupil in St Colman's. He died from cancer before Frank Junior was born. I spent happy holidays with them as well. Helen became our auntie Helen, and she now lives in her own house near Frank, her daughter, Marie, and Marie's husband, Tim. Auntie Helen was like Auntie Lizzie for dispensing hospitality. Both assumed their visitors were too shy to ask for a second helping, so before you could ask, your plate would have a third helping. No matter how busy they were, you had to wait for tea, and tea meant full dinner. Full fare, as they served it, was music to the ears of the lean-fed teenage boarder from St Colman's. Auntie Helen worked very hard after Uncle Francy died. She handed the farm over to Frank and Gutrun to continue. They have a thriving, prize winning cheese company, Fermoy Cheese Company, and export all over Europe. They also specialise in raw organic milk.

We kids never had a lot of homework to do, which was a tribute to the teacher. My mother was most influential in disciplinary matters. She laid down the law, whereas my father was more subtle and psychological in his approach. He told this story about Betty, the hypochondriac who pestered the doctor. When the doctor asked her to cough, she would reply with, 'I can't cough, Doctor.' He would respond with, 'Ah, try, Betty, try,' and she would give a little faint gasp: 'Ahem, ahem.' When any one of us would feign illness, our father would tease us with Betty's cough without saying a word.

Sometimes while we were reading, as we did whatever little homework we'd gotten, Father would request calmly for one us to close the door—he hated open doors—and there would be no response. He would speak a little louder: 'Will somebody please close the door?' And if there was still no response, then his final approach would be more provocative: 'Hmm, close it yourself, Mike, or it won't be closed at all,' at which there would be a rushed response. The winner would be rewarded with 'At least I reared one decent child.' It worked every time, for two reasons: if he got up and closed it himself, we would have to listen to a lecture on the ingratitude of children, and if we obliged, we got the praise.

Our family said the rosary every night after supper. Father was up to the tricks of the older ones, as excuses would be put forward for skipping the long prayers. All excuses were answered with 'That can wait.' During the rosary, he would be always on the alert to somebody nodding off, and he would give such offenders a gentle prod of the stick. One night he began to nod himself and got a verbal reminder from mother, to our amusement.

Our local school was small with two teachers, and we walked to it, as it was only a mile through the fields. My teacher, Miss Halloran, taught me for most of the classes. She was strict but was a very good teacher. Her father, who stayed with her in the teachers' house across the road, died, and my sister Tess, who was two years older than I, was invited to stay the nights with her, so that was great for me and Lil, my younger sister. Miss Halloran was nice to us, but we never pushed our luck. She gave us the basic rules of etiquette. When saluting or greeting someone, you should always address them as Mr or Miss or by their Christian name, and in conversation you should never say 'Ha'; always say 'I beg your pardon.' One Saturday morning, one of the pupils was cycling past Miss Halloran on the road and shouted, 'Good morning.' She answered, 'To whom are you speaking?' He replied, 'Ha.' Two mortal sins of etiquette! We heard about it on the following Monday morning.

My mother decided to send me to the Christian Brothers in Doneraile for sixth class to broaden my education. Doneraile was four miles from Ballyshera, and because I was able to cycle at 6years old, I was expected to cycle to school. It was a challenge at 12 years, but I didn't seem to mind. As the year progressed, I felt in control. Firstly I met new pupils and made new friends, and secondly, I learned nothing new. Our little school with its two teachers was a year ahead of the Brothers in the three Rs. I had a nice easy year, except the brother teaching me didn't take kindly to the 'I did that last year, sir.' I was tall for my age and was wearing long pants at the time. During geography class, he said there were two towns in France which reminded him of Dan Duane's pants—Toulon and Toulouse—to the sound of laughter. Actually I was as tall as he, so maybe he was trying to cut me down to size. I kept a low key after that. He was tough. Recently, I met a fellow pupil and asked him how he had gotten on with that brother.

He said, 'Do you want me to show you the evidence?' I took his word and realised that I hadn't fared too badly in the regime of the time.

Mother had made a mistake, but I never told her the full story. Onward to St Colman's with my hurley and ball in September 1952. And this was no safari. It was to be my abode for the next five years. It was a big change, but not as bad as the situation that one of my uncles described as having happened in his time: the first years (or bonhams) were confronted at the main entrance by the seniors, who would hold them up by the legs and shake all the money out of their pockets. That was scary, but my uncle was talking about the early 1900s.

The biggest adjustment was the act of boarding. We pupils stayed on campus for months at a time, away from home and family. We had to take what we got as regards food and sleep in a dormitory called Japan. There were positives as well, like handball, table tennis, and the playing field. Every class year had their own pitch for hurling and football, and we would practise on these pitches every evening after school. We would organise matches between ourselves. It wasn't long before trouble started, not between us but from outside our first-year group; our pitch was invaded by a group of third years. The term used for this activity is 'horsing'; we were being horsed off our own pitch. The ringleader was a new student who had joined third year and already had a reputation as a 'scrapper'. We objected, and formed a flank to protect the invasion. Because I was the biggest, he attacked me first, with a flurry of punches which connected. Although stunned, I frantically lashed out with a punch which landed on the side of his head, knocking him to the ground. I was the most surprised one on the pitch, but my surprise soon turned to panic as he lay on the ground motionless. Fear took over from panic. I was worried that if 'nix' would arrive, *nix* being the code word for any teacher. If a teacher were to show up, we would all be in big trouble. Fortunately, the lad regained consciousness, to our great relief. The astonishing thing about the incident was the fact that the boy was so small and attacked without provocation. I'd never hit anyone before that, and I certainly, as result of it, would never hit anyone again. Lessons were learned.

Of course my other classmates were never privy to that resolution, so I had a trouble-free run for the rest of my stay in St Colman's. When threats of scraps were brewing from the wounded third-year student, one of my friends would casually address the aggressor with, 'Would you like to wake up with a crowd around you again?' A year later I suffered concussion from a stroke of a hurley. It was a weird experience, because after the hit, I remembered nothing until an hour later, when I woke up (regained consciousness) in the study hall. According to my friends I acted normally during that hour. I had a similar experience at home when I fell off a wall. On that occasion I regained consciousness two hours later at my supper.

I loved the hurling and achieved a moderate standard playing in various positions on the college teams. Life was made a little easier for me in St Colman's by having the luck of having an uncle living within three miles of the college. It was permissible to visit a close relative if such individual lived within the three-mile radius. Uncle Francy was only a mile away in Strawhall, so every third Sunday, either I walked the mile or his wife, Auntie Helen, would collect me and then deliver me back to the college at 6. 30. To them I am eternally grateful.

Boarding school was a tough slog for me. I was very much a home bird. However, it gave me independence and a deeper love for home and for my parents and siblings. Absence makes the heart grow fonder, but absence came at a high price. There were many stories of fellows scaling the wall and lessening the price, but I am glad to have stayed the course. I did make one resolution when studying for the priesthood: that I would never go back and teach there as a priest. Of course that too was broken, but technically, I wasn't a teacher.

I had tasted a little romance before I went to Maynooth, a drop in the ocean, and had heard of the old saying that one didn't need to swallow the Atlantic Ocean to get the taste of salt water—a single drop will suffice. It started with the party in Ballyshera that I referred to earlier. Not long after that, I was alone in the kitchen when there was a knock on the hall door. The hall door was 8 feet in height and 5 feet in width, with a large brass knocker, and when that knocker was used, it would reverberate through the whole house and 'wake the dead'. Consequently it was only used by strangers. When I opened the door I found this itinerant teenage girl of my own age holding a 2-year-old child in her arms. We were both slightly embarrassed by the sudden unexpected encounter, as normally my mother dealt with travelling people calling, who were normally adult women. After an awkward silence, I asked the girl what she wanted. She had her head downcast, and when she looked up, our eyes met and locked. She was beautiful. She bashfully asked for some bread and butter for the child. I relieved her embarrassment by asking if she would like the same for herself, and maybe a glass of milk. She nodded her head with a beautiful smile. I smiled back, and the ice barrier between our cultures began to thaw. I returned with the food and milk, which she gave to the child while awkwardly shuffling about. There was very little conversation but a lot of communication. Having finished eating, she thanked me quietly but gracefully, and slowly departed down the long avenue, occasionally stopping to look back. I returned to the kitchen and pondered the emotional impact of the encounter and the unlikelihood of crossing the Rubicon to appease my new-found unrequited love. Something happened on that day that lingers in my memory to this day. Subsequent to that experience of 'puppy love', others followed, but none of them were ever as memorable. Some of my best friends are women, but I was committed to my call, and even though they would have been suitable as partners in life, the call was stronger and prevailed.

This tug of war between divine and human love is the norm for a normal priest. To be a good priest, one should be firstly a good human being and secondly a good Christian. It's the human being part which causes the constant struggle. Human beings fall in love. The priest is no exception.

I had seven siblings, three sisters and four brothers: Tom, Jim, Gerard, Pat, Mary, Tess, and Lil.

CHAPTER 2

In September 1956, I was on my way to Maynooth, where I would spend the next seven years. The first three years were to be in the university, studying for a Bachelor of Arts, and the last four in the Divinity University, studying theology. I had to dress in a black suit with black hat and black overcoat, but when in the college, we wore soutane and roman collar. The transition from one boarding school to another was easy for me, except here we were addressed as Mister and still treated as Master. Maynooth in 1956 was dreary and strict, a stern test of the human spirit, and many a spirit was broken there. In hindsight, it reminded me of the old Wild West method of breaking a young horse, by pummelling it into submission, with Maynooth's strict regime and stifling culture of insularity. You were allowed to smoke but not to drink alcohol, or eat chocolate, or read the newspapers. It had positives, such as the responsibility to keep your room clean and your bed dressed, and to be punctual, which is essential in all walks of life. Otherwise, it was oppressive and uninspiring.

The Pugin design and structure were greatly admired by the visitors, but living there 24/7 was different. The grey, cold, wet limestone on a winter day was no cure for the mildly depressed and added little cheer to the weary student. It was not only visually cold but also physically cold. However, it had Newman's essential and saving idea of a university, the 'confluence of youth', and in this campus all were dedicated to one vocation. This had positive effects. The first time I met up with my classmates was self-assuring. Here were tall and small, black and blond, serious and funny, diverse and similar, Northern and Southern, all together in pursuit of one vocation. They were all young men taken from the Irish population, answering the call to bridge the gap between people and God. They were very human, having all the hormones that adolescents would struggle with, and the intelligence to discern, and the will to pursue the difficult, grave decision they had made. As we got to know each other, the sense of aloneness began fading and collegiality began growing, merging us into a collage of humanity.

Humour was the safety valve of life in Maynooth. Jokes were as important as learning the serious subjects of philosophy and theology. It was this humour that created the dialect or slang which existed in my time. Everything was described in the slang. If I were to ask a modern student to translate the following sentence, I'm sure he wouldn't have a clue: 'I went up Graf in my sou and gunny shoes to our poz.' Graf was the middle walk; sou was soutane: gunny was 'elite' or big; and poz was the abbreviation for 'position', i.e., meeting place. Every diocese had a poz, a meeting place, where all the students would meet before the bell for lectures and where any news would be imparted. Maynooth had long walks, and students would usually use the walks for exercise and fresh air with their friends and classmates until five minutes before the bell, when they would all split up and converge on their poz. If the bishop arrived in the college, he would know where the poz was, and visit his students there.

There was one walk in the middle called 'Asperges walk', *asperges* being the Latin for sprinkle. This title originated from the risk of crows overhead sprinkling the walkers beneath with their liquid greetings. This was especially prone to happen when unsuspecting Bas (the junior class of senior house, sitting their BA degree) were taken on their maiden walk by night, when all the crows were present, and suddenly the senior host would clap his hands loudly to frighten the crows into bombing his escorts, while he took shelter by the butt.

The college chapel was known as the gun chapel. If a fellow decided to leave, he would be described as 'cutting'. His last night in the college would be celebrated as a 'wake': His closest classmates would call on him in his room, even though it was against the rules, to socialise or smoke in their rooms to celebrate his departure, and the authorities turned a blind eye. A 'screw' was someone who spent a lot of time praying in the chapel. When a screw cut, it would send shudders through the house, but for us lesser mortals, it would bring hope that maybe God wasn't looking for saints, just ordinary men to continue.

There were three houses, junior, middle, and senior, and each had its own dean of discipline. Fr Michael Harty was my dean for almost my whole period at Maynooth. He was fair and sensible and seemed to understand the drawbacks to the obsolete rule, which could not be said of Dr Montpellier, the senior dean, who, in our eyes, was a blast from the past. He urged and aided fellows to exit and appeared devoid of compassion. He, again, was a victim of the times, when the church sought absolute control everywhere, with tight robotic discipline for the clergy and legislation to impel the faithful into heaven—compulsion rather than direction. We clergy and faithful have come a long way since then, but the remnants of power still haunt the hierarchy, which is why errors of judgement still occur.

The Pope, despite his rejection of my appeal, is making progress in the reformation of the antique culture of the Vatican, and particularly the infamous Congregation for the Doctrine of the Faith (CDF). When I visited the Vatican in 2009, Mgr Maurice Dooley, my advocate, reminded me that the building we were entering for the appeal process was the same one where the Italian Inquisition was held, and he assured me the dungeons where tortures were administered were still there. It sent a chill down my spine.

Back to Maynooth of the 1950s and 1960s, where there were no torture chambers except for the anxiety of making the class list without 'irregularities'. If you were on the list, you were called to orders. When a student arrived, he was given a number, and he was known by this number throughout his seven years. Maynooth was definitely ahead of its time on two counts: no smoking inside the buildings—there was a special smoking shed, in case of rain—and you were numbered or tagged before the computer ever came into vogue. You got your place in the refectory, in the chapel, and in the Aula Maxima according to your number. The students on either side were called your 'immediates'. The tea was called 'clam', the porridge was called 'BG', and any legitimate food outside of the 'ref' (refectory) was called a 'flame'.

There was a playing pitch for every two dioceses to share. Cloyne shared a pitch with Down and Conor. We played each other in soccer a few times, and the contrasting styles would be viewed from Graf with great interest. First there was the Belfast style, akin to that of George Best, and second was the *modh díreach* (direct route), the style of the Southerners. Very often the modh díreach would prevail. It was what Jack Charlton used to great effect during his tenure as Ireland manager. High Field was a full-length Gaelic pitch where the class football and hurling games were played. It was a great privilege to be on your class team, and this made for great games. The standard of hurling and football was very high, each team having intercounty players. One particular class had six such players in football and three in hurling; they were a formidable team. But I have a clear memory of our class defeating them in hurling, with yours truly playing at centre forward, out of position, on an intercounty player, and not doing too badly, notching two goals and a point in the process, and nursing a broken finger as well. My preferred position was in the backline, but the captain made the call. The broken finger was the cause of four visits to a hospital in Dublin, a welcome break from college routine.

I had a good time in Maynooth save for a few crises regarding my ability to embrace the demands of the vocation—would I be able to take it on? The longer I was there, the more serious the doubts became. Every time any of my classmates would cut, the doubt would arise. I had a great spiritual advisor, Fr Jimmy Doherty, a Rosminian father and a rock of sense, and he calmed my doubts. He and the other spiritual directors were the unsung heroes. The first three years went smoothly enough, as I was doing a degree which would be a foundation for any career were I to change my mind. I shared a room with Seán Crowley, a fellow Cloyne student, who was also a Harty team player and a pal of mine. We both were of a carefree disposition and enjoyed a good laugh. No. 1 Rhetoric, the room we shared was right next to the famous 'ghost room'. No. 2 Rhetoric, and on the first night of occupation, we kept a vigil with our hurleys by our bedsides.

Later we realised that if the ghost were to appear, the hurleys would be to no avail. We never heard or saw anything unusual during our stay there.

The ghost room in Maynooth was well documented, and the seniors made absolutely sure we got all the gory details before we took up residence. The story goes that a young student in 1841 was found dead in his room in a pool of blood, still clutching a razor in his hand: death by suicide. The room remained vacant for seven years. (At that time students stayed in the same room for the duration of their seven years.) The same tragedy occurred to the next student who occupied the room on his first term, but he jumped out the window to his death. Again it remained empty for seven years. A student occupied it while sitting his matriculation examination and left it; he was later told of its tragic history and decided to go back there. This time the student, before shaving, looked in the mirror and saw a demonic figure which prompted him to cut his throat, which he proceeded to do. Desperate to save himself, he jumped out the window. He lived long enough to tell the tale to the vice president of the college, who ordered the room to be closed permanently and to be replaced with a shrine to St Joseph, but before that happened, a budding psychologist on the staff decided to carry out his own investigation. He decided to sleep in the room with plenty of support from his students on the outside. He didn't sleep very well, but he reported to his supporters that nothing unusual happened, to everyone's relief. He then went to shave himself, and as he raised the cut-throat razor to his face, he lost control of his hand as it kept pushing the razor into his throat. He had no control over his action and began to panic. He couldn't call for help, but he remembered some theories in psychology, such as how matter can absorb strong psychic power, and that where he was standing was such, so he had the presence of mind to move away from where he was standing and regain control. The story concludes with the postscript that his hair turned white within days.

There are many versions of the ghost room story, but this is the one we were given. There are still, to the present day, dark stains on the floor of the original ghost room which cannot be removed. It was the original pool of blood of the first suicide. A prominent paranormal researcher who visited the ghost room in 2011 recorded impressions of a four-legged creature which felt fear and a desire to run. He also found a strong presence around the statue.

There was another ghost in St Mary's, in the sleeping quarters of the fourth divines. It was the sound of footsteps without any presence, and it usually occurred during the weeks before ordination. Students would hear these footsteps on the corridor, and when they exited their rooms to see who was there, they couldn't see anybody.

I mentioned earlier that a 'flame' was a party with refreshments not normally permitted. St Patrick's Day was always observed with a flame, and chocolate was allowed. Seán had hidden a big bar of Cadbury's chocolate in his overcoat in the wardrobe for the big day. Sometimes he was tempted to pre-empt the occasion, especially on a Friday, but he lasted the duration. On the morning of St Patrick's Day, he went to the wardrobe for the contraband to find that a mouse had beaten him to the draw. Gratefully the mouse did leave his calling card, which exonerated me as a possible suspect. We had to laugh; here were young men excited about chocolate and biscuits, silly fellows. From then on we didn't flout the law; we merely justified the supplementation of an inadequate diet. Eventually, chocolate was legitimised and the appetite for it waned. Seán 'cut' and went to teacher training college, where he adopted a career in national teaching. We remained good friends, and whenever we met, we recalled our stay together in Maynooth and shared many a laugh.

There was another annual flame held after ordinations. After one of these flames, I woke up at five o'clock not feeling well, sopping with cold perspiration and a sharp pain in my stomach. Very soon I got an SOS for the nearest toilet and headed for Loftus, the main toilet in the college. I was surprised to discover that I wasn't the only one. The place was packed even though there were fifty cubicles. Not only that, but also there were candidates lining up outside occupied cubicles writhing in agony. I was lucky to get an empty cubicle to dispose of the food-poisoned excrement. Many were still waiting, and as the morning progressed, the toilet got busier. The illness struck one student as he was shaving. With half his face unshaved and a towel over his shoulder, he headed for Loftus to deposit his contribution. He found every cubicle occupied and booked except one. As he waited outside in deep distress, the occupant emitted a groan. He responded: 'I wish that were me.' The occupant replied: 'I do too. I was too late!' That was a very large dose of food poisoning that morning.

Loftus was built shortly before I arrived, and up to then, the toilets were outside, so it must have been horrific in cold weather. When Loftus was opened, one wag posted: 'And from a compulsory task, it has become a privilege and a joy.'

First divine year was the start of theology courses, and it was a new test of the vocation. The top button of the sou was superstitiously called the 'voco button', and if it broke or fell off, it was taken as a sign to reconsider one's call. Nobody took this seriously; nevertheless, they ensured it was well sewn.

'Faith is caught, not taught' was a motto we were familiar with, but faith needs solid evidence to survive. Philosophy and logic were ideal forerunners for this sequence, leading to natural theology, where we were introduced to causality and proofs for the existence of a supernatural being or creator who was not created.

Theology became my faith enhancer; the more I progressed in the courses, the stronger my faith became. Afterwards it was of great assistance when teaching religion. Most laypeople are familiar with the Ten Commandments; they mostly began with 'Thou shalt not'. God was instructing the Jews in plain language, as a parent would instruct a toddler not to put her finger into an electric outlet. The toddler would have no idea of the dangers of electric shock. Later as a student of science, one ascertains that it was good advice. Likewise, in theology and scripture, the commandments will affirm the faith of the student. Jesus condensed the ten to two, love of God and love of neighbour, and demonstrated through his life and on the cross the love which was the genesis of the commandments. They are not mere negative commands but initiatives for the attainment of love.

The Christian faith is generated from Judaism, and the study of the Old Testament is necessary to understand the New Testament. Sacred scripture is the gateway to understanding the faith. The history of the Jews, the chosen race, is illustrating God, as Father, instructing them in trust and loyalty, as a human father would instruct his children. The Christian religion thrives on research and history. Sometimes I hear people say that they don't believe anymore. They haven't explored their religious belief. There are none so blind as those who do not want to see. Faith is a gift given by God, but that doesn't mean we continue to live blindly. I thank God every day for my faith, and I pray for greater faith and the knowledge to strengthen it. There is nothing wrong with blind faith. Blessed are those who believe and have not seen.

My interaction with people is the lifeline of my faith. There are so many great people in our world that the media or world may not highlight who are an inspiration to me, ordinary people living extraordinary lives. There is so much love out there that it is palpable. As is expressed in 'The Ballad of Reading Gaol', I prefer to see the stars than to see the mud. I have been called to minister to all, but there are those who minister to me. This keeps me grounded. The best sermons are the lives of ordinary good people living out their faith; this is more powerful than any sermon. 'Let your light shine among men' is witnessed in the high-rise flats and in the houses and fields of the countryside. In my time in Wales there was this idea among Christians that if they didn't do any harm or injury to their neighbour, they were good people. An Irish Franciscan met that mild heresy head-on during a mission in the parish where I served. He cited it in a homily and continued: 'Neither does many a rat in the sewer; in fact, the rat helps the sewage to flow freely. But Christians will be judged by what good they did for their neighbour, rather than what harm they didn't.' He continued to stress the urgency to be proactive. Being compared to the rat in the sewer wasn't well-received by the congregation, and feathers were ruffled, but I knew the preacher had hit the nail on the head.

Another instance of such shock tactics occurred in London's West End. A very quiet Irish priest was shocked by the lack of response from his affluent congregation to an appeal for funds for flood victims in Bangladesh. He preached the shortest and probably most effective sermon of his life: 'What disgusts me about this congregation is that you don't give a s – – t about the people of Bangladesh. And now you are all shocked at the bad language I used, but you still don't give a s – – t about the people of Bangladesh.' Much truth is uttered in jest, and bad language, when used sparingly, can be very effective.

In 1960, my brother Pat, who was in America, sent me an 8mm cine camera. I was always interested in photography, having won a Brownie box camera which took the early photographs of my family and friends. It was in the house in Ballyshera for a long time, but ultimately it rusted away. My eldest brother, Tom, was getting married, and Pat wanted a movie of the wedding sent to him. I duly obliged and used the camera in Maynooth to film activities there. Two years later, the fledgling RTÉ decided to do a documentary on college life directed by Chloe Gibson. I was given the task of accommodating the TV team. Chloe Gibson was a most interesting person, and her observations of our habits fascinated me. The first thing she noticed was the rush hour for meditation and Mass, the speed of the students coming down the stone stairs at 6. 30 a.m. with soutanes lifted well above their feet and making the chapel in the nick of time. Another habit that she found interesting was the assembly for lunch, when 300 students would converge along the wide corridor, throw their books on the floor on each side, and proceed into the refectory. After lunch they emerged in groups and collected their books without a hitch. There was never a mishap.

I drew her attention to the umbrella culture in the college. Most students had an umbrella, and on rainy days those who had umbrellas would give the less fortunate a 'lift' (shade from the rain); there could be four or five under the one umbrella. You couldn't take the umbrella to lectures or the refectory, so you dropped your umbrella inside the corridor door, to be used on your way back. This is where trust was breached, because your umbrella may not be there when you need it. It's not stolen, merely borrowed. It will turn up sometime, somewhere, perhaps not within the term. An umbrella was never stolen in Maynooth; it was just borrowed on a long-term lease.

The finale of the documentary was ordination. The ceremony is quite long, and the cameras weren't rolling throughout, so my task was to alert Chloe and the crew not to miss the important parts. Most of the crew were on loan from the BBC to the fledgling RTÉ. When I signalled that the actual moment of ordination, the laying on of hands, was imminent, the chief cameraman, with us in the 'crow's nest', a gallery directly above the altar, talked in his intercom to all the others. 'Blimey, mates, let's have a bash,' he said, unaware of the solemnity of the moment. It caused me to give a wry smile, which puzzled Chloe. Later I explained the reason: the following year I would be ordained, and at that moment I would be a priest forever according to the Order of Melchizedek. It would be a little more than a bash! Parts of that documentary are constantly shown on RTÉ as file pictures, and I can identify myself in the footage.

In June 1963, the month and year of my ordination had arrived, and now my mind, after much reflection and indecision, was finally made up. I would be presenting myself for ordination; I would have the freedom to withdraw right up the moment of the laying on of hands. They say that the ghost of St Mary's was perhaps the footsteps of indecision from students in former years, having returned days before ordination. Thankfully, I never heard the footsteps.

A classmate of mine was bothered by human footsteps, which upset his sleep pattern. His room was on the middle floor, and he went to bed at 10 p.m. The student directly over him didn't turn in until 11 p.m. He wore big heavy boots, and he would throw the boots across the room before he went to bed. My classmate had to wait for this to happen before he could go to sleep. Finally, out of frustration, my classmate got the courage to inform his tormentor of his antisocial behaviour, who was unaware of its serious impact. He apologised and promised it would not happen anymore. That same night my classmate went to bed at the usual time. His tormentor turned in at the same, but he forgot himself and had thrown one boot across the room before he remembered his promise. He made amends, placed the second boot softly on the floor, and went to bed. He fell asleep but was awakened at 11. 30 p.m. by loud banging on his door. My classmate rushed in, shouting, 'Will you, for God's sake, drop the other boot!'

The whole class of seventy were ordained together, which limited the guest list for each student. I had seven siblings and their spouses, my mother, and three priests on my list. Pat came from America and filmed the occasion. We remained on to say our first Mass the following morning, and then we departed that day into the world to serve the people of God. I said my first Mass in Doneraile the next day and gave my first blessings to all my friends and neighbours.

Harry Kerr was a friend of mine with a mutual interest in music. I invited him to my first Mass. Because he was Church of Ireland, I made it clear that he didn't have to come to the church, but he was invited to the breakfast afterwards in Ballyshera. He was at the Mass and was first to the altar rails for Communion. He was a big powerful man and a rock-solid friend. I will always remember when my father died and the sympathisers shook hands with me as they went by, many uttering words of sympathy, Harry's handshake spoke volumes. I pray for him every day at Mass, together with a long list of other friends who are deceased.

All the activity of the day was recorded on film, and there in the middle, plain to be seen, is my beloved oak. My youngest sister, Lil, who was manager of the Intercontinental Hotel in Cork, and my mother organised the cuisine. There was an ordination cake which I cut just like a wedding cake. There were 100 guests at the breakfast. It was one benefit of having a Georgian house with its huge rooms to accommodate everyone. My first Mass on a Sunday was in a relief hospital for mildly mentally ill patients. I didn't have to preach, as on that Sunday a letter from the bishop was read instead, to my great relief. I was halfway through the letter when an inmate shouted, 'That's enough!' and walked out. I froze immediately and had a look around; there seemed to be no concern, so I proceeded with the rest of the letter and finished Mass. The matron came into the sacristy and apologised for not having warned me beforehand that the same inmate did the same thing at every Mass. She said that nobody (except me) took any notice.

CHAPTER 3

In September 1963, I was on my way to Cardiff in Wales to take up duty in my first parish, Llanrumney. It was a huge housing estate on the Newport side of Cardiff; it was a new parish with church hall and presbytery. Fr Neilus O Donnell, a fellow diocesan priest, was the curate there, and he helped enormously in my settling down. Double-decker buses passed by my bedroom regularly, causing the building to vibrate. The transition from a Georgian to a modern building took time—but acclimatisation and sheer exhaustion won out and sleeping became normal. I encountered my first culture shock on my first Sunday afternoon when I was asked to take Sunday school at 3 p.m. The All-Ireland hurling final was being played in Croke Park, and here was I in Sunday school. I'd never heard of the term, Sunday school; the idea that kids would come to school on a Sunday afternoon was totally contrary to what I was accustomed to in Ireland. People went to Mass on Sunday, and the rest of the day was spent in recreation events: hurling and football matches, golf, tennis, shooting, fishing, bowling, and every type of sport there was. The contrast between the observance of the Sabbath in Ireland and in the UK was immense. Later on I played golf one Sunday. There were so few on the course that, afraid of being recognised, I withdrew with a certain amount of guilt, even though I knew it wasn't wrong. Sunday was a black day in the UK. I remember a book being published entitled *Sunday, Bloody Sunday*. The English slept late on a Sunday, had rashers and eggs for breakfast, and washed the car. Sunday in Ireland was a fun day with no unnecessary servile work.

Tom, my eldest brother, had alerted me to an immigrant from Castlepook, a woman named Magnier who lived in Cardiff. I told him I'd do my best to locate her, but with the sparse information I'd gotten, I added that it would be 'a needle in a haystack' search. In my first week in Llanrumney, I went on a sick call. My parish priest, Fr Phil Dwyer, and Neilus were out, so I got on my bike. Luckily the house was only a short distance away. Once I arrived, I presented myself to the daughter of the sick woman. Knowing I was new in the parish and Irish, she told me her mother was Irish, saying also that her mother had suffered a mild heart attack and was fully conscious. I administered the last rites, and afterwards the ill woman asked me where I was from. I told her I was from a little place called Doneraile, County Cork. At that she lit up. She was the needle in the haystack. She had gone to school with my father. I spent a long time with her reminiscing the past. She claimed that I made her day, but she had no idea how much she'd made my day. It was an extraordinary coincidence. I had tears of joy welling in my eyes. This made an immense impact on my settling down—a little bit of home so near. The son of a North Cork farmer on the verge of Tiger Bay had cut his teeth in the ministry.

I mentioned already my apprehension about preaching. I didn't have a great voice, certainly not an oratorical one, but I practised my diction. And despite my Cork accent, the congregation understood me. I recall a story about a great actor and orator displaying his skill in a one-man show. At the end, an old man in the audience asked him to recite The Lord Is My Shepherd. The actor agreed on the condition that the old man would himself recite it after him. The old man agreed. The actor delivered the psalm with perfect diction and intonation in dramatic fashion. The audience applauded. The old man began his version in trepidation, but as he progressed he warmed to the task, delivering from the heart with his rural accent. The audience applauded louder and longer for him. In the final analysis, the audience were asked to identify the difference between the two, and the chairperson defined the outcome: the actor knew the psalm, whereas the old man knew the Shepherd! There is no need for the preacher to borrow others' sermons. Write your own, preach what you know, and believe and practise what you preach. Let the head do the writing and the heart do the preaching. I adopted Cardinal Newman's concept of a sermon while in Maynooth: keep it simple, in the people's language; take one point and develop it in full; use no gymnastics with multiple points; and provide a good start and a good finish. Newman was writing before TV and texting came into being.

The modern-day congregation is impatient, educated, critical, and discerning but still expectant of a stimulating homily, which facts make the preacher's task more difficult. The spoken word is still our main method of communication, and the story still attracts as much as it did in Christ's time. Most Irish and English people will be familiar with the comedy *Father Ted*. In one episode Fr Ted describes himself as 'great at saying Mass'. It's a pity that that phrase 'saying Mass' was accepted and used for centuries; from a priest's point of view it should be 'praying the Mass', for that, indeed, is the priest's function. The Mass itself is the most powerful prayer of the church, the essence of our faith, and nothing should deflect from its solemn celebration.

Sometimes it happens that the celebrant feels that his homily or trimmings are the highlight. Nothing is further from the truth; the celebrant can enhance the celebration with music and song and homily. If he were to pray the Mass, the need for these would be less. St Paul puts the priest's calling in his first letter to Timothy: 'Here is a saying that you can rely on and nobody should doubt: that Christ Jesus came into the world to save sinners; I myself am the greatest of them; and if mercy has been shown to me, it is because Jesus Christ meant me to be the greatest evidence of his inexhaustible patience for all other people who would later have to trust in him to come to eternal light.'

The duty to preach is clearly illustrated by Pope Leo the Great in *The Pastoral Rule*: 'For it is a fact that anyone entering the priesthood accepts the office of herald and must by his words prepare the way for the terrible judgment of the one who follows. If, then, the priest neglects his preaching, what sort of a warning cry does he, a dumb herald, give? That is why the Holy Spirit settled on the first religious leaders in the form of tongues: because those whom he fills he fills with his own eloquence.'

There are many stories of priests and their preoccupation with long sermons and ego trips in the pulpit. One such character who fancied himself as preacher was asked to preach the homily at a Jubilee Mass. He went into the church in solemn procession, with chest protruding and head held high. During his homily his notes fell from the ambo. Too proud to pick them up, he made a complete mess of the homily. On his way down the church, he lurched with his head bent low, humiliated by his failure, and as he passed, one woman whispered, 'If you came in the way you went out, you would go out the way you came in!' Another such individual on the morning of his first homily in his new parish had a bad shave and covered his face with little pieces of paper to stop the bleeding. He delivered four pages of foolscap. He asked the sacristan later how he'd fared, and the latter advised him, 'Cut down on the paper, and you will save your face.'

My favourite anecdote is about a bearded preacher who loved to see reactions to his sermons. One Sunday during his sermon he observed a woman in the congregation crying. He decided to meet her afterwards, at which time he asked her by what part, and why, she was so touched. 'Well, it's like this, Father. About five years ago, my husband died and left me nothing except an old goat. Didn't the old goat get up and die on me last week? And every time I looked up and saw you, oh, you so reminded me of the old goat!'

There was this curate who felt he couldn't preach, and he sought help from his PP (parish priest), who told him always to begin with an interesting story or experience. The PP then asked the curate what his sermon would be on the next Sunday. 'Marriage,' the curate replied despondently. The PP told him to introduce it with a light-hearted quip that he used himself: 'My dear brethren, I must confess to you today that I spent many happy years in the arms of a beautiful woman'—dramatic pause— 'my mother.' The curate decided to use this introduction for his next sermon: 'My dear brethren, the PP told me an interesting story the other day, how he spent many years in the hands of a beautiful woman—I forget now what her first name was.' And before he got to say anymore, the congregation were on the edge of their seats.

There's a tale of another curate consulting his PP on the inadequacy of his preaching. He claimed to the PP that his preaching was having no effect on the parishioners. The PP asked him if he put a lot preparation into his sermons. The curate told him that he normally began preparing his sermon on a Monday and finished on Tuesday. The PP chuckled and said, 'That's where you are making the mistake, as the devil knows what you are going to say and is a step ahead of you. Now when I stand up there on a Sunday morning, neither the devil nor I know what I'm going to say!'

I was cutting my teeth in Llanrumney with preaching and ministry. Not long after my first sick call came a second, and this time it was a midnight one to a hospital for recuperating patients which was two miles away in the country. The PP loaned me his car. I had been in the hospital that day, and the usual practice was to meet all the Roman Catholic patients and administer the last rites if necessary, so that we wouldn't have to go there at night. The call at night was very unusual. I administered the last sacraments to the young married woman with terminal cancer.

It was a public ward. I noticed visitors by the bed next to us and was puzzled, because it was late at night. The nurse met me and apologised about the omission and confusion about the dying young woman. She said it was the woman next to us with the visitors who wanted to talk to me. That woman was elderly and fully conscious and wanted to become a Catholic. Her daughter immediately objected; she didn't want any cleric praying over her mother. Her son then spoke up and said: 'If it's my mother's wish, then she should have her wish!' I was now in the middle of a family squabble. I excused myself and said I would return in the morning—timeout being a great healer, I figured. I spoke to the nurse again before I left and asked her to fill me in on the condition of the elderly woman. She told me that the doctors didn't expect her to live the night. This shocked me into a U-turn.

I went back to the elderly woman, who seemed very pleased at my return. The son and daughter had agreed that she should have her wish. We talked, and it emerged from her conversation that this was not a snap decision and that she had been considering it for a long time. I baptised her and gave her the last sacraments and promised to call the following morning. I called the following morning, and both patients were dead. It took a while to absorb what had happened, but after reflection, I was reminded me of the parable of the workers in the vineyard. Some were called in the morning, some were called during the day, and some were called at the last hour, but they all received the same pay.

My first funeral was for an infant. I was collected by limo and, with altar boys and thurible, was driven to the cemetery. We were met on arrival by the undertaker on his own. I didn't see a hearse or coffin, and was biding my time, when the undertaker asked if I was ready. I nodded, and to my surprise, he produced what looked like a boot box from under his overcoat. This, I figured, contained the little corpse. It was the pomp that preceded that seemed incongruous to the boot box.

My first wedding was a quiet affair. I was in the presbytery with the PP, and we both saw a woman in advanced pregnancy coming to the door. We both anticipated it was a future baptism booking. The PP answered the doorbell. After the woman left, he told me it was a wedding she had booked in a week's time. I was delegated to perform the wedding, which was private with no fuss and no confetti.

My first Mass in the parish was a Saturday evening Mass. I noticed when Mass ended that there was very little movement in the congregation and very few people left. Before I reached the sacristy door, these huge partitions began to close outside the altar rails. It was a church, and now it was a hall for bingo. The idea of a church hall finally registered in my head.

The sacrament of reconciliation

I have strong personal views on confession and how to behave as confessor. Since my first reading of the parable of the prodigal son, as a child in fourth class, which had a serious impact on my understanding of God as Father, and since my scriptural exploration of the parable's content in theology, I had a very clear idea of what a confessor's responsibility should be. While adhering to the canon law procedure, I found there was room for discretion and latitude. We heard a story in Maynooth about a missionary priest meeting a nun in the wilderness who needed confession. Worried about canon law, which obliged him to have a grille between them, he turned his bike upside down and heard her confession through the spokes of a wheel. Since then things have changed, but there's still need for a grille. (Canon 964 §2 still requires the grille: 'As far as the confessional is concerned, norms are to be issued by the Episcopal Conference, with the proviso however that confessionals, fitted with a fixed grille between the penitent and confessor always be available in an open place, so that the faithful who so wish may freely use them.') My canonical advocate, Mgr Maurice Dooley, in an article in *The Furrow*, advised that before a priest 'takes his saw to his traditional confessional, he might consider the disadvantages as well as the advantages of the face-to-face confessional room. It is a wise saying that you should never take down a fence (or a grille) until you know why it was put up!')

The penitential rite was reviewed and ameliorated and focused on the administration of the sacrament, making it easier for the penitent. Unfortunately, there was little effort to focus on the confessor's attitude. Open confession was always available in Ireland at house Masses or the 'Stations', so nothing was new when that was introduced. The theology in the past focused too much on the penitent's duties in confessing sin, with huge emphasis on mathematical accuracy, as recounted in the song 'The Croppy Boy': 'I cursed three times since last Easter Day, at Mass time once I went to play.'

The parable of the prodigal son describes the prodigal as being sorry for his debauchery and fornication and wanting to come back to his father with a prepared confession. He approached his father, who ran to meet him, and before he could finish his confession, his father ordered a celebration in response to his decision to return. Much theological discussion centres around a 'firm purpose of amendment' of the penitent. In this parable Christ is saying that the decision to come back is a decisive factor of the prodigal son's purpose of amendment, that is his sincerity to repent and be reconciled. When penitents come to confession to me as confessor, they will be considered as having purpose of amendment and a desire to change.

Compassion and reticence are requisites of a good confessor. Confession is not an easy task for the faithful, and we confessors should always be aware of their apprehension and put them at ease. We must be very patient and understanding with children's confessions, as a bad experience could have lifelong consequences for them. I remember watching Alfred Hitchcock's movie *I Confess* in 1954, which is about the 'seal' of confession and how a priest should be prepared to die rather than break the seal of secrecy of confession. As a young teenager, I found this gave me great confidence in confession, and when I was ordained, I willingly accepted this responsibility. Recent suggestions by child protection agencies that this seal be removed horrified me. In our world where nothing is safe with whistle-blowing and tribunals demanding highly personal information, some people now want the seal of confession (under pain of death to the accused priest) to be removed, while ironically, data protection laws are being strengthened. I am fully committed to the protection of children from abuse of all kinds, but within the law. (Mgr Dooley wrote in 1976 that it is not impossible that neurotic penitents might project their fantasies onto their confessors, and the confessor's best defence is one inch of mahogany between him and the penitent.) I prefer the 'one inch' of mahogany in the sacrament of reconciliation over the one-to-one form for the protection of confessor and penitent. I like rite 2, where confession is in the church as a community rite.

Visitation of homes was the biggest and most time-consuming duty for the curates. The aim was to visit all the families in the parish and take a census every year. I was given a visiting book which had been filled in by my predecessor. Each estate was entered with house number, family names, and details He had used a code word *caveat* for 'beware'; it could refer to anticlerical or violent tendencies. Visitation was interesting and rewarding, and I met many lovely people on my watch. There were one or two blips also. Only 5 per cent of the population was Roman Catholic. Mass attendance was 85 per cent. With 90 per cent of the population being Church of England, the church attendance was thirty people.

There were high-rise flats in the parish, and my experience of them was horrific. It was baffling that planners would approve of them as adequate and proper for human living. There was one thing sure: those who planned them never lived in them. A home should mean more than a roof and walls up in the sky. These flats were breeding pads for all that can go wrong in society, such as depression, antisocialism, psychosis, and neurosis. On one occasion I visited a flat (with a 'caveat' tag) in fear and trembling. A woman answered the door. She seemed very friendly and innocuous. After a while her teenage son came out of a bedroom. They both sat on a dilapidated couch and were amiable and chatty. The flat was in bad shape and had a musty stench, but I had seen worse. They spoke with a strong Welsh accent. I kept wondering what the caveat was about. I was about to leave when the husband arrived. He saw me, and then he looked all round the flat. Looking at me again, he said in a slow Dublin accent, 'There's a smell of s – – t here!' I felt the reference was to my presence. I could feel the adrenalin rising within me, wondering if this was a bad case of anticlericalism. I stood up. At six feet I would have a height advantage in the argument. The man came closer, looked at me again, and said, 'Isn't that right, Father?' I was dumbfounded and didn't answer right away. I started: 'Ah, well, it's not Buckingham Palace.' He interrupted: 'I've pleaded with my wife for years to clean up this place. Am I wrong?' Without another word, he then went over to the sink, put the kettle on, and proceeded to make his own tea. The woman never batted an eyelid and sat there all this time. I made the excuse that it was teatime and departed into the fresh outdoors, noting that things are never what they seem.

My first confirmation was only weeks into my ministry. A 12-year-old girl dying from leukaemia needed confirmation and the last sacraments. Only a bishop confirmed in Ireland, so this was all new to me. The girl's dignity, calmness, and courage made a deep impression on me. The sick room was alight with candles and had an aroma of perfume. Even though emaciated, the girl looked radiant dressed in her confirmation dress, like a cherub in the bed. I could sense great faith, hope, and love in the room. Her parents were naturally upset, and yet she smiled as I administered the sacraments. I think she could sense my shock (which was visible) and sense of inadequacy rather than her own impending death. She died two days later; it was my first time witnessing a young person dying. The picture of that room that day will always be part of my special memories. 'The child is father to the man' from William Wordsworth crossed my mind. This little girl could discern between my inadequacy as a human being and the power vested in me as a priest.

An important part of pastoral ministry is monthly visitation to the sick with Holy Communion. I had a lovely elderly couple on my list. The husband was from West Cork, and his wife was a Welsh convert. He was very deaf, and she would be the medium of communication. When it came to confession, she would shout: 'Any sins, Dad?' Canon law is very specific on the confidentiality of confession and especially on 'the seal'. This situation was very unusual to a raw tyro like me, but there was no alternative. He would say his piece, and she would help him. I was very taken by their relationship; they were in their nineties and madly in love. One day I called and found him sitting in the sun chair. I shouted at the top of my voice: 'Killing the time?' 'Nah, time is killing me,' he replied with a smile. The couple were still alive when I left the parish.

The birds and the bees lesson

A young couple arrived to arrange their wedding. She was pregnant, so instead of having them attend premarriage courses, the priest decided to instruct them individually. The man came first. During the instruction, he seemed hesitant and doubtful about the pregnancy. It emerged that the couple had not had intercourse, yet the medical tests proved positive and the woman displayed all the symptoms, including a swollen abdomen. The groom-to-be said something that caused me to doubt his responsibility for the pregnancy: they'd only kissed, and he never thought kissing could cause pregnancy. This was Cardiff in 1963. I had assumed the couple would be well informed on the birds and the bees.

I contacted the woman's doctor and informed him of the problem. He hospitalised the future bride for extensive tests, and lo and behold, the result was negative. It transpired that the bride had assumed that kissing could make her pregnant, and this belief led to 'phantom pregnancy' with all the symptoms of real pregnancy. I was dumbfounded, even though an old sheepdog bitch belonging to my brother portrayed symptoms of pregnancy and ultimately chose an old shoe as her phantom pup, protecting that shoe as if were her pup. I have never heard of phantom pregnancy since.

Catholic instruction

A soldier who had survived the two world wars wanted to become a Catholic, and during instructions he told me that he had faint memories from childhood of his mother with rosary beads in her hand. He was a child of a mixed marriage in Liverpool, and his mother died when he was 6. He needed assistance in investigating the possibility of his being baptised a Catholic. He gave the name of the district in Liverpool where he was born. I wrote to the archdiocesan offices with his name to see if anybody by that name had been baptised. I assumed it would be a needle in the haystack, and anyhow, he would get conditional baptism. I got a reply, and to my astonishment, he had been baptised—and a certificate was included with the letter to prove it. I nonchalantly gave him the news, and this tough-as-teak soldier broke down unashamedly. When he regained composure, he explained how important it was for him. During the wars he'd witnessed Irish soldiers clutching their rosary beads as they went to battle; he wished he could share their confidence. One day he borrowed a rosary beads and could sense the same confidence in himself. He always sensed that he had some power within him protecting him. Later he felt guilty because he felt he had feigned religion. Now he felt fully justified for what he'd done as he was a Catholic during all that time.

A nurse wanted instructions to become a Catholic, and during her sessions she revealed the thing that had so inspired her. While the nurse was on duty one night, a dying woman asked her for help. The woman could not face death and was extremely agitated. The nurse held her hand and calmed her down by telling her to close her eyes and look for bright lights and angels singing. As the nurse was doing this, she was reading another patient's medical records, and when she looked at the woman again she realised she was dead and wearing a beautiful smile on her face. It startled her because she didn't believe a word of what she had said to the woman.

Marriage counselling

A man arrived upset one day because he was having marital problems; his wife wasn't satisfied with their relationship. Judging by the evidence he presented, I found him to appear as a very good, loyal partner and an excellent provider, but dull in romantic affairs. I suggested to him to try to spruce up his and his wife's personal relationship with a fresh approach, rather out of my inability in marital affairs than knowledge in marriage counselling. Everybody has a streak of romance in them, and I thought this might work, as I ran short of solutions to his problem. I suggested buying flowers and socialising more. He objected and said it would be a waste of money. I couldn't offer anymore advice, and he left disgruntled. A couple of weeks later he returned with the good news that all was well again, after he had reluctantly followed my advice. It would be difficult to differentiate who was the most surprised; I was certainly taken aback at the outcome! I wasn't convinced that I was a miracle marriage counsellor.

Prison counselling

It was 1963. Sonny Liston was heavyweight world champion boxer. A man of similar stature called one day and needed my advice. He began by saying he had a problem: he had a wife and a child in Swansea, he had a girlfriend in London, and he had another, pregnant girlfriend in Cardiff: 'My problem is, I'm being charged with larceny,' he said. Needless to mention, there was no easy solution to his problem, and unfortunately, he left in the same condition as he arrived.

———

After a year I was moved to a new parish, St Brigid's, Crystal Glen, an affluent part of Cardiff. My new PP was Fr Brendan Morris from Omagh, County Tyrone. Our housekeeper was Sally O'Neill from Kildare. I enjoyed my stay in St Cadoc's, Llanrumney, my first parish, and was grateful for the experience of pastoral ministry and the friendships I took with me to St Brigid's. I wasn't long there when another marriage problem arrived. A Belgian man presented the problem that he'd been married and divorced six times and now had an Irish girlfriend and young daughter. He wanted to get married in the Catholic Church. This was definitely a first for me and for the PP. Firstly, he had to present the decree nisi for each divorce as proof of dissolution, and then I had to have letters of freedom from all his domiciles to ensure he wasn't married in the Catholic Church. Having obtained all this documentation, he then casually told me he had changed his surname. The whole process had to be repeated. When all the papers were completed, I sent them to the archbishop for approval. The man and his girlfriend were married in private; the church was locked with only me, the PP, Sally, and the wedding pair. The PP officiated, and Sally and I were the witnesses. It was a beautiful wedding for the couple. He had no children with his previous wives, and he had a little girl now, except she had a hole in the heart, which was serious then. He believed it was God punishing him for his past behaviour. I had assured him that God wasn't to blame and the future for his daughter's well-being would be in the hands of God and medicine. His new wife was a staunch believer and a big influence in his change of heart.

The penny press

The PP decided that a weekly bulletin with all the parish news would commence. I was made editor, my first venture into journalism. The bulletin had Mass times and other news but was a little piece of homemade stuff. Fr Tom Dunne, the PP in the next parish, had similar ideas. He was a good friend and golfing buddy of mine, and we used to joke about who would have the best 'scoop' in the penny press. We nicknamed it 'the penny press' because there was a charge of a penny for it. I stole a dance on him one week, not on the scoop, but on the readership. In my visitation rounds I called to the house of Julian S. Hodge, a huge financier. As we were talking in the room, I saw a copy of the penny press on the mantelpiece, and I drew his attention to it. He read it every week and complimented the author or authors for its content. Mr Hodge was a good Catholic and attended Mass regularly in his Anglia car, even though he had a Rolls also. He was also very generous to priests, and anytime he noticed us in restaurants, he would prepay our bill.

Sport

I always had a keen interest in all sports, and especially golf. We, the Irish priests, played golf on our day off, every Monday. Radyr Golf Course was our normal venue, but we moved 'on tour' to other courses. Two little instances come to mind from these outings in Radyr. Two high-ranking army men were sitting behind the first tee as we prepared to hit off, and Fr Stephen O'Mahony, a member of our group, was practising his swing when a divot flew from his club head and landed plumb on one of the forehead of one of the army men. There was an awkward silence while the man removed the clay from his forehead. He relieved the tense embarrassment with, 'It could be worse, old boy; it could have been a ball!' Greatly relieved, we all laughed. On another occasion, as I was putting on the last green, a white dove landed on my shoulder. For a moment I wondered if it was the Holy Spirit or just a normal 'birdie'. It was neither the Holy Spirit nor the birdie, which I'd duly missed; it had just escaped from a house nearby, and the owner came shortly afterwards to collect it.

Horse racing was another of my sport interests. I persuaded four of our group and a layman, Jim, well known to us all, to go to Chepstow Races. We travelled in Neilus O'Donnell's black Volkswagen, fondly known as 'the black Beetle of Llanrumney' (Volkswagens were rare in England so soon after the war, and everywhere Neilus's car went, admiration followed). One steeplechase is etched clearly in my mind. I can only remember the name of one runner, Dick Whittington, and the reason why is easily understood: all five of us had him backed to win. We stood between the last fence and the stands viewing the progress of the race. Most of the runners had fallen, and only three survived. Dick Whittington was way ahead, heightening our anticipation of a winning wager, when, at the last fence, he didn't just fall but went spectacularly head over heels, causing Jim to exclaim a list of expletives. Realising his embarrassment, Jim ducked out of sight, leaving the four of us white-collared clergy with red faces, taking the blame in the full gaze of a scandalised crowd.

When I was living in Wales, rugby was never far from the news. The Welsh loved their rugby, and international matches were big events. I attended some of these in Cardiff Arms Park. I was friendly with the O'Donovan family, and Paul got me a ticket to the Welsh–Irish match. We walked the short distance to the pitch, and the atmosphere was electric. Inside the stadium we could hear 'Bread of Heaven' sung in four-part harmony by the crowd; the Welsh were brilliant singers and not afraid to display song and harmony at any event. They excelled at big rugby internationals, which inspired their own team and intimidated the opposition. They were the victors on that day, but we had our revenge the next year. The rite of Benediction was so different from the Irish version. In Wales, if you had 15 people present, you had a four-part choir, whereas in Ireland, if you had 100 people, you sang on your own.

Mother pays a visit

My mother decided to come to St Brigid's at the kind invitation of Fr Brendan. She flew from Cork to Bristol and then on to Cardiff. She had no fear of flying, having been to visit Pat in America. Aer Lingus flew the Cardiff route with a twin-engine DC-4 (a prop jet), and before one trip home at Christmas, Cardiff Airport and Wales were covered in snow. I rang to find out if the flight was to go ahead. There was no snow in Cork, and the flight would go ahead as scheduled, so my PP drove me, or rather we skidded our way to the airport. I boarded. Only seven others made it to the airport. The pilot didn't use the intercom but just pulled back the curtain (just a curtain separated the cockpit from the passengers) and addressed us: 'Welcome aboard, you brave ones. Cork is clear for landing, so if we get out of here, we will have no problem.' I don't know how the other passengers interpreted his statement, but I was worried about the 'if' clause. However, we made it safely.

After her stay in St Brigid's, I drove Mother to the airport and bade my adieu. Halfway to Cork, the plane lost power in one engine. A state of emergency was declared at Cork airport, where Tom was waiting to collect our mother. The flight was half an hour overdue in what was a one-hour flight; nerves were frayed on the flight and at the airport. Tom was nervous but pretended not to be. He was next to the girlfriend of a passenger on the plane and asked her if she had insurance, telling her that his mother was on the flight too, saying that he had her insured and wasn't too worried. The woman didn't know whether to laugh or cry, and before she could decide which, the plane came into view to all their relief. Tom didn't tell the worried girlfriend that he had spotted the plane before he made the infamous insurance gibe. Later, a passenger whom I knew who was on that flight told me that he was sitting next to my mother, who identified herself to him, and said that when the pilot announced the bad news about the failed engine, the crew gave out extra food and refreshments. My mother chose ham sandwiches, while he, being a good Catholic, took cheese sandwiches because it was Friday. (It would have been a mortal sin to eat meat on a Friday in 1964.) I laughed heartily when he told me the story, which confused him even more, because I knew Mother never ate meat on a Friday. She must have been very scared and confused to have done so. I explained the mistake, adding that surely she wasn't fully aware of her actions. I used to laugh and tease her about the awful scandal she caused on the plane.

We all teased her on another occasion when she greeted the local curate at the back door with 'Get out, you whore.' The local curate was on his way in as the thieving whore of a dog was on his way out with stolen bread. *Whore* and *feck* were he only 'bad' words Mother used. She was always looking for some 'fecking thing' which she left in some 'quare' place. My father used *whore* in a different way. If he called anyone a 'whore's ghost', then that was as bad as it could get. My grandfather sometimes uttered the same expression and used it one day in the presence of Canon Sheehan, the famous author and parish priest of Doneraile. The revered canon told him that the phrase sounded bad but meant very little. My grandfather provided the canon with the material for his novel *Glenanaar*, in which Nora Curtain is the heroine. She was born in the existing ruins where my great-grandfather lived; Glenanaar is a townland situated a few hundred metres from the present ruin.

———

My stay in Cardiff was coming to an end, and even though I was returning home to Ireland, I was sad about leaving so many friends and acquaintances.

I am grateful for the valuable experience I gained in pastoral ministry. The parishes where I served presented me with tokens of their gratitude which I still have today, and they also left me fond memories. I had read *My New Curate*, another novel by Canon Sheehan, in which he describes the priest leaving the parish with all his bits and pieces, including a goat which thieved the parishioners' gardens of cabbage and other vegetables, and yet the parishioners found a tear for the said goat despite his faults and those of their pastor.

For the priest, leaving a parish is like pulling a plant from the soil and severing the roots that were established in pastoral care and human ties. Priests too have flesh and blood while ministering to the spiritual needs of the faithful they serve, and they form friendships with their parishioners. The interaction between priest and people is mutually beneficial in the growth of a Christian community, and this is temporarily suspended when one leaves, but it is resumed and ameliorated by the coming of another. In one way the priest, in his interaction with people, is privileged to meet the cream of society, the beautiful people of this world, and also those on the margin who are as beautiful but less fortunate. And these yield valuable relationships. The unique trust of people in their pastors dates back to Christ and his apostles and must be maintained and fortified from generation to generation. I placed great emphasis on trust in my pastoral experience.

On one summer holiday while I was a student in Maynooth, my sister Tess asked me to tend to a flock of chickens in deep litter which she was preparing for the food market. They were permanently locked indoors and fed morning and evening; my job was to release the food pellets at these times. On my first visit, I noticed one chicken not eating and detached from the rest, so I moved towards her to see any signs of injury or sickness. I noticed that she was unaware of my movement; she was blind. When I lifted her, I discovered she was only skin and feathers. What could I do for a blind chicken in the midst of 200 healthy ones? Pull her neck? Pity won out, and I decided to take her out. I got an old used bean tin and filled it with mash and put her head into it. It didn't work at first, but to my surprise, after a few attempts, she ate it all. I put her back into the house and repeated the same method in the evening. One morning I forgot the old bean tin. When I left her out I had nothing to put the mash in, so I decided to go back down the yard for the tin. To my astonishment she followed me down, staying very close to the wall and then walking through the yard to the coach house, where I found the tin. I now realised this blind chicken had formed a trusting bond with me. When she finished her food, she would perch on my shoe and cackle her gratitude. Some of my siblings were suggesting to play games like hiding, or keeping silent to see if she could find me, but I refused in case it would damage the trust and bond I and the chicken had.

I went back to Maynooth in September. By then, Tess had taken on the task of feeding 'Chicky'. Ever since, I've known how to establish bonds with humans and animals. Trust is the vital variable in both cases, and breach of trust is not easily repaired. Say what you mean and mean what you say. Animals know when you hurt them accidentally, say, by stepping on their toes; humans vary in their responses and are less forgiving.

CHAPTER 4

Ireland beckoned. I bought a car, a banger, a green Anglia, UBO 380, which I thought would be more than adequate to transport my belongings to the ferry in Fishguard and, from there, across the Irish Sea to Rosslare. My first appointment was a temporary posting to Mourneabbey for a month. I baptised a child while there and saw my uncle's name entered in the baptism register forty-six years previously. Having spent my period in Mourneabbey, I was moved in November 1965 to Blarney parish, where I resided in a hotel as temporary priest to the parish. The financial arrangements were£200 to the hotel for my upkeep per annum for full board and lodging, which included a bedroom and a sitting room with a fire, and a personal salary of £300. Dr Forrest was my host and proprietor. It was an idyllic situation. After Mass I got my breakfast in the kitchen, hot porridge and cream and whatever else I needed. The other meals were brought to my sitting room by Catherine and Joan, and they looked after the fire as well. Fr Tom Corcoran was my acting PP, as Canon P. Sheehan was on sick relief. Fr John O'Shea was the other curate residing in Whitechurch.

Blarney was only twenty miles from Ballyshera, and yet I had never kissed the Blarney Stone. The castle and stone were straight across from the hotel, and there was no excuse for not kissing it. Pa Byrne was the man who helped me to bend backwards and downwards to kiss the famous stone. After the ordeal, Pa drolly said, 'I suppose now we won't be able to shut you up next Sunday, Father.' I loved to go into the castle grounds and read my office. The green pasture, the grazing sheep, and the gentle sound of the nearby stream was the perfect backdrop for 'The Lord Is My Shepherd'.

Trees of every variety formed a magnificent background to the castle and its famous stone. Blarney was a small village then with the woollen mills being one of the few industries. Many tourists passed through it on their way to Killarney, leaving the village unaffected, enabling it to retain its old world character and charm.

The people were witty and warm. I settled in the parish very easily. There were great characters there, like Bacchus, called after the Roman god of wine, and Amber, who will figure in a few stories. One of the stories I was told was that Amber spent some time every day on top of the castle, viewing the tourists kissing the stone, and on one particular day a woman tourist was in deep distress because of her psychological inability to kiss the stone. When she saw what she would have to do, she couldn't overcome her fear. She had travelled 5,000 miles to kiss it, and now she couldn't. Pa allayed her concern by suggesting that if she kissed somebody who kissed the stone, the effect would be the same. She approached Amber and asked him if he had kissed the stone, to which he replied, 'No, ma'am, but I sat on it.'

One night on my way into the hotel, I saw Amber in the toilet urinal, and after five minutes, on my way out, he was still there. I shouted at him, 'Are you all right, Amber?' 'Yerrah, I am, Father, but I can't stop.' Judging by the slurred reply, I gathered he was well inebriated, so I thought that I should alert him to the broken water pipe which was dripping noisily, in case he was playing by hearing rather than sight. On my way back in, after a few minutes, he was gone. Problem solved.

Muskerry Golf Course was only a five-minute drive away, so I joined. Most of the members were from Cork city and were very welcoming. I usually played in the four-balls on a Saturday afternoon. On one Sunday evening I decided to play a few holes, and when I arrived, Timmy McElligot, the professional, asked me to join two visitors for a few holes. The two were Jack Lynch, Minister of Government, later to become Taoiseach, and Denis Law of Manchester United. The World Cup had finished shortly before that, and Denis was describing the skill of the great Pelé who excelled for Brazil. Jack Lynch could play left-handed and right-handed, and he carried a couple of both types of clubs in his bag.

Blarney was surrounded by wooded glens with mature trees, and even though it was only a ten-minute drive from the city centre of Cork, it was a peaceful country village, unaffected by the tourist throngs that visited the castle and famous stone. Major Hilliard, the owner at the time, invited me into his adjoining residence to see his Irish wolfhounds. They were truly beautiful dogs, so graceful as they trotted around the grounds. The house itself was a magnificent limestone building. I took my trusty cine camera with me to record the sights. I also filmed the tree-lined glens in the middle of May with their forty shades of green.

Card playing was another social pastime which the local clergy engaged in during the long winter nights. Two of these games had unusual outcomes which stuck in my memory. Fr Jerry Ahern, a local PP, invited Fr Tom Corcoran and me to a pre-Christmas dinner and a game of cards. His brother, Bishop John Ahern, was there, as were six other priests. I was the junior one, so I kept a very low profile. And I was a pioneer (teetotaller) without any source of Dutch courage. The 45 card game began by casting knaves for partners. I was cast with Tom. After having played five games, we found the spoils were evenly divided, so the last game, the rubber, would decide the richest pairing. The fee was a half-crown (about €4). I was the dealer and turned the jack of diamonds as trump. When the play came to me, with the king of diamonds winning, I robbed the jack and took my trick with the ace. I had four trumps including the jack and joker, so I pondered my next move, decided what to lead with. During this pause, Tom was making positive noises towards me to lead, which our opponents interpreted as prompting and strongly objected to, but I figured the best play was to lead the jack, which I did. It survived, and I led again with the ace, and it survived. And again with the queen, and it survived. Finally I led with the queen of spades, but it was immediately beaten by the king, to the relief of our opponents. When it came to Tom, he produced the five of diamonds, the best trump, to win the game. Consternation followed, with our opponents suggesting that Tom had cheated and the game should be declared void. Tom maintained that he had not cheated and that he was just clearing his throat. The argument continued for some time with Tom maintaining that he'd said nothing to me, that he was only clearing his throat, when the bishop intervened, offering Tom a drink to help him 'clear his conscience'. Tom reminded the bishop that his conscience was clear and refused the drink. Eventually, Tom's persistence about his innocence prevailed, and our opponents reluctantly produced the half-crown fee. Then Tom dramatically interrupted in a solemn tone: 'Sorry, now, but it's doubles for jinks.' And the whole argument erupted again. It was never serious, just tongue-in-cheek—a lot of tongue and a little cheek!

Tom always drove his black Volkswagen to the card games. One night after a game in Cloghroe, as we drove home on a very frosty night, we both thought we heard a cat meowing in the car. Tom kept driving, while I searched the car for a cat with no success. Tom doubted his sobriety while I doubted my sanity. The following morning I called on Tom at his house, as previously arranged, to celebrate a Station Mass, and when Tom opened his garage door, he was greeted by a very confused cat which dashed into the shrubbery. And that's when the penny dropped: the cat must have been under the car, availing of a little warmth on a frosty night, when we drove off. It had created a puzzle for us while enduring its midnight nightmare to Blarney.

Tom was a real gentleman with a great sense of humour, which made my stay in Blarney blissful. He was a shrewd mentor and well versed in human nature. One day in my room I was listening to one of a certain type of tourist who frequented Blarney and every other presbytery in Ireland, 'a knight of the road' (con artist), spinning out his tale of woe: he was an English Protestant wanted by the Gardai (Irish police) for crimes he didn't commit. He had a very convincing story. He said that he knew he could trust a priest. He also knew that being a Protestant at a time in Ireland and England when ecumenism was gathering momentum would put a Catholic priest in a predicament. He was very convincing. But his request to get a ticket for the Innisfallen, the daily ferry service between Cork and Fishguard, which cost £30, a large piece of my annual income, stalled my charity from responding when. As if it had been arranged. Tom knocked on my door and said he wanted to talk to me for a minute in private. In that minute, Tom explained his plan to help my visitor. He invited my visitor to join us in his Volkswagen and assured him he had the ideal solution to his desperate situation. He drove straight to the residence of the Protestant bishop of Cork and told my visitor that he would receive refuge and sanctuary there. My visitor, whether he believed Tom or not, knew he had been outfoxed and got out of the car. I thought it was a bit harsh at first, but Tom assured me the visitor was a conman. Two weeks later we met Fr Scriven, a Sacred Heart priest, who told us the story that we were so familiar with now, saying he had donated the price for a ticket for the Innisfallen ferry to our visitor and, on the following morning, nearly tripped over his drunken beneficiary on Lapp's Quay. Tom chuckled and winked at me, as in, *I told you so.*

Tom was great with visiting the sick. He took me frequently to the hospitals in Cork. On one of these visits to the mental hospital on the Lee road, we were waiting in a long corridor for our parishioner patient to be located, when an inmate came helter-skelter down the corridor like a witch on a broom and stopped in front of us. Tom whispered out of the side of his mouth, 'She's mad,' not realising where we were. A nurse appeared and, with a gentle but firm command, ordered the woman away, and the latter took flight again. It would be funny but for the sadness of a human mind gone slightly awry. These mildly insane patients and special needs people are beautifully described by the Gaelic term 'duine le Dia', meaning a person very close to God.

Tom decided to bring the aged canon to a funeral. As is customary, we went ahead of the funeral cortège in the black Volkswagen to Dunbullogue cemetery. While waiting for the hearse to arrive, we heard the last post being sounded on the trumpet at the funeral of a soldier inside the cemetery. The canon, who'd been dozing, was alarmed when it woke him, and Tom had to explain the phenomenon wafting in our direction. We surmised the poor canon must have thought it was Armageddon. He didn't live long after that, and my term in Blarney came to an end. I headed down the road, with all my possessions in the car, to my new posting as chaplain in De La Salle College, Avondhu, Mallow.

De La Salle was a secondary boarding school for young aspirants to the order of teaching brothers, and my duty was to say daily Mass and hear confessions. My salary jumped to £380 per annum, and I had my own house within the grounds. The house was in bad repair, reeking with dry rot, but the kitchen, one bedroom, and sitting room were habitable. That was more than I could furnish with my two suitcases. The brothers very kindly had a bed ready for me, and one of them said he might call back later as I settled in for my first night in this new abode. I still had my hurley stick with me, and I figured that this would be my last line of defence should I be invaded by thieves. I managed a smile at imagining their disappointment, if it did occur, and was dozing off when I heard footsteps coming up the stairs. Assuming it was the brother, I shouted, 'I'm fine, Brother. See you at seven in the morning, DV.' I got no reply. Curious to know the reason, I went to investigate. Having searched all the rooms upstairs, I found nobody. I thought, perhaps, the hurley may be needed. And in case of a ghost, I got the holy water ready. I went back to bed rather restless and was not looking forward to a sleepless night when I heard the footsteps going down the stairs. With the adrenaline pumping overtime, I leapt out of bed and, with hurley in hand, rushed to the staircase, where there was nobody in sight. But my hearing solved the mystery. There was a house next door, semidetached, and the people next door were going up and down their stairs; the houses were divided down the middle of the stairway by a thin partition. I breathed a sigh of relief and felt embarrassed at my overactive imagination. I had a good sleep that night, but the second night had another surprise. Unafraid of night raiders, I went to sleep the second night like a baby, only to be awakened by the sound of mild thunder shaking the house; it sounded like a running, panicking crowd of people. I got up and went to the window, from which I saw a bunch of cattle stampeding out of my garden. I was grateful for a natural explanation but still puzzled by what could have caused the fright and flight. All became clear the following morning, when I saw the upturned beehives belonging to my predecessor in the garden. Those cattle had good reason to run.

The dry rot eventually won the battle of occupation, and I had to leave and reside in the college. The brothers decided to build a new house adjacent to the Church of the Resurrection, which was under construction. I moved into that house in 1969, and my mother decided to housekeep for me. She brought some furniture with her from Ballyshera, and Tess made the curtains and other items to help to feather the very bare nest. I enjoyed my term in the college and had plenty of exercise on the playing pitch and in their fine handball alley.

The boys were from all parts of the country, and the school was excellently run, way ahead of its time. I enjoyed the meals with the brothers who were specially chosen for the juniorate college and were excellent teachers. When I moved into the new house, the parish priest, Mgr Richard Ronan, asked me to become an assistant curate in the parish and teach religion in the technical school to supplement my salary. I was paid by the hour by the Education Authority. It was a well-toted adage at the time that a chaplain was the lowest rank of the clerical ladder, so my transition to assistant curate was a petty promotion, but a promotion nevertheless. Mallow was an expanding town, and a second church was needed to accommodate Mass goers in the south side of the parish.

At the opening of the new Church of the Resurrection, Mgr Ronan said in his address that history was being made, as it was a first time for a church and clergy in the south side. I very delicately reminded him afterwards that such may not have been the case, referring to a short story called 'Remanded' by Canon Sheehan, in which he describes the betrayal of a priest, Fr Duane, by the mistress of the captain of the yeomen. The mistress was to testify that the priest was a member of the Whiteboys, an illegal organisation and forerunner of the IRA, but on the eve of the trial, she drowned herself in the Bullworks (a popular swimming place in the Blackwater), still clutching the blood money she'd received for her false testimony. This occurred in the early nineteenth century when victims of suicide were refused burial in consecrated ground, and parishioners wanted her remains buried elsewhere, but the priest insisted on breaking into the cemetery and burying her there with the help of his friends. When the captain, who was ill in bed, heard of the tragedy, he refused to believe that his mistress was dead. He ordered the body to be exhumed and brought to his sickbed for identification. He requested a few minutes on his own with the corpse, and this was granted, but after one minute the yeomen waiting outside heard a shot. And when they returned, they discovered he had taken his own life by a shot to the head. The legend emanated from this act that the bloodstains on the ceiling could never be eliminated, echoing shades of Maynooth's ghost room.

Sandfield House, the residence of the captain, was where this occurred. It was a ruin about 100 yards in front of the bungalow where I lived. Mgr Ronan wasn't convinced and shrugged off the authenticity of the story by claiming, 'Sheehan was a writer, not a historian.' Canon Sheehan was a native of Mallow and may have collected traditions and stories for his writings. He was a thorough researcher. Evidence of this can be seen in his history of the PPs of Doneraile, which still takes pride of place in the sacristy of Doneraile Church.

I was the youngest priest in Mallow, which had three curates and two assistant curates. I soon got embroiled in many organisations, becoming chairman of local Red Cross branch, chaplain to the Pioneer Total Abstinence Association, and chaplain to the Boy Scouts. And I produced dramas for the Marian Players. There was no suitable hall or premises for a youth club or for community concerts, so instead of asking the parishioners for premises for each organisation, we amalgamated into one committee for fundraising. The fruits of this joint approach rendered a huge community hall with annexes for the Red Cross, the Boy Scouts, and Meals on Wheels for the senior citizens. I enjoyed every moment of my ministry in Mallow, making many lifelong friends, too many to mention them all. Everyone was kind and cooperative to me and my mother. It suited my mother very well, as she was very near the church for her daily prayers, and she could exercise her culinary art looking after me.

There were four other housekeepers who formed a card school and chat school with her, and my siblings and their families called regularly, so my mother had plenty of company. My grand-nephews and grand-nieces stayed with us for holiday breaks, and my brother Pat came every year in November from the United States for the pheasant shooting. I had two dogs, an Irish red setter called Grouse and a cocker spaniel called Prince, and my mother loved those dogs. Fr Séamus Corkery lived next door; he was a senior curate, and we both ministered in the Church of the Resurrection while I was chaplain at De La Salle as well. There were a lot of young boys and girls calling, and these would be eager to get any messages from the supermarket for my mother.

One of these became a regular caller, and I felt she had a more interest in me than in shopping for my mother. (In fact she later became the most hostile of all the complainants who levelled accusations against me. She appears in the Cloyne report under the pseudonym Donelle. I shall return to her later to recount all the trouble she caused me.) It all started after she called with a Mass card on a Saturday evening, and the following Sunday morning I said the early Mass in St Mary's, the church in the town centre, and she was at it. Her usual Mass would be the 10 a.m. Mass in the Church of the Resurrection, which was only a hundred-yard walk from her house. This aroused my suspicion, which was confirmed in the following weeks, that she might have a schoolgirl crush on me. She called regularly over the next few weeks with Mass cards and messages for the Red Cross. I discouraged her by advising her to concentrate on her studies. She only called when I was at home, and I wondered how she knew. One day I met her mother and referred to her daughter's calling, and her mother informed me that she could see my car from her bedroom window. I began to park my car outside my garage door, and her visits ceased for a while, only to resume later. I confronted her again on her unnecessary visits, but she continued calling on the pretence that she was shopping for my mother. I was uneasy with her undue attention and was exploring a remedy when the opportunity arose: the bishop and the president of St Colman's, College, Fermoy, asked me to pursue further studies in University College, Dublin, in counselling and career guidance, with a view to taking a post in St Colman's College, Fermoy. I thought about it long and hard. The pact I had made on my departure from said school not to return as a teacher was about to be broken, but not without the guarantee that my term would end after twelve years, and with the promise that I would not be involved in discipline, which would hamper the role of counsellor. The conditions were agreed, and I was relieved because I was due to be moved, and now I knew my destination. Also, I would be free of my uncomfortable position with uninvited visits from my smitten caller.

CHAPTER 5

Back to school

In April 1971 I was destined for Dublin for a year's diploma course, believing I had made the right choice, as professional counselling would be very helpful in my pastoral ministry once I left St Colman's. I spent a lot of time commuting to Dublin in preparation for the course, which commenced in September. From then on I stayed in a religious house in Rathgar. The course was new and groundbreaking in that it was established by and run by the Department of Psychology under the aegis of Revd Dr Feichín O'Doherty, a professor, with strong emphasis on the psychology of adolescents. We studied general psychology, child psychology, and the art of counselling. We interviewed drug addicts in a Dublin hospital. Dr Jim Chamberlain was the director of studies, and students were assessed individually on their performance as interviewers. There were written examination papers at the end of the course. I received my diploma in July and waited to start work in St Colman's on 1 September 1972. The president of St Colman's notified me that because of lack of accommodation in the college, I would have to commute from my base in Mallow to Fermoy.

Fr Dónal Leahy replaced me in Mallow, and he invited my mother to stay on as housekeeper, as there were three bedrooms in the house. However, my presence in the house was very limited due to the fact that I was studying for my H. Dip. Ed. in Mary Immaculate College, Limerick, working a full school day in St Colman's, and also teaching one class in St Mary's Convent in Charleville for teaching assessment. I graduated in

1973, and given the time-consuming effort in establishing a career's library in 1973-74, I remained a lodger in Mallow.

There was a complete change for me in weekend activity; I was used to working weekends as a curate, and now I was free at weekends like other teachers. Nevertheless, I offered to say Mass in the parish. There was no obligation that I do so, but I wanted to stay in touch with my pastoral ministry.

My golf handicap was 9 in 1971, and by 1976 it had dropped to 4 because I could play regularly at weekends. Fr Leo Trace, a spiritual writer, once stated that if a priest could only shoot over 80, he was neglecting his golf, and if he could shoot under 80, he was neglecting his parish. Well, I had no parish to neglect, so I played golf. When I resumed pastoral duty in 1986, my golf steadily declined. I am grateful for the experience of meeting so many people and forging lifelong friendships. There is nothing more refreshing than a game of golf after a tough day at the office, to tread the green turf and fill the lungs with refreshing oxygen and wonder at the beauty of nature, so different from the dull wallpaper of an enclosed room, which prompted Oscar Wilde on his deathbed to utter, 'One of us must go.' I will continue to play for therapeutic reasons until time will beckon and not count the shots, as an old friend, Walter Bennet, used to say, 'Counting the shots spoils the game.' Old golfers never die; they just simply lose their drive. They say the game is played in heaven.

There is tell of this famous four-ball in heaven consisting of Bobby Jones, Moses, Jesus, and an old man. They come to a par 3hole measuring 200 yards, pitched on a tiny plateau surrounded by water and brush. Moses is the first to strike, and he hits a fat shot destined for the water. When he outstretches his hand and splits the water, the ball rebounds off the bottom and bounces onto the green four feet from the pin. Bobby Jones is next up and hits a beauty landing three feet from the pin. Jesus then hits an excellent shot, but a strong gale suddenly blows with Satan's initials on it. Jesus raises his hand and calms the wind, and the ball ends up two feet from the pin. Lastly, the old man hits off. Barely able to lift the club, he half hits the ball, and it dribbles down off the tee, where a crow picks it up and flies away with it. Then the crow is ambushed by an eagle over the green, causing the ball to fall into the hole. Moses and Bobby Jones are dumbfounded, but Jesus turns around and says to the old man, 'Nice shot, Father.'

St Peter is fascinated with golf as well, as another tale from heaven will confirm: A young man goes for golf lessons, and the advice the professional gives him is to practise with a driver and wedge. He hit a drive 300yards at a par 5, but unfortunately the ball ends up behind a tree. He then uses the wedge to get over the tree, but he catches it thin and the ball hits the tree, rebounds, and hits him a fatal blow on the head. He arrives at the Pearly Gates and meets St Peter, and the first thing St Peter asks him, because he saw in his CV that the man played golf, is 'How far can you hit the ball?' And the young man replies: 'Oh, I don't know, but I got here with a drive and a wedge.'

Fr Dónal Leahy played golf as well. He also played the guitar and had a lovely singing voice. He was very kind to my mother, and she liked him, so we lived in harmony until he was moved. Fr David Herlihy replaced him in 1976. Dave was fresh out of college and stood 6feet, 5 inches tall, a gentle giant with a beautiful tenor voice and a great sense of humour. I was standing on a chair one day, hanging the curtains in the sitting room, when Dave arrived and helped me without the aid of chair. It was then that I realised how tall he was and the extent of his reach. On another occasion he used this reach to great effect for a bit of fun at a carnival in the town park. The stand where you got six wooden hoops to test your skill at casting them around prizes about eight feet away was supervised by a nice, quiet woman. I bought six hoops and gave them to Dave, knowing that with his reach he could literally drop the hoops on top of the prizes. Dave reluctantly agreed. While the woman was not looking, he dropped the hoops over the six prizes. We were both wearing Roman collars. I drew the woman's attention to the prizes Dave had won, and she was flabbergasted, telling us that it was the first time it had ever happened. And then it was time for open confession. Dave demonstrated how he had achieved the feat. There was no cheating, but he refused to take the prizes. However, the woman insisted we take one each as a souvenir in appreciation for the bit of fun. Dave played golf as well, and we had many games together.

My mother's arthritis was worsening, and she was hobbling around the house with a stick. One day she fell and broke her hip, ending up in a hospital in Cork, where they inserted a plate into her femur. She had a further operation to stop internal bleeding and was recovering. She suffered a pulmonary thrombosis and died the very morning she was to come home. It wasn't unexpected, but it was a hammer blow when it did happen. She had great faith and had had it tested during her young life. Her two teenage brothers, both clerical students, and her teenage sister were buried within the space of three years. The family of two surviving men, her, and her parents would pray after Sunday Mass at the graveside just outside the church in Ballhooley. On one particular cold, wet Sunday, the local curate advised my mother and her family to go home and pray there, because her children were not in the grave, only their mortal remains were. They took his advice. My mother never visited my father's grave after he died, but she never failed to pray for him and all her relatives and friends everyday of her life. Her prayer books were bulging with mortuary cards which she thumbed through every day. She tended to her younger brother Francy before he died from cancer; she tended to my father in his long illness; and her wish was to be taken quickly, which was granted.

There were occasions when her simple, strong faith surfaced, such as when I arrived back in 1977 from the All-Ireland colleges hurling final and she casually said, 'Ye won.' She hadn't heard the news on radio, so I asked how she knew. She told me she was in the church and, after praying, sensed her prayers were answered. On another occasion, my nieces Deirdre and Maura were staying with us, and Deirdre lost the key to the house, which troubled my mother. She left the three of us playing cards to pray in the church to St Anthony; she returned home later and sat in her favourite armchair, watching us at the cards. After Deirdre won a game, she jumped for joy, and the key fell out of the fold of her jeans. Deirdre was very relieved. She shouted the news to my mother, who coolly said, 'You can thank St Anthony,' feeling fully confident her prayer had been answered.

I have strong faith but not that type of strength. I would hope rather than believe my prayers will be answered, and I constantly pray to try to achieve a stronger faith. In my ministry I have met people of strong faith, like my mother, and I always ensure to ask for their prayers. If you can't draw water from the well yourself, beseech those who can. And that is why I'm still a priest surviving the ordeals and trials of spurious allegations. The title *In the Shadow of the Most High* is from Psalm 91, which describes God's rescue in face of trials and persecutions. In my case, the ordinary people whom I've served have rescued me by their prayers, so that in the height of desperation and trepidation, and in the surreal nightmare I was living, I felt airborne and euphoric, secure in God's hands, like being on eagle's wings. He protected me from the results of 'undue process' and still protects me from having the executioner's sword ultimately falling on my head.

Looking back over my whole life, I believe the predestination and realisation of God's plan, as I recount near-fatal accidents. I was catapulted out of my pram and uninjured, I was nearly drowned twice, I fell on my head from a ten-foot wall, I was concussed by the stroke of a hurley, I had a tractor accident, I had numerous escapes in the car, I survived one bad car crash without a scratch, I was shot accidentally twice, I had several falls with my arthritic hips, I had false and unfounded allegations thrown at me, I was tried twice in the criminal courts and found innocent, and I was tried by my beloved church's canonical tribunal in the face of zero evidence and found guilty and threatened with removal from the clerical state, but I'm still a priest according to the Order of Melchizedek, 'in the shelter of the Most High'. It has been an extraordinary life for just an ordinary country boy, but survival was ensured with God on my side in the comforting presence of my guardian angel. Sometimes, I could sense the angelic aura around me, like when I was in the dock on trial and very ill in bed.

I got very ill in 1989, a recurrence of hepatitis A, which I previously contacted, and which confined me to bed. It took six weeks to recover, and when I did, my recovery didn't last long. The symptoms I suffered were similar to those of ME (myalgic encephalomyelitis, or chronic fatigue syndrome). One of these was fatigue; little tasks took a major effort. Some mornings during Mass I thought I would never finish. When I urinated I had to sit on the toilet, the ultimate insult to the once athlete who had never witnessed fatigue. Fatigue is totally different from tiredness; you go to bed with fatigue and get up with fatigue, whereas you go to bed tired and you get up fresh. Fatigue feels like the physical body cannot recharge energy like a tired body can, so the patient is stuck in this circle of endless periods of inertia. I fought it off with elixirs and large doses of protein to help the body to recover, and then I might get a year respite, but I always dreaded the first signs of a relapse. My GPs, Dr Barry Condon and Dr Cormac Lyons, were very understanding of my condition, but there was no known cure. However, they took great care of me and were available at all times. Cormac insisted I take antidepressants, which was a wise move. To this day he is still my medical rock and friend.

I spent Christmas in hospital. I attended many medical consultants, but they found nothing wrong with my body, which raised a question about my mental state, but I can assure them now that I still suffer from ME, although not as bad. And my mental state despite the plethora of false allegations, is still stable, thanks to God, Cormac, and Barry. I also want to thank Patricia Murphy (Pat), my trusty housekeeper and friend, who looked after me in those dark days of sickness. Pat helped me to move to my present abode and patiently bore my faults and failings for ten years. I also want to thank my sister-in-law Lil for the times she nursed me back to health in her home in Sycamore.

There were periods in my sickness when I thought I would never return to normal living again, but my family and friends helped enormously in the return to near normal life and to them, I am most grateful. I can do most things now, but I must keep a constant watch on my energy levels. Since my forced retirement in 1995, I have improved in health thanks to having found ASEA, which I take daily, along with other supplements to my diet regimen. The fact that I can stop and rest when I feel my energy low is also beneficial and nips the fatigue in the bud. When the energy is low, the brain slows down, making it difficult to find words for the crosswords which I love completing. On good days I would spend less time completing my puzzles, and on bad days I would have to rely on the dictionary too much, so gradually I have acquired a system of control. Gardening helps immensely, and the fruits of the earth are a joy to eat. I am enjoying my retirement in the maelstrom of stress and humiliation created by the church I love and worked for. As St Paul wrote to the Corinthians: 'Not that it makes the slightest difference to me whether you or any human tribunal, find me worthy or not, I will not pass judgement on myself. True, my conscience does not reproach me at all, but that does not prove I am acquitted; the Lord alone is my judge.' Since my forced retirement, my celebration of the Mass and Eucharist in private has become more prayerful; I don't have to say Mass for stipends, so I have more freedom to offer it for the whole church and for my family and friends, which was the purpose of my ordination. I have ample time for private prayer and thanksgiving and to contemplate the immense privilege of my vocation as agent of God's salvation to his people.

While I was in St Colman's, I taught religion, and on one occasion a bright young boy asked a question: 'What, or why, is there need for church and priests, because Christ saved us all on the cross? Why not cut out the middleman and go straight to the Boss?' When you get questions like that, you have to use simple and similar language in answering, so I found the simile between the oil well and the motor car useful: What good is an oil well in Africa if I want petrol for my car? I can't go to Africa, and if I could, I would still have to refine the crude oil for my car. So all the oil in the world is no good to me for my car; the oil needs to be refined and distributed through petrol stations to my car. Christ died on the cross to win favour and grace for us with his Father, but he also left the apostles and the sacraments as the dispensers of that grace. The apostles appointed priests to help them, so we all depend on priests to deliver Christ's salvation. No priest, no Eucharist; no priest, no penance. Both priests and laypeople need the church. That is the way Christ established his Kingdom on earth.

The role a priest fulfils both comforts and terrifies me, a sinful man taken from sinful people, appointed by God to intervene on their behalf, a mediator between God and humankind, ordained to celebrate the Eucharist. God knows I'm not a saint, and still he called me to this august office. I heard a humble colleague say once that he could do things that the most powerful leaders and scientists of the world could not: he could say Mass.

There is no retirement from this office, there are no union laws, and it is forever. Shortly after I was forced to retire, a friend of mine, Tim Mullane, requested that I minister to his terminally ill daughter, Jenny. The Mullane family lived between Kanturk and Newmarket, and I had the pleasure of calling to their home in happier times, enjoying the home baking and banter of a very happy family. It started when Jenny was working in the Vintage Pub, only a few houses down from where I lived, and where I usually went for my daily lunch, so I got to know her well. She was a light-hearted, bubbly teenager, only 17, when she was diagnosed with cancer. The family were very upset. Because the prognosis wasn't good, they wanted Masses said for her recovery. She lost her womb, and for a young girl this news was devastating. She recovered after months and returned to the Vintage; I was as shocked as the family were at the tragedy of a lovely young girl almost losing her life and being deprived of the opportunity to have a family of her own someday. Jenny never lost her bubbly personality and was undaunted by her illness. A few years later, I officiated at her wedding to Dónal. It was a very joyous occasion for her and both families. When she introduced me to Dónal, I knew straightaway that he was the right man for her. I remember saying at the wedding how she was giving me my dinner every day before he ever met her and that he would never be hungry again while she was around. Not long after the wedding they adopted a little Romanian girl, Amy, and soon afterwards they adopted her little brother, Timmy. The family had a lovely house in Newmarket, where I visited them. Jenny and Dónal did everything for those kids, including a trip to Disneyland, and transformed their house into a happy home. Sadly it wasn't to last, as the cancer returned with terminal consequences. That's when Tim contacted me to express Jenny's wish to see me. I cleared my intrusion into Newmarket with her PP, Fr Anthony Cronin, and tended to her spiritual needs.

I would say she did more for me than I could ever do for her; she still had the bubbly personality and was very calm and brave in the face of death, planning her funeral. Only days before she died, she got rid of all the tubes and went to the church for Timmy' first confession. She joked to me afterwards how everybody thought they were seeing a ghost. She decided to have Mass in the house only days before she died with all her family present—siblings, spouses, and children—totalling forty or more, all of whom were in tears except her, who smiled as if it was her wedding Mass and not her last Mass. I had brought her Holy Communion during her last few days, and afterwards she would sit on the couch and discuss her funeral plans. She had arranged that her kids, Amy and Timmy, would not spend the full time in the funeral home during her removal; it wouldn't be right to have them endure the trauma. On the penultimate morning she stayed in bed, and when I took the pyx containing the Holy Communion out of my pocket, my favourite rosary beads came with it. After Communion, she commented on the beautiful beads, a present I'd received years previously, and I just said casually that if she would like, she could take them with her. She nodded her delight. I added that she might present them to Our Lady when she got to heaven, and she promised she would. I realised it was selfish of me, but I believed I was privileged to witness a living saint! I attended Jenny's funeral, which was so sad for Dónal, Amy, Timmy, and the Mullanes, but for me it was the celebration of the birth of a saint who would put in a good word for my wretched self in the kingdom of heaven, I pray to her and for her every day.

A couple of years later my sister Mary died of cancer too, and she also was very brave and dignified in her last days. She spoke to each of us individually of her impending death and was calm and content. Her husband, Joe, had died six years previous. We used to go on holiday together to Spain or Lanzarote for a week. We usually stayed in a B & B and would search out the local restaurants for our evening meals. Mary loved her wine, and each night she would sample the house wine before ordering a glass. One night she was sampling the wine with the waiter in attendance, and suddenly her face contorted in discomfort as she spat the wine out, leaving the waiter dumbfounded. With the reaction of both of them at once, I was in uncontrollable convulsions. The poor waiter's worst nightmare was realised as he stood there motionless and speechless; Mary's worst nightmare was realised as she signalled to me to taste the wine. I was very embarrassed at my uncontrollable burst of laughter that I muttered, 'Perhaps there was a mistake.' It transpired that the rejected and ejected wine was vinegar; the cork had shrunk and let the air in. The waiter returned with a new bottle. I couldn't look him in the face, because by now the poor guy must have been peppering in his shoes and wishing he could make amends. While Mary lifted the glass very gingerly to her lips, and I was holding my breath, until she nodded approval. The head waiter came over to us, apologised for the mishap, and very generously offered us the meal for free. I laughed all that night, and so did Mary when I recounted the poor waiter's reaction. I jokingly suggested that she should repeat the same reaction in the next restaurant and get another free dinner!

Two nights before Mary died, my nephew, Michael, Tess, Pat, and I were chatting with her in her bedroom, and she, as if in a casual conversation, told Michael that she would have very good tips for next year's Cheltenham Racing Festival. Joe and she had racehorses, and when Joe died she gave them to Michael. I excused myself to go to the restaurant for something to eat, and on my way out Mary said, 'Be careful of the wine!' I don't think the others really understood the humour, but to me it was astonishing, knowing that she would be dead within hours. She died, and a part of me died with her. She was my older sister who practised her maternal concern for her youngest brother, always looking out for me. She had begun work in Cork while I was still in St Colman's, and whenever we played hurling matches in Cork, she would meet me and treat me to a meal, which was very much appreciated, to supplement my meagre diet. And she would add £1 to boot for pocket money. These were big acts of kindness and love which forged a strong bond between us. She was great fun and an extrovert and loved a bit of adventure, but she was very nervous behind the steering wheel. Pat taught her to drive, though only for a while. One day when he was giving her a lesson, as they approached a pedestrian with a loose dog, he warned her to be ready to stop if the dog decided to cross the road. As the car approached from behind, he shouted to stop because he thought the dog was going to cross the road, and instead of stepping on the brake pedal, she hit the accelerator, with the result that the car shot past the dog and man like a rocket, as in the cartoons. Pat said later, 'The pedestrian felt wind and heard the noise but saw nothing, she went past them at such speed.' That was the end of Pat's tuition; he said he was too young to die. Mary displayed some of the boss's genes in her driving endeavours. She was his first daughter, and Pat said she was his pet, so he used her to gain favours from the boss.

Ballyshera was a Georgian building with large rooms and windows, which created natural air conditioning in the summer and deepfreeze in the winter. There were three bedrooms in the front. The first was shared by my father, my mother, and the youngest, Lil. The second was the girls' room, and the third was our room. The girls would sometimes have one of their friends staying for holidays in their room. Our room was next to theirs, and their window was about twelve feet from ours but could be easily reached with the help of a fishing rod. We would give them time to go to sleep and then suspend a gruesome face mask from the rod, extend it over to their window, and give a few loud bangs on it until we heard a scream. Then it was time to retrieve and conceal the mask and feign sleep before all hell broke loose. Soon the boss would be out on the landing. We could hear him muttering, 'Which one of ye had the nightmare now?'

That gaffe could not be repeated, but other ones followed. One time a wounded curlew was placed in the room before bedtime, and we boys were waiting for the reaction when the girls discovered this long-beaked bird, but there was no reaction. Disappointed, we drifted off to sleep, only to be awakened in the early hours by more than an expected loud reaction. The curlew must have gone under the bed and stayed there until all was quiet before moving and terrorising the girls. That was not passed as a nightmare. Our plot went badly awry, as the boss was not amused. He gave us the warning threat of sharing sleep with the cows if there was a repeat. All 'hostilities' ceased immediately.

As the sisters left the nest to go out to work in the world, Ger and I were promoted to their room, and then a different game commenced between him and the boss. Mother was the alarm clock and alerted the boss to 6. 30 a.m. cow time; the boss would shout out to Ger to rise and shine, and of course I was directly in the line of fire. I would awake immediately to the call. I still don't know how Ger could answer in his sleep, 'I'm up.' There wouldn't be a stir about him. Silence would follow for about ten minutes before the second shout: 'Is that whore up yet?' This would reawaken me, and the shout would be accompanied by the boss rattling his walking stick on the floor, feigning he was coming to check. Ger would reply again, 'I'm up,' and rattle his boots on the floor to counter the boss's pretence. At the last call Ger would be on his feet and up, rather than suffer the indignity of being pulled out of his bed by the boss. The whole pantomime might last twenty minutes. This game went on for ages, until one morning, at the first call, a chorus of voices joined with the boss's: 'Ger, will you, for God's sake, get up and let us all get a few winks of sleep?' Democracy won out in the end—and all in good fun.

The boss, very shrewd, was seldom fooled, except on one occasion: Pat was a great socialiser and went to dances every week. The dances in the 1950s lasted until 2 or 3 a.m., and on this particular morning, after being at a dance, Pat was sneaking up the stairs at six o'clock when the boss appeared on the landing above him. Pat, seeing him first, turned to go down the stairs. The boss said, 'You are up early this morning,' not noticing Pat's good clothes. Pat went for the cows and milked them in his Sunday best.

Mike Morrissey was part of the family and was privy to seeing interested suitors come and go, but he would never whistle-blow on us. Pat told us that after a 'good few drinks', he was coming up the avenue very early one morning on his bike and tumbled over Mike, who was lying prone on the avenue after a good few drinks. They ended up on top of each other and staggered all the way up to the house. At breakfast the following morning, Pat said to Mike, 'You were in great form last night, Mike,' and Mike denied everything. It wasn't a plain lie, just a broad mental reservation— no tales out of school. His room was at the end the annex, and the maids' rooms were next to his.

I can't remember any resident maid in those rooms, which remained vacant. The middle of those rooms had a reputation of being haunted. The previous owner had taken his own life there in 1860, and suicide at that time was shrouded in mystery. He was building a ten-foot wall around the orchard, and the project ceased at his death, leaving the wall incomplete. The jagged edge of the unfinished wall is still there, never touched. Mother told us that when Tom and Jim were born, she employed a nanny to help her; the nanny left after a few months. The same happened with the second nanny. And when the third nanny gave her notice of leaving, she asked her what was wrong and why was she leaving. The nanny told Mother that there was nothing wrong with her or the work, but she couldn't sleep in the room. Mother got the local curate to say Mass in the room and bless it. She got another nanny. That one stayed five years and was very happy in the room.

It was a beautiful room directly over the kitchen, making it the warmest room in the house until the old range in the kitchen was replaced by one with a back burner to produce hot water. At that point, Mike moved to the middle room while his room was fitted with the hot water cylinder, making that room the warmest in the house. Mike never moved back and finished his days there. I liked the cylinder room during the Christmas holidays but reverted to the air-conditioned room during the summer.

CHAPTER 6

St Colman's College

The change to St Colman's College was timely and life-changing. My work now would be Monday to Friday from 9 a.m. to 4 p.m. It didn't always work out like that; a qualified priest counsellor was a rare entity in the early 1970s, and soon the Mallow and local parishioners were making appointments for personal counselling. It was a free service which attracted many who could not access or afford other services. It kept me in touch with pastoral life and helped to fulfil my call to serve others for which I was ordained. I didn't agree with the cynic who said, 'We were told that we were put here to love others, but what I want to know is, what are these others doing?' Later, when I was interviewed by the Dublin Commission of Enquiry, the presiding judges could not understand the free service offered to people. The legal profession are not known for free or even cheap service.

I never wanted money as remuneration for services rendered, cognisant of what Jesus advised: 'You have freely received, give freely in return.' Ironically, the free service was ultimately the cause of my downfall, as will become clear once we progress towards my forced resignation. I enjoyed my work in St Colman's, and the constant interaction between my adolescent clientele kept me young at heart. All the fear of parents and elders about adolescent irresponsibility and rebellion disappears when youth are separated from their peers and in a one-to-one situation. They knew they could trust me, and I trusted them and ensured that their trust would not be broken. There were plentiful vocations to the priesthood, which was very encouraging.

Some of my extracurricular duties entailed the management of the tuck shop, assisting in hurling coaching, and managing the concert hall. I believed in delegating responsibility to the students and acted in a supervisory way, and they responded to their duties. Sometimes they would be only second-years. One particular afternoon there were rehearsals in the hall, and the young boy who had responsibility for collecting the microphones called on me at my office for the microphones. I warned him jokingly to have those same microphones on my desk when I arrived in the morning or I would take his life! He was a day boy and lived two miles away. I arrived the following morning to find the microphones on my desk in a neat bundle and was happy with his performance. Minutes later I heard news of his accidental and tragic death; he was hit and killed by a car as he was crossing the road to get his school bus. A few hours later I called at his house to sympathise with his parents. His remains were laid out in his bedroom. I will never forget the heart-rending experience of his parents sitting alongside, numb and inconsolable. I felt so helpless and couldn't respond in a meaningful way. I could only let go of my pent-up sorrow in tears and shake their hands. I went back to the college to visit the boy's classmates, who were in tears. They must have seen my red eyes. Together we went to the chapel and celebrated Mass for him and his family. The death of a peer at that age had traumatic effects on his classmates; it gelled them into a closer and more compassionate group.

On another occasion I delivered Intermediate Certificate results to the parents and family of another boy who was killed in a tractor accident during the summer holidays. I could feel their pain, but all I could do was to stay with them in their anguish; words are inadequate in those situations.

There were very happy times too, such as when we won the All-Ireland colleges final in 1977. Such a victory generates great morale for the student body and lasts for a long time. Then there was the night Dennis Taylor won the World Snooker Championship from Steve Davis. I was watching from my room, which was across from the recreation hall where the boys were watching it; the fact that there were so many watching and cheering made it seem like being in the actual arena. The same atmosphere would pervade during the Cheltenham Festival. Fermoy and North Cork had a huge interest in horse racing, and many great horses like Cottage Rake, Denman, and Monty's Pass were bred and trained in the area. Coolmore had a stud farm in Grange, and Liam Cashman had some of the leading stallions in National Hunt racing in Rathbarry Stud. Cheltenham was a special time in St Colman's. I have already referred to the steeple of the Church of Ireland in Doneraile as the origin of the first steeplechase, and the St Leger's were the sponsors of the oldest flat race, the St Leger. The biggest horse fair in Ireland and Europe was held at Cahirmee, where Napoleon's famous charger, Marengo, was purchased.

I resided in Mallow until 1984, when I moved into the college, where I stayed until 1986. The night shift in Mallow consisted of receiving callers and clients of both genders and all ages, some of whom were school goers visiting the priest of the parish. About seven of these became clients of mine after the curate left in 1983, four of whom were teenagers who later made allegations of sexual abuse against me in the first decade of the new millennium. I will address the allegations and their lack of substance in future chapters. Apart from those, I met hundreds of people and formed friendships that still last.

There were times when I let people down because I didn't hear their cries for help, something which bothers me to this day. One Saturday night I went to bed at 11.30. The house was a bungalow, and my bedroom was in the front. I went to bed and tried to sleep despite the constant banging of a car door outside on the road. I got up again and alerted my priest housemate. Agreeing there was something unusual about it, we decided to investigate. I went out and walked past the car, which was all steamed up. I could see nothing because of the fogged windows, but I heard groaning. We rang the Gardai (police) and informed them of our concern. They arrived within minutes. All the car doors were locked, so the Gardai broke a window to gain access and discovered a young man in critical condition. They informed us when we arrived at the car that the young man was still conscious and recognised my voice. It was then that I recognised him as one of my callers; he had shot himself at close range in the car, and with the aid of a pillow had silenced the gun report, which was the reason we didn't hear the shot. He had consumed a lot of alcohol and couldn't be sedated, which complicated remedial surgery, and it ended in his death.

This young man had been calling on me and talking about general things and also about the break-up of a relationship. He had hinted, saying, 'I will do it,' but he never specified what he was going to do. That was the mistake I made: I should have explored what was on his mind and what he intended to do. He might still be alive today if I had detected his intention. I didn't know him that well before he arrived the first time, but he told me that I had visited his primary school a few times.

Later I encouraged my colleagues to visit schools and get to know the kids. The risk assessor in his risk assessment of me after the allegations were lodged labelled this as 'grooming'. Has the pendulum swung out of control in the protection of children, with common sense having been abandoned? Every priest who visits primary schools could now be accused of 'grooming' according to that risk assessor.

That experience of missing the cue in the sad death of the young man intensified my efforts to be more watchful for similar cues in future. One Saturday while I was the races in Mallow, I got an SOS from the secretary to report home immediately. As I drove home, I kept wondering what could have happened. When I arrived at the house, my fear got worse. I saw my mother's shoe at the open door and rushed into the sitting room, where my mother was sitting on her chair. Bridget, the housekeeper from next door, was there too. Both of them were smiling. I was told that my mother had answered the door, and as she opened it, a young man collapsed on top of her, causing her to fall. He was unconscious, and my mother crawled to the phone and rang Bridget next door, who came to her assistance and rang for an ambulance. I arrived when the whole episode had ended. Seeing all was well with my mother, I joined in their obvious relief.

The same young man had arrived on a previous occasion with slashed wrists, and I rushed him to hospital. I also went to see him in the hospital after his second suicide attempt, and I was told he had taken an overdose. I was called to a bad accident outside the hospital a year later. It involved a car driver intent to commit suicide who ran into a truck and was killed, but a passenger in the back seat of the car escaped unscathed. It was the young man of two previous attempts, who told me that he had thumbed a lift at Two Pot House, where he was picked up by the driver, who told him he was going to crash into the first truck they would meet. At that, he thought that if he went into the back seat and lay prone, he would have a chance of surviving. I pleaded with him not to make any more attempts as his guardian angel was working overtime!

I was sound asleep on a Saturday night when the doorbell rang. I stuck my head out the window and could see a man at the door. I asked him what he wanted, and he said he was very upset and wanted to talk. At first I thought he was on drugs and reminded him of the time, 1 a.m., but I gave him the benefit of the doubt and let him in. He was from Dublin and camping in the park with his brother. Earlier that night he'd been with a girl, but his brother had double-crossed him and stole his girl. They had a very serious row over the girl, and he decided to walk out of the park. He was so upset that he walked onto the parapet of the bridge and contemplated jumping in. The Church of the Resurrection caught his eye, and he decided to get off the bridge and head in that direction. Seeing it was closed, he headed to the nearest house, hoping it was the priest's house. I put on the kettle, and we had tea and chatted for a while. He had calmed down by now, so I told him I would drive him over to the park and try to locate his brother. We found his brother alone in the tent, in a very upset state, guilty and wondering where his sibling was. The two of them had a happy reunion. I was glad I read the score right on that night.

When people call late at night, they usually need help. Of course there are exceptions, like the knights of the road wanting lodgings or money, but that is a rare occurrence. Quite a few of them are regular callers looking for money to feed their drink problem, and others are hoping to subsidise their homelessness. I treated them all the same with a small subscription. If I were to give a large sum, they would be back for more.

A parishioner told me that as she was getting supper one night, a knight called looking for a slice of bread and butter. She shooed him off saying she was busy. Her husband, hearing her, said that the knight could be St Joseph in disguise. She gave him the man bread and butter and returned and said to her husband, 'Your St Joseph wants jam on it now!'

One of my regular knights called three times in one week, and I gave out to him, pleading, 'Do you think I am the Bank of Ireland?' to which he replied: 'Sure, I might be the cause of getting you into heaven.' He was a character and had a middle-class background, but alcohol had taken control of his life. He knew my schedule of commuting to Fermoy every weekday morning and would be waiting outside the house for a lift. He told me a story of theft and treason one morning: He had gone to his favourite pub in Fermoy one night and found it closed, so he went to the back entrance to find it open, but there was no one inside. He couldn't believe his luck when he found bottles of vodka, whiskey, and gin, which he pocketed, along with a considerable amount of loose change from the till. He headed for Cork and met up with one of his fellow knights, and they drank themselves to sleep. When he woke up in the morning, his 'friend' had gone with the money and booze. I said, 'What a miserable ungrateful wretch,' but he replied, laughing, 'No! The Gardai pinned the Fermoy robbery on him.' My caller had a tragic end in Leitrim in a fire accident and was only identified by his teeth.

Another frequent caller, Rodney, had a tragic past, having lost his entire family in the Aberfan disaster in Wales in 1966. He left Wales and got a job in Tara mines, where he worked for many years. He met his fiancée there, who died shortly after their marriage. This loss tipped the scale for Rodney, and he took to the road, ending up in Fermoy and surrounding area. He was always very pleasant and would have a joke or funny story to tell. I lost contact when I moved out of Fermoy, but I heard he passed away. The lifespan of knights is short because of their lifestyle and the effects of alcohol on their health. I had sympathy for them, even though, being a teetotaller, I could understand the grip the demon alcohol can have on a victim. I joined the AA group in Mallow, at their invitation, and learned a lot about alcoholism and its addiction. I had great admiration for the members who were so honest and brave in revealing their experiences of their addiction and struggle to 'dry out'. They were some of the finest and kindest people one could meet. If a person with a drink problem called on me looking for help, I would recommend AA, knowing the help and advice and support such person would receive. I also had a friend from my golfing days, John O'Riordan, who was excellent in one-to-one consultation, if a person preferred that style of assistance. John was selfless, compassionate, and tireless in his work with addicts and did extraordinary work regularly and discreetly. When he died, I was deprived of both a friend and fellow counsellor.

An unusual caller was the 12-year-old son of settled travellers and was attending school. He was happy with a tanner (sixpence), and I encouraged him to do well in school. This day he called looking for a half-crown (which is five times sixpence), and I asked what he wanted it for. He told me he was going to the pictures with his school friends and that he would never bother me again if I gave him the half-crown. I was sceptical of his promise, but I believed his story and forked out the half-crown. That boy kept his promise and never came back for money again. When I arrived in Buttevant, I learned that it is part of the travellers' culture to treat promises very seriously.

The annual Cahirmee Horse Fair is held in Buttevant every twelfth of July, and it was the meeting place for Irish travellers, who came in their throngs. The men folk would call and ask to be 'lifted', which bamboozled me the first time, until I discovered the request was that they be lifted from the solemn pledge they had taken not to drink alcohol. They honoured that pledge and wanted it lifted during the fair day, and for them only a priest could do the lifting.

Buttevant

I left St Colman's College in 1986 and took up residence in Buttevant. The year 1985 was very wet, the wetness culminating in a huge flood in August. It was also the year of the 'moving statues'. Public grottos with statues of Our Lady were drawing big crowds to witness them moving. One such grotto was in a small community in Ballinspittle near Kinsale in County Cork. My sisters Mary and Tess were down from Dublin, and together with Tom we decided to pay a visit. Tom's daughters, Liz and Bernie, had already been there and saw the statue move. Tom was very sceptical and questioned his teenagers' objectivity. We arrived at Ballinspittle in very heavy traffic around 6. 30 p.m. on a beautiful August evening. It was reported that twenty thousand people had gathered on 15 August 1985 to witness the statue moving. We were stunned at the number of people from many parts of Ireland gathered in front of the statue. Nearby fields were used as car parks. There must have been a few thousand people there. I brought my binoculars to get a close-up of the statue.

We stayed together and prayed the rosary and sang hymns, but mostly it was quiet, and we only whispered to each other. I spent a lot of the time looking through the binoculars to see what may be causing the phenomenon, should it shake, which I doubted very much. A man behind me asked if he could have the binoculars for a few minutes to analyse the background of the statue. When he returned them, he told me he was a psychologist from County Carlow and was trying to find natural explanations for the 'shaking'. He thought it could be caused by staring too long at the statue, and I agreed. I asked my sisters if they noticed anything. They hadn't. We were there for at least an hour, and then I thought I saw movement. I didn't panic. I decided to look away and then look back again, and once I did, the statue was shaking. I rubbed my eyes and looked through the binoculars, and the statue was rocking. I looked away again and looked back, and I thought the statue of Our Lady would fall off the pedestal, it was rocking so much. I then got a tap on the shoulder from my psychologist friend for a loan of the binoculars. He was telling me at the same time that he had seen the statue shaking violently. It shook for a long time and then stopped as mysteriously as it had started. Neither of us got excited. We wondered what caused it, as we certainly hadn't expected it, but we were left to ponder on.

On our way home, I and my family members stopped at a pub at the request of Tom (doubting Thomas), who was very quiet up to that point. He ordered a double whiskey for himself while we had minerals. After one whiskey he announced solemnly that he had seen the statue moving. It was clear he was in shock. I told him that I had seen it moving also, and that calmed him a little bit. The two girls saw no movement and were disappointed.

I arrived in Buttevant in late September 1986. The curate's house was between the PP's house and an old castle, Lombard's Castle, belonging to an Italian family who settled there as wine importers and wool exporters. Buttevant had as many priests as people in the thirteenth century. Ballybeg (small town) Abbey was established by the Augustinians in 1229, and the oldest and only columbarium (pigeon house) still stands there near the ruins of the monastery. The Franciscans established another big friary in 1251 in the middle of the town, and the ruins are still there behind the church. The war cry *Boutez en avant* of the deBarrys, or Barrys, the Norman dynasty, gave the town its name. The same motto is written on the gates of Fota Island, East Cork, where the deBarrys lived previously were first established. The curate's house was old and had no central heating, only an oil-fuelled range in the kitchen. Bridie O'Donnell, the matron in St Colman's and a native of Buttevant, helped me to set up house; she made the bed and put two pillows on it. Normally I like only one pillow, so I removed one from behind my head and wondered, as I tried to go to sleep, how many soldiers had been killed in the old castle and if it was haunted. As I lay there for some time and was dozing, I felt this cold hand gently touch my face. I jumped up in panic and slowly discovered it was the pillow I had put aside gently falling on my face. Imagination can create ghosts.

I settled in well. One man said to me, 'Everybody knows the stranger, but the stranger don't [*sic*] know anybody.' So getting to know the parishioners started all over again. Buttevant has a great tradition of music and song, and the celebration of the Eucharist was enhanced by the magnificent choir and chanters. The Church of St Mary is one of the most liturgical-friendly buildings to celebrate the Eucharist; its cruciform and compact shape lends to intimacy of celebration as the congregation is close to the altar. Canon Michael Cogan was the PP, and his cousin Fr Micheál Cogan was my fellow curate. The Convent of Mercy was across the street from my house, and the nuns kindly invited me to lunch every day. It was relaxing and easy-going compared to the schedule in St Colman's, and it was a joy just to visit the schools and not have to stay in them all day long. The people were welcoming and friendly. I spent three happy years there.

The twelfth of July was the busiest day of the year in Buttevant as the medieval Cahirmee Horse Fair was held on Main Street. The fair was held in a huge field at Cahirmee, halfway between Buttevant and Doneraile, until 1921, when it moved into Buttevant. All the houses in the town and surrounding area became hostels for the three days of the fair. A local explained to me the difference between a penny bed and a halfpenny bed. One could only sleep on one's back on a halfpenny bed, and there was room to turn on one's side in a penny bed. It was and still is a meeting place for the Irish Travelling Community, who arrived from all over Ireland and England. The Cahirmee event's reputation as a horse fair has dwindled, but it was once one of the biggest horse fairs in Ireland and beyond. Napoleon's horse Marengo, and Lord Wellington's horse Copenhagen, were purchased at Cahirmee fair.

In 1752, fifty years before Marengo's purchase, the first steeplechase was run between Buttevant and Doneraile, a challenge between a Mr Blake and Mr O'Callaghan cross-country from the steeple of the church in Buttevant to the steeple of the church in Doneraile—hence it was called a steeplechase, and later called point-to-point. It's no wonder that racehorses abound in the surrounding countryside. The legendary Vincent O'Brien hailed from nearby Churchtown. The limestone-base land is perfect for the bones and tendons of young horses.

The local community organised a busker festival in the town during the summer which attracted musical talent from Ireland and England and some who were not so musical. One of these latter was a character named Sinan from London who claimed to be related to the Synan family and pretended to play a ukulele without strings. The Synan family were a noted landed Catholic family who lived in the area in the sixteenth century but were now extinct. This Sinan, who was being pursued by the local sergeant after the committal of a crime, ran into the church seeking sanctuary from Canon Cogan, saying, 'I seek sanctuary in your church, sir.' Canon Cogan was very witty and replied, 'Don't 'sir' me and you might get it.' But Sinan turned back and gave himself up. He accused a local publican for 'pinching his ukulele', which mysteriously turned up in another pub. I advised him to visit the last two brothers of the family in Doneraile, and on return he told me he was not impressed with their humble abode. The medieval family built Castle Pook, which still exists but is of no great value, so with no fortune to claim, Sinan returned to London.

Donkey derbies were regularly run in Buttevant for charity. One of these events stands out in my memory. Well-known jockeys were willing to participate. On this occasion they were given bed and breakfast by the local organising committee the night and morning before the race. Anne Marie Crowley was a successful National Hunt jockey, and she and another woman rider were assigned to stay in my house. The derby was held in the GAA pitch, the track running all round the perimeter of the pitch. It ended after three rounds of the pitch. I was standing at the corner of the home straight when the two leading donkeys approached upsides. Philip Fenton, an accomplished amateur rider, was on the outside of Anne Marie, whose mount was tiring but staying on, while Philip's mount was full of running and ready to pounce. To encourage his beast more, Philip produced the whip. But instead of accelerating, the donkey veered sharply to the right and sent Philip sharply to the left while Anne Marie's donkey slowly but surely crossed the winning line. When it comes to donkey racing, patient persuasion beats physical force. Anne Marie is now the wife of Aidan O'Brien, master of Ballydoyle and maestro of horse racing.

Three years is a short time in a parish, but I got to know most of the parishioners and made many friends. I helped out in the secondary school at the request of the nuns, as there was no career guidance counsellor there. The students came to me in pairs during their free classes. Many adults called by appointment for counselling and chats. When I arrived back from my holidays, Bishop Magee requested me to move to Kanturk.

Kanturk

I arrived in Kanturk in 1989 as junior curate and served in that parish until 2005. My health began to deteriorate with the condition known as ME or CFS, resulting from a virus I contracted in Buttevant. I suffered from long bouts of flu like symptoms with severe fatigue. The clergy and people were very kind and understanding of my lack of energy in their service, and despite my illness, I have very happy memories of my stay there. Kanturk has its own unique character and tradition. It is the capital of Duhallow, a large rural area between Mallow and Killarney in north-west Cork, and while it nurtures traditional family values, it also is an independent, self-sufficient, thriving commercial centre and has produced more than its share of entrepreneurs at home and abroad. It is a great business town for shoppers from hinterland areas. It had its own ice-cream shop and still has its bakeries, award-winning butchers, creamery (producing milk and butter), and jam makers. The founder of Southwest Airlines in the United States, Herb Kelleher, has family links with Kanturk, and Michael O'Leary, a native of Kanturk, went to meet him and based Ryan Air on Southwest Airlines. The great Olympian Dr Pat O'Callaghan was from Kanturk. The people are warm and welcoming and have a strong traditional faith, which was evident during Lent and other church seasons.

I lived in Egmont Place on the Newmarket road with neighbours on either side, which is more homely than a detached presbytery. The parishioners were very generous, and I never wanted for anything while there. I spent eighteen years in the parish, and I loved every moment, which is the best tribute I can pay to the people I served there. I had the impression that it was a happy relationship, even though my health had deteriorated by 50 per cent and I could only offer a fraction of my service. There were times when I started Mass and only hoped I could finish. Even standing was demanding on the little strength I had. But I would do it all over again because the people were so considerate and supportive. From senior citizens to the schoolchildren, I felt accepted by all and privileged to share in their sorrow and happiness.

There is a phrase describing a priest as a member of every family who belongs to none, but in Kanturk and Lismire, I was a member of every family and belonged to them all. It was a home away from home. Maybe there is wisdom in not leaving a priest in a parish for too long, but from my point of view, I was lucky. I would have qualified for a position of parish priest in 2000 but for the unfair restrictions placed on me. And when Bishop Magee removed me from public ministry in 2005, I had no option but to retire. After my retirement, I decided to vacate my residence to facilitate my successor, and I moved to my present abode.

I was sad leaving Kanturk with so many happy memories. I had planted a grapevine in the garden and, with the help of Sheila O'Callaghan, made wine in 1999. The wine wasn't too bad, but it was the fun and experience of making it which was the memorable part. I put it on display in the Vintage in 2000 under the label of Egmont Sauvignon 2000, explaining that there were only three bottles in the world. And did that create problems for Stephen, the proprietor, who had numerous enquiries in the first months of the new millennium! It was a bit of fun.

I had great neighbours around me, and the houses were so well constructed that they were literally soundproof. Despite my house being on the main Newmarket road, the traffic didn't impact too much on the inside. There were four bedrooms and a nursery, a roomy kitchen, a dining room, and a sitting room. Sitting in the kitchen and looking out the back window at the trees was like living in the country.

I became involved with the Red Cross by agreeing to be chairman of the local branch and helped out by driving the ambulance in my spare time, as I had the required driver's licence. The Kanturk and Millstreet branch was responsible for supplying first aid and ambulance cover for the surrounding area, and the Green Glens complex in Millstreet hosted many national and European sports events, including the world middleweight boxing title bout between Stephen Collins and Chris Eubank; the Eurovision Song Contest in 1995; and the Millstreet International Horse Show every year. It was fun attending these events. There were many other events as well, such as the many point-to-point race meetings held in Dromahane and cycling races. Kanturk was a great sporting town and fielded winning teams in every code. I was involved with the Senior Citizens Committee in setting up the Mercy Day Centre in Church Street with the financial assistance of the Mercy Sisters, who donated the premises. I liked going there on a Friday to relish the tasty cuisine served up by Sr Helen, Margo, and the staff, and I liked to deliver meals to other clients in the country in the minibus. I remember many trips in the minibus to Lisdoonvarna, Killarney, Mount Melleray, and Craggy Island.

Christmas was always a special time in Kanturk. The annual assembly of the family emigrants would swell the town's population. Midnight Mass would be thronged with the united families together for the celebration of the birth of Christ, and the crib very simply depicted the baby in the manger, the story of God's love for us. I remember the Taizé Masses in the latter part of my ministry, celebrated amid candlelight and with sweet-smelling incense, conducive to prayerful worship. Lismire had its own unique character in the northern end of the parish with its own church, school, and playing pitch. It was always a joy to visit the school and get to know all the children and share in the fun. The community staged their own variety concert every year, and there was no shortage of humour.

I remember a story about Donie Murphy, a member of a notable family; his brother, Con, was ombudsman for labour relations. Donie came home one very frosty night, and in an effort to warm his behind, he fell into the fire on his ass. He presented himself at a hospital the following morning and calmly told the doctors that he was suffering from AIDS. There was consternation until he explained that it was 'arse in a desperate state' and not the lethal virus. Lismire had plenty of historical sites like Poll an Fhiaidh and Kilmacow.

Even though my health was debilitating in my ministry, the support of the community and Dr Cormac Lyons kept me ticking over to do most things. But I would have loved to be able to do more. Cormac was both friend and doctor and understood my condition. Later when I was removed from ministry, he took particular care of me, and both he and Sheila, his wife, were available for medical and mental support. Later he was joined by Dr Brian O'Connell, who is now my GP. Brian and I have the same interest in horse racing. I have known him since his school days. He continues to provide excellent medical care, going above and beyond the call of duty.

Kanturk was different from the other parishes that I served in, in that the senior curacy would rarely be contacted after teatime, which provided time for socialising and house visitation. Every house became a friendly haven, so much so that I can't mention them all. In the wintertime I played cards on Monday nights with eight friends in their respective homes, which was a great social experience. Leo, Lyn, Conor, Derry, Celeste, Jane, Joe, and I formed the card school. The rules were as follows: (1) start at 8 p.m. and end at 11 p.m., and (2) refreshments were restricted to a cup of tea and biscuits, with a biscuit being defined as the content of a packet or tin. But the rules were lifted for special occasions. Eventually every Monday night became a special occasion, and nobody objected. It ended when Leo, Lyn, and Celeste died. May they rest in peace.

Egmont Place, my place of residence, was named after Lord Egmont, the explorer, who had strong historical connections with Kanturk. My next-door neighbours were Andy and Peg Keating and Michael and Noel O'Brien. My house was once occupied by Dr Matt Twomey, who won the English Greyhound Derby with his greyhound, but the kennels had been demolished when I arrived. There was a beautiful garden at the back where I grew strawberries, raspberries, grapes, and tomatoes. It was soothing to visit the garden after a day's work and admire nature's growth. There were wild cats there. After a lot of effort, I managed to tame one, and just when I had it tamed, it abandoned my garden to frequent the Vintage for better fare. I spent sixteen happy years in Kanturk. I still like going back there.

The first inkling of trouble surfaced in 1995 while I was in Kanturk. The vicar general of the diocese wrote to me in connection with an allegation of sexual abuse made against me by a participant of a retreat I gave in Cork in 1981. This person, who appears in the Cloyne report under the pseudonym Caelan, claimed that I abused her in confession by touching her inappropriately. I was absolutely dumbfounded and could not remember anything untoward happening at the retreat. She made the claim in a letter to the bishop, who commissioned the vicar general to interview me about the alleged abuse. I discussed the issue with him. The term she used was *abuse* (not sexual abuse). She said that I made her lie on the bed and then put my hand on her tummy. I told him that confessions were held in a bedroom with only one chair, so I would sit on the bed while the penitent would sit on the chair. It was a retreat for adult youth and was charismatic in nature, so confession would begin with a charismatic blessing consisting of my hands touching head, shoulders, and face of the penitent.

It wasn't what happened that mattered, but the more serious canonical transgression of confessional solicitation (soliciting a penitent in confession for sexual favours). I was again dumbfounded by this accusation. I hadn't said anything to the penitent other than the blessing, which went like this— 'May God the Father, the Son, and the Holy Spirit bless you'—while simultaneously placing both hands on her head, shoulder, and cheeks. The vicar general was worried because she made a statement to the Gardai.

I assured him that the evidence I gave him was my side of the story and suggested that we wait for the Garda enquiry. I was interviewed on the statement 'Caelan' had made to the Gardai. She had been asked by the interviewing Garda, 'Did he touch you on or near your breasts?' to which she replied, 'No.' 'Did he touch you on the genital area or near it?' She replied, 'No.' I was asked by my interviewing Garda if I touched her on or near her genital area or breast area, and I replied, 'No.'

The DPP (director of public prosecutions) returned a nolle prosequi, with a subscript detailing the reason— 'no clear evidence of physical or sexual behaviour'—but the diocese persisted with the allegation of solicitation in confession despite the lack of evidence. They refused to let me have a copy of the original letter in which Caelan claimed abuse, which I requested because I wanted to take a civil case of false allegation. They barred me from having any contact with children, even though Caelan was over 18, and relieved me of visiting schools. She later claimed to the Cloyne tribunal that I sued her, which was incorrect, and that I threatened to take half of her farm. Later the Cloyne ecclesiastical tribunal found me guilty of sexual abuse in that case (even though what Caelan alleged would not fulfil the canonical definition of *solicitation*, even if the allegation had been true; solicitation means urging the *penitent* to commit a sin and has nothing in common with the *confessor* doing something inappropriate).

Another allegation of sexual abuse surfaced a few years later, arising out of another counselling client, who appears in the Cloyne report under the pseudonym Ailis. She alleged together with her parents that I gave her alcohol and sexually abused her in my house in 1986. What actually happened was that she was referred to me by her mother after Christmas in 1988. The mother was worried about her daughter's forthcoming Leaving Certificate examinations. 'Ailis' wasn't studying and was disruptive, and the mother thought I might be able to help. I knew the girl from school and street meetings, and I knew that she had been thrown out of her local school and had to transfer to another school. The first time she arrived to my house, she was smoking and confrontational, but she settled down and began to reveal her tempestuous relationship with her father. Her inordinate hatred of him was disturbing. After I'd probed for the reason why she held such a distaste for him, she told me of his violence towards her and her mother. She said her mother was all set to leave him, with her cases packed, but she was too afraid. She also referred to his extramarital affairs with three different women, including the mother of her best friend.

The reason soon emerged why all this was occurring: Ailis was boisterous and unmanageable because she had been molested as a 12-year-old. This is typical behaviour of victims of early childhood abuse, to attract attention to their problem. The molestation was well known as it happened in public. Her parents didn't provide her with counselling, and now it was on my watch.

Ailis called by appointment of her mother four or five times, and each session was conducted in my kitchen, which was the only warm room in the house. On one of these sessions I went to answer the phone, and when I resumed the session, Ailis had a bottle of beer in her hand, which she had gotten from the fridge. Even though I felt it was forward, I asked her if she drank alcohol in the presence of her parents, to which she replied, 'No.' I took the bottle of beer gently from her hands and told her she would not be allowed to drink it here, which rule she reluctantly accepted. In her statement to the diocese she said I had offered her the beer. When she admitted the historical molestation, she broke down and wept; I put my hands on her shoulder in empathy and, as was my wont in these circumstances, put the kettle on to allow her space to recover her composure.

One effect of childhood abuse is the impairment of trust. I gradually encouraged Ailis to begin to trust men and to repair the damage without committing herself to a full-time relationship. What I wasn't aware of at that time was that she had a crush on me; this was later confirmed by a witness whom she told that she was in love with me and that I was in love with her. I did stress to her that my friendship was not an emotional one. We are all very wise in hindsight. I would have acted differently had I known her intentions then.

Before I went to the United States on vacation, Ailis rang me from the United States, where she was on an au pair holiday, pleading with me to contact her when I arrived. She contacted me in Connecticut from Long Island and asked me to meet up with her in New York. My sister Lil pleaded with me to enjoy my vacation in Connecticut and to let parish business alone until I got back to Ireland. It was my practice every year to spend a day in New York, to walk the length of Fifth Avenue and purchase the newest electronics on sale, so I told my sister I was getting the train to Grand Central anyway. There was no inconvenience as Ailis was getting the train from Long Island. We agreed to meet outside St Patrick's Cathedral, where I said Mass. I showed her the main sights before escorting her to Grand Central to catch her train back to Long Island, and on the way she asked me to hold hands, which I refused, reminding her that we would go down Fifth Avenue as we would walk down the main street in her native town. I could sense her pouting at my response, and I then realised she was expecting more than a professional friendship between us.

Ailis was still in the United States when I moved to my new parish in 1989, and the next communication from her was a letter from London, where she lived for some time, and in which she described a traumatic break-up of a relationship she'd had with a Muslim man. She ended the letter with 'Why can't we get back to where we were?' insinuating a renewal of counselling. Because there was no forwarding address, I didn't reply. I was led to believe they were actually married and that she left him.

I heard no more from Ailis until she made an allegation of sexual assault against me in 1996, claiming that I had sexually assaulted her on my couch. In fact there was no couch in my kitchen, only ordinary chairs, and she was never in my sitting room, where there was a couch. This was the initial allegation. She embellished it as the years progressed, stating in her claim form that during the alleged assault I would leave the room and come back, insinuating that I masturbated while away. She also claimed that I told her that I had inappropriate relationships with boys in St Colman's.

I was unaware that she went to the senior curate in my parish, accompanied by her mother, to try to prevent me from leaving their parish. She alleged that there was kissing going on in my house but made no reference to sexual abuse. The reason her mother gave to the bishop for making the allegation was her discovery of love letters between her daughter and me, which she said she immediately burnt because of the shock it caused her. In fact I never wrote any letters to her daughter. This allegation was given eleven pages in the Cloyne report, mostly dealing with Ailis's age and the manner in which the diocesan personnel dealt with the matter.

My account of events which are contained in the above page got little mention, and my full-day interview with the Commission was given a few short sentences, which included three substantial factual errors: (1) I arrived in the parish in September1986; (2) Ailis was born in May 1970, so she was over 16 at the time, and (3) her mother first phoned me in December1988 to make the first appointment. Her daughter had been to my house once with another classmate to discuss her career choices, but she was over 18 when she began to call on her own. Most of this data was omitted. When my legal team sought sight of the Commission's data in the High Court, they were refused by the Commission, which claimed ownership of said data.

When one scans the Cloyne report, one finds that my name leaps off every page as guilty. The allegations are clearly stated in their entirety, while my defence is condensed to mere denial in a single sentence. This is the chief reason why I am encouraged by my legal team to write this autobiography and redress the justice that I was denied by the Cloyne report and the Cloyne church tribunal. I am stating the allegations and my defence in full so that the readers can make their own judgements.

A perfect example of this is contained in Chapter 9, paragraph 9.13, which just says, 'Fr Ronat "strenuously" denied it.' It will be difficult to be objective but my training in philosophy, logic, and psychology will be of some help.

Sadly, the above claimant died ('Ailis') in November 2006. She was in psychiatric care for bipolar depression and developed cancer. She made a statement to the Gardai in 2005; I was never interviewed by the Gardai in regard to this young woman's allegations, but after her death, the file was sent to the DPP, who returned a nolle prosequi in 2007. Her parents persisted with upgrading her allegation in the media, insisting that 'she and another girl were hypnotised, plied with wine, and repeatedly raped', for three years by me in my house and in various other places. They spoke on radio (*Morning Ireland* and *The Marian Finucane Show*), and Ailis's father appeared on RTÉ 1, *Nine O' Clock News*. Prior to that, her father was the source of an article by Justine McCarthy in the now defunct *Sunday Tribune* (20 Apr. 2008), claiming his daughter was devastated by the DPP's nolle prosequi of 2007, when in reality she had died in 2006.

I was stationed twenty-five kilometres away when these alleged rapes allegedly occurred. Ailis was over 16 when I arrived in her parish and over 18 when she first called on her own. Diocesan records corroborate this evidence.

Her parents told the bishop that they weren't interested in money but wanted to get me out of circulation in the interests of protecting children. Nevertheless, they sued the bishop for monetary compensation in 2001, and whereas all the other claimants sued me, they did not. Readers should realise that, legally, the claimant must prove the allegation with corroboration beyond reasonable doubt; there in no onus on the accused to produce evidence. Ailis's parents and Donelle united in conducting a public campaign of vilification against me in the media, which I will outline later.

The third allegation: The mother of a young boy complained to the vicar general that I sexually abused her son, Mathew. I was friendly with the family and called periodically. I was saddened to hear that they had separated, but I kept calling. The mother asked me to talk to her son, who was suffering from depression and was attending Dr Paddy Murray, a consultant psychiatrist in a psychiatric hospital. He recommended counselling, and as he already knew me, he recommended my services. I knew the boy well. He was only 8 or 9 at the time, so it was a different challenge from the adolescents I was accustomed to. I took a keen interest in his welfare as he was well behaved and bright and deserved a good future. The mother stayed in the kitchen while the boy and I chatted in the sitting room. During one of these sessions, I asked him if he missed his father much, and he immediately responded by dropping his bottle of Tanora (lemonade) and literally jumping from his chair across from me into my arms in floods of tears, reclining on my shoulder. I let him be for some time. His mother entered the room, and I explained to her the extent of his anxiety over the marriage split. When he recovered and went to bed, I showed her my drenched coat where he had wept to illustrate the depth of his anguish.

He recovered completely over a period of time, and I kept in contact, concentrating on enhancing his self-esteem. He wanted to go to St Finbarr's College, Farranferris, for his secondary education, and I arranged with the president, who needed a priest's recommendation for him to gain entrance. Mathew settled in well and was achieving high standards. I didn't see anything inappropriate in our relationship. His mother encouraged it and invited me to his confirmation 'afters'. She advised me what present to buy him, which was a small reading lamp, costing the meagre sum of £4. His mother wanted a loan of £400 for dental bills, which I gave her, and she was paying it back in instalments every month. I received a letter from her, out of the blue and without any expectation, one morning with a cheque enclosed for the final instalment and a note warning me not to call or see her son anymore. I was stunned and saddened at the letter, and I rang to say I would fulfil her wishes.

She rang back after a few weeks to apologise and asked that I call to see Mathew, since he was asking questions about my absence. After much deliberation, I decided to call and discover for myself what the problem was. I met her son in the sitting room as usual, and during our conversation I asked if he was comfortable with my presence. He seemed puzzled at my query and wanted my reason for asking. He was in Intermediate Certificate class and mature enough to understand what sexual abuse was, so I next asked him if I had sexually abused him in any way. He denied that any abuse had ever occurred. I assured him that I could not replace his father, but I would be his mentor and confidant for as long as he wished. I was now satisfied that he had not complained about me to his mother and that the contents of the letter were her ideas. I called again with a more cautious and distant attitude since the first letter arrived.

Another, final letter arrived with delicate phraseology requesting me not to call anymore. I did as requested, but the son called from a phone booth and pleaded with me in broken tones to call. These calls were recorded on my answering machine when I wasn't at home. One evening when I returned home for an appointment, I played the messages of missed calls, and the person who was with me heard one of these plaintive messages from the boy and urged me to attend to his request. Naturally I couldn't explain the circumstances and said I would do my best. The calls stopped and I heard no more until the vicar general mentioned the allegation of sexual abuse that Mathew's mother made against me, allegedly on her son's behalf. He knew that it was on dangerous grounds and didn't constitute sexual abuse, and he was aware that I could cite false allegation against her from the evidence I had. On that account he protected her rather than wading into uncharted waters. She already had done considerable damage to my reputation in Cork, where she worked in a hospital, by broadcasting the alleged abuse to all and sundry. She convinced a priest colleague of mine in Cork that I was guilty. I was told this by several colleagues who didn't believe her story.

When her son reached 21, he made a statement to a Garda, who didn't consider it as sexual abuse and didn't pursue it by interviewing me. Her son didn't want to pursue the case but did wish to record it on the PULSE system. Despite this specific request, the Cloyne report berated the Garda for his lack of action and ordered that I be interviewed. I was interviewed. The allegation was that on one occasion when Mathew bumped into me fully clothed, he sensed what he thought was an erection. I had no recollection of ever having an erection in his presence. He could have been confused about objects in my pocket. He later sued me for money which I didn't have. This was very hurtful and ungrateful, but I hold no ill will against him or his mother.

By now I was being treated by the diocese as damaged property, even though there was no credible evidence to support the allegations. I should have long been offered the office of parish priest, and even though I didn't miss it, I challenged the diocese to define my status. I was restricted from seeing children even though there was no credible child abuse allegation against me. The three allegations thus far were made by adults. My position was that I could associate with over-18s but not under-18s where there was no allegation. I went to see the bishop and told him that his treatment of me was untenable, adding that if things didn't change, I would be coerced to sue the diocese for injustice. I was refused any documentation from my diocesan file with the excuse that the documents were private and could not be used in court. The irony now is that those private documents were published to the whole world in the Cloyne report and did little to help my cause in the format of their publication. 'Quote me in full, or don't quote me at all' was the motto of a famous archbishop which illustrates the danger of dealing with documents and quotations.

The Cloyne report's remit was to analyse whether sexual abuse claims made against priests in the diocese were handled appropriately. As I pointed out already, they didn't have priests' interests at the same level as the claimants' interests, giving an imbalance of documentation by quoting the allegations in full and not quoting the defence in full, and justifying this by claiming that they were not judging the veracity of the claim. A half story is a dangerous story.

In August 1999 I was offered a parish miles away from my doctors, and I refused because of its distant location. I was offered another parish in 2000, but the same problem prevented me from accepting. I nominated another parish which was free, but I was refused because it was too near the claimants' parish. I knew now that Ailis's case was far from being dormant as I was led to believe, so I was set on litigation to break the impasse.

The bishop told the Cloyne report that he offered me 'an insignificant parish' knowing that I would refuse. He cynically repeated the process in 2005. The Cloyne report concentrated on the treatment of claimants; it was conspicuously silent on the treatment of priests. It seemingly accepted all allegations as fact and seemed to be unmindful of the right of the accused to the presumption of innocence. It concluded that this case, without the slightest corroboration, was credible, while ignoring the overwhelming evidence I presented.

All this activity was taking a huge toll on my health. Stress is not good for the healthy, but for somebody with ME, it became life stopping. My energy levels would drop with each ill fortune. I was slipping gradually into the valley of darkness, and if it had not been for my doctor, family, and friends, I would have succumbed and retired. Indeed, I would have retired but for the cloud of ambivalence around my reputation. I wanted to prove my innocence, but I was frustrated with failures and restrictions on every side. My mind was made up; I was going to invoke the civil law to clear my name. Near future events, whether predetermined or accidental, would stifle my plan once again.

The fourth allegation came like a bolt out of the blue. Donelle, who had been dormant for a few years because of her familial duties, as she had a partner and family, phoned me one night, and we chatted until she abruptly hung up. Then the phone rang again, and her partner was on the line admonishing me not to be phoning her. I found this rather strange because I didn't have her phone number, which was ex-directory (private).

I moved to another parish shortly afterwards, and Donelle rang again from her mobile. She phoned regularly from phone booths and her mobile discussing her children and exhibitions of her pupils' works. She rang to make an appointment to see me, but she said she wouldn't come to the front door and needed directions to enter by the back door. When she arrived, she explained that her partner, who was a truck driver, might see her calling at the front door. She called a few times before revealing her partner's controlling habits. He was suspicious of all her male friends; he checked the car mileage and her phone calls every night, and he checked the household bills. She was afraid of him, even though he never abused her. This explained the phone calls from phone booths. When she arrived each time, she insisted that I lock all doors.

One day she said that she was on the verge of a breakdown because of having to pay off an old debt to the bank before she was married. She had kept it secret from him. She was paying out of the household funds and from private art tuition and was afraid he would find out. She looked for a loan of £1,000 to bail her out of a desperate situation and promised faithfully to pay it back. We discussed her plans to pay it back in instalments. She insisted the loan should be cash, saying a cheque would arouse her partner's suspicion. I went to the credit union where I had an account, and the manager, with whom I was friendly, thought I was mad to use cash for a loan. I couldn't explain my reason. In any case, I delivered the loan to her house as arranged. She kept calling, and each time she was getting more familiar, bringing CDs of her favourite music and a DVD entitled *Quills*, in which she compared the hero and heroine to 'our' relationship. She also wrote letters with risqué allusions to 'our' relationship, and in one letter she openly expressed that she wanted 'to make love' and outlined her preferred practice in lovemaking.

This letter broke the boundaries of our relationship. When she called again, I told her that her proposal was indecent and unacceptable and that I didn't want to discuss it any further. She tried to justify it by reminding me that her relationship with her partner was finished, saying that they slept in different rooms. She didn't pursue the matter any further, but she did keep calling and sending letters. She phoned me in Lanzarote on one occasion and sent her regards. She wrote to me on another occasion, requesting an anonymous Christmas card and asking me not to post it in my parish. She discussed her life and how she'd spent years in counselling and still wasn't happy. Her domestic situation was in turmoil. I understood that she needed support, but I surmised she was seeking sexual solace, which I could not and did not entertain. She said she could 'chill out' in my house in minutes, whereas at home, she was under constant tension.

By now I was extremely cautious and suspicious about her visits, deciding that the next time she called, I would deal with it. She phoned and asked me to pick her up from outside the nursing home where her mother, who suffered from Alzheimer's disease, was cared for; this was a change of her normal routine. When she got into my car, I queried the reason for it, and she explained that it would deflect her partner's interest if he phoned her and that her sister would cover for her by pretending she was with her for the duration of the time she spent with me. This cloak-and-dagger stuff put me on high alert.

Sure enough, Donelle got very amorous and reminded me that the coast was clear. I turned down her advances and told her that all the secrecy of her visits was disconcerting and that she should let her partner know she was calling on me. On the way back to her car, she held my hand and said, 'I will never forget those hands.' I knew she had gotten the message, but I didn't expect the horrific and extended response that followed.

She rang me in July to tell me that a priest friend of mine rang her asking for a huge favour, and she wondered what it was. Three months later she made an allegation of sexual abuse, including full sexual intercourse at 13 years of age, against me. I was sick when the vicar general informed me by phone of her allegation. I told him of my illness and my inability to meet with him and proffer my defence, but I said that I had no case to answer and would deliver my defence when I recovered. He had been in contact with me earlier in the year and wanted me to retire, but I assured him that I would not retire under a cloud of suspicion. I also told him that I would strive to clear my name in the civil forum, if necessary.

He believed me then, but this was a fresh opportunity to remove me from public ministry, which was executed without a canonical enquiry. The bishop and he either believed my illness was feigned or real and refused to wait for a canonical enquiry, leaving me with no alternative but to retire, which I duly did in November 2005.

Donelle was successful in her first quest for revenge. Others would follow. I was interviewed by the Gardai, and my file was sent to the DPP and returned with a nolle prosequi and a footnote declaring the reason, that 'there was no evidence of criminal sexual behaviour'. I gave a deposition to the vicar general and the bishop, and I noticed that there was no note taking. I reiterated my defence to them as it was presented to the DPP, but I did not include the letters and other evidence mentioned. I have never seen the resume of that evidence; whether it mysteriously disappeared or never noted. I mentioned the lack of note taking by the bishop during my interview with him, but he said he would write the notes later. There were dates and times crucial to my defence which would stretch the boundaries of normal recall, but he will have my full credence only if I ever actually get to see those missing notes. Canon law specifies the need for a preliminary enquiry of an allegation before any decision is taken on it; I leave it to readers to judge if this occurred.

The Cloyne tribunal were given all the evidence by me, including letters and items, but I was found guilty. The distinguishing factor in the judgement was that, in their view, Donelle was the more credible witness in her graphic description of the sexual abuse allegedly perpetrated on her by me, even though she admitted to being horribly abused by at least three other men. As well, I could identify twenty-four lies and other discrepancies in her deposition. The reason the church tribunal gave for claiming my lack of credibility was my refusal to answer an unlawful question which entitled me to invoke canon 1728 and not answer. This canon is similar to the civil law which acknowledges that an accused has no obligation to incriminate himself and that a leading question which could self-incriminate can be barred by the judge. This situation arose three times in my deposition and annoyed my advocate, who had to intervene on the three occasions to point out to the judge that he was violating canon 1728. Nevertheless, I was deemed a liar by the tribunal because of my refusal to answer. I will deal with the Cloyne tribunal in full later.

Another allegation of sexual abuse was made against me in 2008 by a woman with the pseudonym in the Cloyne report of Edana, one of the three classmates. She alleged that I rubbed against her crotch area while we were fully clothed. She claimed she 'blocked it out' for years and recovered the memory when in counselling for an unrelated illness. She was also friendly with 'Ailis' and was described as a 'schoolhood friend' by Ailis's father. The two were also in psychiatric care together. 'Edana' came forward after Ailis died in 2006, and her allegation bore a resemblance to that of Ailis. She later claimed that I masturbated while rubbing against her, which did not appear in her statement to the Gardai, as Ailis also claimed for the first time in her claim form in 2000. The DPP returned a nolle prosequi because of the lack of evidence. The Cloyne ecclesiastical tribunal found me guilty even though it was uncertain of Edana's age. Edana rang a friend, 'Naveen', and told her of her alleged abuse, and Naveen and her friend 'Muirin' made an allegation against me and against another priest. A fourth classmate also made an allegation of sexual assault. I was interviewed by the Gardai, and the files were sent to the DPP. There are two more complaints made by adults.

I have dealt briefly with the above allegations, and now I will give details of each case as it was presented to the DPP and the Cloyne tribunal. I will explain the frenzied atmosphere that pervaded in Cloyne and the Irish church in 2008 until 2013 in regard to child protection and discuss how much of it was the result of the vicious, mendacious publicity propagated by Donelle and Ailis's parents.

CHAPTER 7

Public campaign of vilification and intimidation

PRIEST ACCUSED OF GIRL'S RAPE, BUT GARDAI NOT TOLD FOR TEN YEARS (*Sunday Tribune*, 20 Apr. 2008)

The public campaign began with an article by Justine McCarthy in the *Sunday Times* sourced by Ailis's father. In it, he claims a priest (Fr. Duane) abused his daughter and her friend for 3 years. The man and his wife are telling the story on behalf of their daughter who is unavailable to discuss it. (Ailis is deceased.)They tell how she was severely and frequently abused by the priest, who had access to their rural school in an official capacity. How it went on for almost three years, beginning when she was in transition year. *How the curate used ply her and her friend with alcohol spirits and hypnotise them before raping them* usually in his own house, or sometimes in theirs. ... The abuse was perpetrated in the mid-1980s but it was not until she had left school and her mother happened on a letter alluding to the priest that the daughter finally confided in her parents. ... The daughter gave the Gardai a sworn statement around Christmas 2005 and an investigation file on her complaint was sent to the DPP. It came back with the instruction that there was to be no prosecution. The daughter was devastated. (The daughter was deceased before the file was sent to the DPP.) Asked what was the current status of this complaint, a spokesperson for Brendan Smith, the minister responsible for children in the department of health, replied: 'Any issues in relation to the Cloyne diocese have been referred to the HSE, which is currently in discussion with the church authorities in relation to this matter. The HSE will advise the minister as to whether any referrals to the Dublin Commission are warranted.' Barry Andrews did refer this case to the Commission in 2009. Prior to this article, her father and Donelle had taken the allegations of rape and physical abuse to the CEO (NBSC) after both files had been returned with a nolle prosequi. (This is outlined in the Cloyne Report)*The allegations presented to the CEO were unsubstantiated and untrue, nevertheless, he accepted them as credible without a proper investigation, and without checking the diocesan files.* This prompted Barry Andrews (the then Minister for Children) to chide: the normal channels of reporting allegations had been bypassed. The Elliot Report then led to The Cloyne Report. Ailis's father continued to source the local press, the national press, national radio and TV with the false allegations. After the Cloyne website published the Elliot Report, he identified Fr B. He said on TV and Radio (*Morning Ireland* and *The Marian Finucane Show*) that Fr B raped his daughter at 14 … and that he knew of 10 other cases of girls he abused urging them to come forward. As a result it was being publicly perceived that Cloyne had a serial child rapist at large, and that the church authorities were doing nothing about it. This campaign was aided and abetted by Donelle, posing as a 13- to 14-year-old under pseudonyms. The following is a brief outline. Fr Michael Mernagh marched from Dublin pro Cathedral to Cobh Cathedral amidst huge publicity.

Trish O Dea bragged in the *Corkman* that she was the first to break the 'Cloyne clerical sex scandal'. Ailis's father had contacted her in 2002 and Donelle in 2005. He is given headlines by Trish O Dea: 'I'm not talking about revenge; I'm talking about Justice'(*Corkman*,23 Dec. 2008). He 'was full of praise for ... the CEO and Sean Sherlock'. ... However, it has been, this man said, an extremely difficult week. They were simply unable to read the detail of the report relating to their daughter. And their pain is matched by a female victim of Priest B, the woman who contacted the *Corkman* in 2005 *and has been pushing for Priest B's prosecution ever since. 'I know of four other victims; I didn't know about any of the victims in the report.* This is only the beginning. But for the likes of CEO and Sean Sherlock,' she said, 'the silence may have continued indefinitely. *I have been told by other victims* [of Priest B] *that complaints were made as far back as 1980.* 'The Cloyne report identifies Donelle as citing the vicar general as the source of this 'dating back to the 80s'. He categorically denied it in the report.

NB: Both Donelle and Ailis's father had been with the CEO just days before these articles were published. A text from Donelle confirms their collusion.

PARENT: I KNOW OF TEN OTHER CASES
(*Irish Examiner*, 24 Dec. 2008)

———

Ailis's father sourced this article.

> 'I know of five for certain and suspect three,' he said. 'And of one of the five I know of, they know of another five,' he said.

Morning Ireland, 22 Dec. 2008

Ailis's father interviewed by Aine Lawlor:

> ['Ailis'] was an innocent 14-year-old. She met up with this Fr B. ...He plied her with wine. ... She couldn't get away from him for some reason I cannot explain, went from groping to full-blown sex ... Aine ...a 14-year-old girl. ...Yes. It went on for 3 years. ... I wanted to get him out of circulation. ... The dogs in the street know who the perpetrator was in our case. ... Molesting a child, an innocent body, an innocent mind that is affected for evermore.

> (Fr B is now touted as a serial child molester. ... Cloyne diocesan personnel are under suspicion for covering up his abuse. Fr Michael Mernagh marches from Dublin to Cobh in protest amidst great publicity. The media are agog. Politicians join in. Donelle and Ailis's father fuel the quest for more scandal. Even Christmas was hardly over when the press tsunami erupts again. He appears on RTÉ 1 (*Nine O'Clock News*) interviewed by Paschal Sheehy; he repeats his allegation and that *there are at least 10 more out there and urges them to come forward*. Fenella (friend of Ailis) and Keita (friend of Donelle) make allegations. Later, A. W. and Naveen, classmates of Edana (RTÉ 1, *Nine O'Clock News*, 9 Jan. 2009). Five fresh allegations follow in as many months.

The Marian Finucane Show (10 Jan. 2009)

> Ailis's parents repeated the allegations of child rape and violence on radio again ... claims his daughter is 14 when hypnotised, intoxicated and raped repeatedly by Fr B. He wanted to be the 'voice' for victims. He subsequently sent numerous complaints to the church and state authorities about Fr B. (A friend of Fr Duane told him that she

had been asked to make a complaint against Fr Duane by his associates. She said she had nothing to complain about, but the answer she got was: 'You were calling there.' Another friend of his had the same experience. According to a third friend he (Ailis's father) talked about 'rounding up the troops' in the local pub.)

FATHER CLAIMS ACCUSED PRIEST WAS LIVING NEAR SCHOOL AND CRÈCHE (*Irish Examiner*, 10 Jan. 2009)

'A close friend of mine observed him while shopping that he was by his chat obviously trying to recruit a person (a very young woman) in the shop.' (The shop was in Mallow; the very young woman was thirty something; she was the checkout clerk. Fr Duane was head of a large Q and he just smiled and said thank you to the shop assistant. This was interpreted as grooming by Ailis's aunt, his sister-in-law, who was in the next line and obviously thought he didn't notice her.) The girl's father who wished to remain anonymous said he was highlighting the issue because *he wanted to be to be the voice for victims. 'I want justice for victims. I am their voice.'* He said: 'Terrible perversions were perpetrated' against his daughter. 'It cuts to the core of our beings. It is with us morning noon and night.' The father said some families wanted to sweep abuse under the carpet because of loyalty to the church. However, he said they should report such incidents to the Gardai. He maintained the priest served in other parishes where there were further victims. (In the radio interviews he also claimed to be the voice of Fr B's victims.) He repeats that he is aware 'of at least 10 more victims of Fr B'.

(Donelle completes the same page (broadsheet) with her story.)

THAT MAN WAS A PERVERT AND THEY PROTECTED HIM ALL THE WAY (*Irish Examiner*, 1 Jan. 2009)

Every time she is out for a walk or driving around town and a certain model car in a particular colour whizzes past she freezes—unable to lift an arm or breathe—and is rendered speechless. It doesn't have to be his car. It doesn't have to be him. All it takes is the possibility that it could be that car. She has spent years in counselling outpouring the torrent of emotions that her tormentor has forced her to face all the days of her life. (She was in contact with Fr Duane until weeks before the allegation in a friendly cordial way. She discussed her problems with him ... she sought help and got it. She *confided* in him that she had been in counselling for years.) While calling to his house for advice and counselling, up to weeks before she made the allegation, she requested that the doors be locked while discussing her problems in a friendly cordial manner.

Her counsellor is a rock to her. ... While the CEO won her over as 'he was committed to getting to the truth', other alleged victims have told her they can't sleep unless every door in the house is locked. Sudden noises at night make others jump in their beds. Another woman cannot be alone in a room with a man. *These women had their lives savaged by a priest.* The bishop of Cloyne and his senior clerics caused unending heartaches to victims by not reporting. ... When Sinead told the Gardai herself, the Church stonewalled all the interaction with her and other authorities. ... 'They are a disgusting disease, that diocese ... that man was a pervert and they protected all the way,' she said. (A Canon Lawyer assured her that they did everything according to the book in her case.)

FURTHER DOUBTS OVER HSE AUDIT
(*Sunday Times*)

A Woman whose child abuse by a priest is documented in the Cloyne report sought intercession from an Archbishop, but was assured ... by the child protection delegate in his archdiocese, who told her that Cloyne did everything 'according to the book' in relation to her complaint. ... 'I don't have notes of the conversation (on the phone), but I would have said that the Bishop had under-utilised his canonical powers and he could have done more to restrict the priest' (the alleged abuser).

ABUSE VICTIM'S PARENT SAYS CLERIC IS UNSUPERVISED
(*Irish Examiner*)

A priest alleged to be a serial sex abuser has not been properly supervised. The claim has been made by the father of one of the alleged victims [Ailis's father].

CHURCH HOLDS CRISIS MEETING OVER CLOYNE
(*Irish Examiner*, 23 Jan. 2009)

The Catholic Church is to hold an emergency meeting today to address the continuing fallout following the mishandling of child abuse claims in the Diocese of Cloyne. Cardinal Sean Brady, as president of the bishops' conference, called the meeting ... after it was alleged that the handling was 'inadequate and in some respects dangerous'.

ABUSE VICTIMS WANT THEIR DAY IN COURT
(*Corkman*, 29 Oct. 2009)

The CEO of the Catholic Church's National Board for Safeguarding Children, told a new North Cork group that he would welcome the opportunity to talk to the DPP's office about why complaints of clerical sex abuse are largely returned to Gardai with directions not to prosecute. The CEO met on Thursday night with a new survivors' support group which is made up of, so far, of seven survivors of alleged abuse at the hands of one particular priest and both parents of an eight, deceased, survivor. The group is evolving continually as survivors become aware of each other through the Gardai. The priest was identified as 'Priest B' in the CEO's explosive report ... 2008.

During Thursday night's meeting, survivors indicated that they are determined to issue a legal challenge. ... 'He (DPP) can't take the burden of proof into account,' one survivor said. 'There were witnesses to these crimes. God was our witness, the DPP is our witness.' ... The CEO said after the meeting: 'At some stage I would welcome the opportunity of talking to the DPP to help to understand why these matters don't proceed and people don't get their day in court.' ... Ahead of the proposed Canonical Court hearing, *informal meetings have been held between the group and legal representatives of the Diocese of Cloyne and one of the survivors said on Thursday night: 'They told us they would welcome a prosecution.'* The DPP at this point in time had issued reasons why there was 'nolle prosequi' in all files returned. [Donelle: 'No evidence of criminal behaviour'; Ailis: 'deceased'; Caelan: 'no clear evidence'; Edana: 'insufficient evidence'; Fenella: antiquity; Keita: antiquity.]

CLOYNE AUTHOR OFFERS TO MEDIATE FOR VICTIMS
(*Sunday Times*, 25 Oct. 2009)

The author of the Cloyne report on child sexual abuse has offered to act as an intermediary to restart a stalled church tribunal into a priest named as Father B.

The CEO (NBSC) met seven abuse complainants in the north Cork diocese last week to hear their concerns about the private canonical tribunal. The women who said they were abused by Fr B as schoolgirls, want the inquiry's outcome to be announced. They want Fr B's real identity and the accusations made against him openly recorded if the tribunal concludes there is evidence to support them. A church spokesman confirmed that the tribunal has been 'paused' pending talks with the women. ... He said: 'I've no role in the process but I'm happy to help resolve this as a channel of communication.'

CLOYNE SAGA BEGAN WITH COMPLAINT TO ONE IN FOUR
(*Irish Times*, 9 Mar. 2009)

On April 7th the NBSC was contacted about another Cloyne case, this time by Faoiseamh. ... *It involved regular rape by a Cloyne priest over a five and a half year period from when she was 13*[Donelle], which also had been reported to the diocese. ... The CEO sought 'an unconditional indemnity' (when handing on his report to Barry Andrews for publication). No indemnity was forthcoming. Andrews forwarded the report to the HSE, as the appropriate body.

On December 19th, the weekend before Christmas, the NBSC report was published on the Cloyne diocesan website accompanied by a statement from the Bishop in which he apologised, and took responsibility for what had happened. ... Fr Michael Mernagh on a walk of atonement from Cloyne to Dublin received a lot of attention.

WOMEN: PRIESTS SHARED US FOR ABUSE
(*Irish Examiner*, 27 Mar. 10)

I have made official complaints to Gardai that they were both abused as children by the same two priests. One of the priests is Fr B, the alleged serial paedophile. ... Two women believe there are more women who were sexually assaulted and raped by these men twenty years ago. The two priests know each other and 'were aware of what the other was doing' (Naveen and Muirin).

Muirin claimed sexual abuse when stroked on the cheek in the presence of a witness.

SHOCK AS 'PRIEST B' LET OFF THE HOOK
(*Corkman*, 4 Nov. 2010)

Naveen's file was returned with nolle prosequi. It was recalled later after Donelle and Ailis's father applied political pressure by picketing the DPP's office.)

> A ripple of shock spread throughout North Cork this week with the news that the DPP has decided not to prosecute a priest alleged to have committed sexual offences against at least seven people. This despite the fact that a number of people who have made allegations about the priest have already received apologies from the Church. The decision has led to disbelief among the victims. 'The Cloyne Report is due out in the first week of December, but the DPP's office seem to be saying he's innocent,' said one woman who has made allegations against Priest B. 'The church has apologised to me, yet the DPP is saying no. It's crazy at this stage,' she told the *Corkman*. 'They are making us feel like we all made up the same nightmare and we were wrong and he is fine,' she added. [The woman source is Donelle.]

DPP URGED TO MEET CLOYNE VICTIMS
(*Irish Examiner*, 26 Nov. 2010)

> The Rape Crisis Centre has said the DPP should meet the victims of clerical abuse in Cloyne [it must be noted that there were no victims as such in Cloyne; nobody had been convicted] to discuss his decision not to seek prosecution against the alleged serial paedophile in the 2008 Cloyne Report.

The victims, who are all adults, are 'livid' at this latest refusal, as they say 'there are such clear similarities between all their cases'. A Rape Crisis Centre spokeswoman last night said 'it is most unfortunate' that the DPP does not give reasons for his decision not to prosecute. ... His latest decision has caused huge anxiety again for them. ... Having met with the three canonical judges ... his victims refused to co-operate with the trial until their criminal cases had been dealt with and the archdiocese report published.

DPP OUT OF STEP WITH ABUSE VICTIMS
(*Irish Examiner*, 28 Dec. 2010)

For the ten victims who have made Garda complaints about the horrific abuse they endured at the hands of 'Father B' in Cloyne, Co. Cork, the expected publication later this year of the Dublin Archdiocese report is certainly another important milestone in their hard-fought battle for justice ... how this abuser was enabled by the Church to continue his rampage of sexual abuse and rape. But nine criminal investigations into Fr B's actions hit a brick wall with a thud once they reached the DPP's office. A decision is still outstanding on the tenth file. For the women *who were systematically groomed, abused and raped* by this supposed pillar of the local community, the DPP's failure to take on any of these cases is not just frustrating or anger inducing, it just does not make sense. ... Still Fr B walks around his local town, sniggering at their hurt and anger. In recent weeks one of the women encountered him in a local supermarket and such was her trauma that she had to abandon her trolley and flee the building as fast as she could. (The woman was Keita, accompanied by her taxi man partner; she was already at the checkout when Fr Duane arrived. Fr Duane left the shop and they left after him. The source of this story was Fenella. She texted Fr

Duane that night.) Another man, whose daughter was a nervous wreck because of his abuse, couldn't control himself and started to berate him when he saw the priest stroll over towards him in a north Cork shop. The priest's response? 'Imagine that a man can't shop in peace?' He tut-tutted to onlookers. (The shop was in Mallow, the date Feb. 5th 2008. Fr Duane was at the checkout when he was verbally assaulted by Ailis's father; 'This man is a paedophile all over North Cork.' ... He repeated it twice. Fr Duane went straight to the Garda Barracks in Mallow. ... A Garda advised him to get witnesses. ... The girl at the checkout heard everything but did not want to risk her job. ... She did not want to get 'involved'. ... Another woman said she wasn't sure what he said. ... The Garda said, 'Waste of time without two witnesses.' The father also shouted across the shop: 'I'm not finished with you yet, Duane.' Weeks later the article on alleged rape and sexual abuse of his daughter appeared in the *Sunday Tribune*.) The victims describe him as outwardly 'very charming, very funny and very witty. ... He just sucked everyone in with his gas stories, being the funny man. But really he is a narcissistic ego who has no shame whatsoever for what he did to us and how he destroyed our lives.' All of the victims contend that there is a *lot of similarities between their cases*, whether it is the physical description of where the abuse took place, how they were groomed, how he ingratiated himself to their families and even of the abuse itself. 'The pattern of abuse is exactly the same,' one said. (*They were all allegedly raped as children ...* North Cork Ten.)The group met with the State Solicitor recently and he agreed that the DPP should meet with the women to discuss their cases. They also met with Labour party justice spokesman Pat Rabbite. One victim, Maria [Donelle], says, 'Every time another abuse complaint was sent to the DPP's office, I sent in a letter reminding him of my case and the many more that have gone through his office. And every time I received the same letter that the position remained the same as outlined in previous correspondence, the position is unchanged.'

Maria has received apologies for her abuse from the diocese of Cloyne, as well as compensation. The diocese sought to defrock the priest before they were forced to postpone the canonical tribunal. A written copy of a diocesan apology was sent to the DPP's office. The extent of the evidence that the women have amassed is astounding. 'The files were so strong. There were presents that he bought for us, diaries from that time. We remembered things about the physical environment so clearly, it was like a written photograph' [Maria, alias Donelle].

DPP WARNS CLERICAL ABUSE SUPPORT GROUP TO HALT CALLS FOR PROSECUTION
(*Irish Examiner*, 27 Nov. 2010)

A support group for victims of clerical abuse have received a letter from the DPP warning them to halt their campaign seeking a prosecution of the notorious Father B in the Cloyne report. The group called Religious Abuse Truth ... On their Face book page, Religious Abuse Truth, they advised people to write to the DPP about the lack of prosecutions around clerical abuse in Cloyne. ... The DPP did not react too well to this recent campaign informing the group that he must be 'impartial and independent' in making a decision and how he 'cannot therefore consider representations made by members of the public with the purpose of influencing prosecutions of criminal cases'. 'He told us we had broken the law. But look at what Fr B did and what the Bishop did in protecting him and other paedophile priests.'

Fr B 'still danger' to children
(Sunday Times, 19 Dec. 2010)

Survivors demand that one of the alleged abusers be charged

Allegations of child sexual abuse by the priest, known as Fr B have been the subject of 10 Garda investigations. The office of the DPP has decided not to press charges in nine of them. The 10th file is still under consideration.

Fr B was psychologically assessed this year for the Murphy Commission and found to continue to represent a risk to children with whom he has contact [the flawed risk assessment].

Three women have received out-of-court compensation from the diocese. [None of them were hypnotised and never referred to it in their statements to the Gardai until Keita mentioned it first and was followed by Naveen in the last of the allegations.] Several complainants have accused the priest of using hypnosis to molest them. A delegation of Cloyne abuse survivors visited the Dail on Tuesday to protest about the lack of prosecution of Father B. One woman showed Pat Rabbite, Labour's justice spokesman, a written apology she received from the diocese as part of her settlement. 'The case they made was very compelling and the facts are very disturbing,' Rabbite said. 'I would have thought the letter (of apology) has to raise a presumption of sustainability of the case in the DPP's office.' Fr B has denied the allegations to Gardai.

(Pat Rabbite, Shadow Minister for Justice, made the above statement one week before the general election with the polls predicting a landslide victory for the Rainbow Coalition.) The North Cork Ten had picketed the DPP's office only hours previously. The DPP, having warned RAT only weeks before to lay off pushing for Cloyne priest's prosecution, changed his mind and recalled all ten files on Fr Duane. The outstanding file [A. W.] and one other [Naveen] were selected as probably the strongest cases for a prosecution. After the 1st case was dismissed by the judge, many clerical and legal friends of Fr Duane expressed their surprise at such an obvious weak case reaching the courts. The media which anticipated a conviction in a pretrial frenzy was left stunned.

As Horace wrote, 'Montes parturient nascetur ridiculus mus' (The mountains will go into labour and give birth to a little mouse).

NO CHARGE FOR PRIEST OVER ABUSE AFTER 9TH ACCUSATION
(*Sunday Times*, 31 Oct. 2010)

WOMAN WHO RECEIVED APOLOGY FROM THE CHURCH AND WAS PAID COMPENSATION BY THE DIOCESE QUESTIONS DECISION NOT TO PROSECUTE 'FATHER B'

The Church has apologised but the State still turns a blind eye. ... Fr B escapes prosecution. One woman [Donelle], whose case was rejected for prosecution in 2006 but who was paid compensation by the diocese last year, wrote to the DPP. 'Why are you not charging this dangerous serial abuser?' she asked. 'The church has apologised and accepted responsibility but the state has continued to ignore, turn a blind eye and deny us justice. How will you justify your decisions when the report on Cloyne comes out?'

I GO THROUGH THE PAIN EVERY DAY BUT I DON'T CARE ANYMORE. I'M NOT AFRAID OF HIM
(*Irish Examiner*, 4 July 2011)

The story of abuse victim Aoife (alias Fenella):

Home wasn't a good place for Aoife (not her real name). She knew she had to escape for her own sake and back in those days (1988), there were only two ways out. 'I could get pregnant at 17 and escape into a bad marriage or I could escape into a convent. To be fair I liked it there and the nuns were good to me. You know, if it wasn't for what happened with the adoption, I'd probably still be there,' she muses.

Aoife's life and Aoife as a person changed irrevocably when she found out she was adopted at 20. Suddenly her life had been shown up as a lie. She couldn't function or cope with convent life. The only solution seemed to be to leave. 'I was very upset at that time, very vulnerable. He said that he'd talk to me about it. And someone said, "He'd be good at that." ... I was all over the place. I was so hurt. So I went to his house and he plied me with drink and ... then he anally raped me.'

[Fenella called by appointment to me for two years after the alleged rape in a friendly, cordial counselling relationship until I remonstrated with her over her drunken behaviour. There are several witnesses who can testify to this.]

'He' is a priest who was loved by his parishioners. One and all described him as a 'great man', a fantastic asset to the community, a parish stalwart. 'He' is a priest from the Diocese of Cloyne. 'You know, he was delighted with himself when he did that to me. He wanted power over me and he knew for a long time that I had absolutely no time for him.' Aoife couldn't go to the toilet properly for three weeks after she was raped. ... A year later she tried to kill herself. (She attempted suicide in 1990, and was calling to Fr Duane until 1992.)

(Aoife's story re power is baffling. She made appointments, came and went as she willed. There was no control, no coercion. She believed Ailis's father's and Donelle's story about this strange power Fr Duane had, and the allegations of rape.)

BOND OF TRUST WAS BROKEN SO YOUNG I COULDN'T TRUST ANYONE
(*Irish Examiner* 14 July 2011)

Maria [alias Donelle] was repeatedly raped by a priest in the diocese of Cloyne from the age of 13 to 18. [There is no mention of rape in the Cloyne Report.] Her life has been derailed ever since she says—even though on the outside she looks like a normal middle-class woman in her 40s [she was in her *mid-50s* at the time of this article]. 'I see what happened to me as being like dealing with a disease. ... Can you believe it, they didn't have the decency, the Church or the commission, to send me a copy of the report?' ... When she told Vicar General about what she endured as a teenager, she was told 'there's always the civil route'. On another occasion he patronisingly quipped: 'My, my. How articulate we are.' ... 'They are a disgusting disease, that diocese. ... That man was a functioning pervert and they protected him all the way,' she said. ... (The Cloyne Report found no evidence of a cover-up. ... A canon lawyer assured her that they did everything according to the book in her case.) The priest had an open friendship with the young girl but secretly she was being subjected to the most savage abuse. (The DPP found no evidence of criminal behaviour.) Locals where she lived used to refer to her as his 'little friend' as he wanted to bring her everywhere with him. ... Nothing was done. 'I was told at one time that he was on restricted ministry when I knew full well he wasn't. It was all lies and more lies. My God, they had plans for a retirement party for him—even after my complaint—and were urging people to give money towards his retirement fund. I threatened to picket it.' Maria's case was not prosecuted by the DPP and a civil case was settled in recent years.

FAMILY VINDICATED AS BISHOP RESIGNS
(*Corkman*)

> The family of a North Cork clerical abuse victim said they feel vindicated by the resignation of the Bishop this week. The parents of a young woman [Ailis's family] whose alleged abuse was reported to the Bishop in 1995 have been fighting since her tragic death at a young age to have the perpetrator brought to justice.

Facebook

> Support the North Cork Ten (Election Special) (27 Feb. 2011)
> Who is Fr B? (12 Apr. 2011)
> Newsflash (27 Jan. 2011)

> The North Cork Ten win a first victory against child-raping church and state in Cork, Ireland.

> A handful of survivors of priestly rape and torture in Ireland, called the North Cork 10, have forced a reluctant Irish government to reopen a case against the notorious child rapist, 'Father B.', after a prolonged campaign of picketing and protest.

> Virtually alone, the North Cork 10—seven women and one man who were victims of 'Father B.' as children—confronted the DPP for his failure to prosecute the priest. They were assisted by members of Religious Abuse Truth (RAT) and the International Tribunal into Crimes of Church and State (ITCCS).

> The DPP initially threatened legal action against the survivors and their supporters for demanding action against the rapist, but continual protests by RAT members

Kevin Flanagan, Dave O Brien and Gerry O Donovan, the DPP relented on his threats.

This past week, the DPP announced that the Gardai were resubmitting files on 'Father B.' for his examination, and that he would be reopening the case. 'I'm very pleased the DPP has come to his senses, and it shows you can get results when you confront these criminals,' commented Kevin Flanagan of RAT today in Dublin.

'We aren't calling them abusers anymore. They're criminals and need to be prosecuted.' RAT and ITCCS members will continue to campaign until 'Father B' and all child rapists are brought to justice.'

North Cork Ten (27 Feb. 2011)

Description: There are ten brave women living in Co. Cork. They were sexually abused as children by a R. C. priest referred to as 'Father B' in the Cloyne Report. They made their complaints to the Diocese about the atrocities inflicted upon them. The Bishop at the time was made aware of 'Father B's' activities but failed to act appropriately. Because of his failure to act 'Father B' was free to continue his reign of abuse. ... The Vatican has written to these women and apologised, it has also paid them financial compensation. The Vatican has also since defrocked 'Father B' and he is living freely in the North Cork area.

———

'A picket will be placed on the offices of the dpp in support of the mallow 10 and the jailing of dan duane.'

———

'Father b, evil bastard, getting away with wot he an all the other dirt got away wit. peado animal. Father b ur dirt. Vermin scum of the earth dwn 2 very last.'

———

'now that fa b name is out dan duane hold your hands up the dpp wont save you now he was also member of all priests show with cleary walsh and another who we hope to name soon what a team touring the country scum.'

———

Reply from the DPP:

'Under Section 6 of the prosecution of Offences Act 1974 it is against the law to write to the Director to ask him to either stop or not to prosecute a case. In addition writing to the Director to persuade him to bring a prosecution was considered by the High Court to be against the law.'

———

PRIEST CLEARED OF SEXUAL ASSAULT FACES NEW TRIAL
(*Sunday Times*, 3 Dec. 2011)

> A secret church trial, which began in Cobh two years ago, was suspended when several women who alleged Duane sexually abused them when they were children withdrew their co-operation until the state's criminal proceedings were completed. ... 'There is no doubt we intend co-operating with the tribunal,' said one of the women [Donelle], who has received compensation and a letter of apology from the diocese of Cloyne.

Criminal court trials

First trial, May 2011

In the first trial, the trial judge, Seán Ó Donnabháin directed the jury to find Fr Duane not guilty. He said, 'The delay by the woman in making her complaint was inexplicable, given that she was trained and worked in a profession which encouraged victims to make complaints, and which emphasised that complaints would be treated seriously when they were made.' The judge added that he had a worry about the delay, given that Fr Duane had established to his satisfaction that he shared the house with a housekeeper and a curate. 'If the complaint had been made earlier, these people could have been asked to make statements. Given the likely presence of these people in the house in the afternoon and their ability to give a statement … is worrying.' The judge outlined other worries: 'no corroboration … no witnesses … broad spectrum of time, 1 September 1980–1 April 1982'. He couldn't understand why that period of time could not be narrowed down. He also referred to 'talk' about exams and 'study' and Intermediate Certificate, which indicates that it was either before or after the Intermediate Certificate.

As the judge was revealing these 'serious worries', Donelle stormed out of the courtroom, causing him to pause, and seconds later Naveen stopped proceedings by shouting, 'This court is a farce!' The judge ordered her arrest for contempt of court.

Second trial, November 2011

The trial judge was Seán Ó Donnabháin, who received media criticism from Rape Crisis for the first case. Fr Duane's legal team were of the opinion that no matter how strong a case they had, it would go all the way to the jury. They interjected three times with legal argument, but it still went to the jury. The jury, despite coming back to the court on two occasions seeking clarification, took only an hour and twenty-five minutes—thirty-five to forty minutes of deliberation.

'I would trust my memory very well,' Fr Duane said in his evidence.

Naveen's recollection did not impress the judge: 'People remember circumstantial evidence if something traumatic happens in their life, like what time of year, the day of the week, the people who were there, whether they walked or got a drive.' All of these were missing in her account. Witnesses for Fr Duane corroborated his evidence, and as they were giving evidence she interjected: 'That is not true.' In one of her written statements to the Gardai she painted all priests as 'scum'. Her reason for coming forward was, in the judge's summary to the jury, 'to save the world'. (Her outbursts in court did not impress the jury, according to Fr Duane's legal team.)

She maintained she went to three priests with her allegations. All three had no recollection of her mentioning the allegations. She applied for compensation on three occasions but denied having done so in court.

Abusive texts

In June 2011 Fr Duane went to Kanturk Garda Station to make a complaint about anonymous, unsolicited, and abusive texts being sent to his phone from multiple sources. A detective took details and also his phone for X-ray, to establish the origin and authenticity of the texts for presentation as evidence for possible court proceedings. Later he revealed their origins and the identities of those involved. There were five people involved: Donelle, her partner, Naveen, Fenella, and Keita. He interviewed all (except the partner, who was seriously ill then and who has since died) and warned them. Fenella and Donelle ignored the warning and continued to text Fr Duane. The detective advised civil litigation as a solution. Fr Duane wants to wait until the tribunal is completed before making a decision.

———

The following texts are certified as authentic and approved as evidence for the civil forum:

Donelle
<u>2008</u>

'I'm in bits ... very near losing now ... am I there? ... Can't why don't ever love me ... was a game only. Why?' (19 Jan. 2008)

***

'All my life ... I loved u ... always laughing ... I did everything for love of u. I'm so tired. Is God real?' (19 Jan. 2008)

***

'I often wonder where my deepest hurt lies ... it's your utter dismissal and rejection of me ... and it stays and hurts to this minute.' (04. 40. 26, 21 Jan. 2008)

***

'Finding it very hard to sleep. Do you sleep well? I was in Bandon ... the river was so high ... so dirty and so fast. I felt so drawn to it ... almost teased by it. I'm still frightened by the slyness of it ... the ugly gasping sounds. I hate full-flooded rivers ... their compelling power horrible ... the sneaky beckoning power that could take you away, away, away.' (02. 47. 42, 23 Jan. 2008)

2010

'Stay away from all ceremonies for E. S. U have blood on your filthy hands ... you sack of shit.' (15. 18. 57, 15 Nov. 2010)

***

'Do u know what happens to bastards like u in prison?' (8 Apr. 2010)

***

'U deserve to rot ... and u will.' (14. 44. 16, 27 Apr. 2011)

***

'U can hide from the truth so long and then the truth finds U.' (10. 49. 08, 26 May 2011)

Fenella
'Dan u saw a closer friend of mine today in Aldi. She very upset. I still forgive u but think others pain. bad for her this night. Please be honest.' (20. 15. 50, 21 Dec. 2010)

***

'Dan ur next.' (22. 26. 55, 17 Nov. 2010)

***

'Hi Dan walsh on tv and radio all day … ur day near … member holy show Urself … Report out … people will know by march. God is good. This text is power like u had over me. I can forgive. forget is different. God bless ur soul.' (22. 23. 38, 17 Dec. 2010)

***

'Dan hope u read the examiner 2day, page2.' (21. 12. 00, 28 Dec. 2010)

***

'Would be happy to face u.' 353863663014, 15. 24. 55, 14 Jan. 2011.

***

'Hi Dan. all ur cases against u going well. … New thinking new Life for us all. DDP will act Dan. All my forgiveness for me and M.' (22. 55. 48, 26 Jan. 2011)

Naveen
'U lied with ur hand on the bible … U keep killing children like me.' (12 Dec. 2011)

***

'Who are ur contacts duane who save u? What secrets do u hold over others who know what u are but too afraid to tell the truth because of what u can do to them?'(15. 03. 06, 12 Dec. 2011)

Ailis

Fr Duane contacted Telecom Eireann in 1999 re nuisance phone calls. MB was assigned to scrutinise his phone. Kanturk was one of the last regions to be upgraded and the first to receive digital phones which had the technology to trace and identify phone numbers. The nuisance calls were traced to a hotel in Lahinch and a phone booth in a nearby town. MB cautioned the caller to cease. No names were given. Ailis was working in the hotel and was a quasi-resident in the town. The calls ceased for two or three years. They started again about 2003. Fr Duane contacted a Garda in Kanturk Garda Station and requested a trace.

The calls were traced but not identified. The reason given was that they were probably from an unregistered mobile phone. The calls ceased when he left Kanturk in 2006.

Fr Duane's elderly brother was the recipient of late night and early morning calls for a year. One morning when his daughter, Mary, was home on a short break, she answered the phone at4a.m. Ailis's father identified himself and asked to speak to her father. She refused and said to ring at a more civilised time. The calls ceased.

Post–Cloyne report media comments

REACTION OF GOVERNMENT TO THE CLOYNE REPORT
(*Sunday Times*, 17 Nov. 2011)

> When they found her comatose from an overdose of whiskey and pills the year after a Cloyne priest raped her, they also found the glass she had drunk from. The words she had written on it with lipstick were still legible: 'I hate myself.'

She had been a novice nun in the large rural Cork diocese but had left the convent. As a teenager, she had gone to the priest for advice. He plied her with alcohol until she barely understood what was happening. She reported the rape to the diocesan authorities. Nothing happened. Nobody in the church informed the gardai or the health service. No prosecution was taken, although the diocese paid damages. ...

'I've no doubt people in the Vatican know where the Bishop is,' the former novice said. 'He's gone back to the rat's nest. He's a shameless coward.' ... After last week she will not feel so alone. 'They have no power anymore halleljiah,' she said.

Fenella (in her own evidence) attempted suicide in 1990. She was calling on me until late April 1992. Several witnesses can testify to this.

Her reason for going forward was to protect other children (*Irish Examiner*, 14 July 2011)

For Liam and Bridget, Ailis's parents, today is an extraordinary poignant day. Their only daughter was a victim of Fr Ronat but has since passed away. ... 'The Bishop listened to us and that's all he did. He listened to us but nothing else,' said Liam. 'All I can say on the Vicar General is that he was a charlatan, a phoney.' A couple with a profound faith ... 'For our daughter, her whole reason for going forward was to protect other children. It was her commitment to being Christian and it is our commitment to being Christian and that stands to this day,' said Liam.

'We never knew the real extent of the abuse. We found out about it in a letter afterwards that we found.' (Ailis's father and mother on their only daughter, Ailis. They have two other daughters. Ailis was 18 when she began to call on Fr Duane.)

VICTIM'S FATHER: 'IT'S VERY DIFFICULT TO READ'
(*Evening Echo*, 20 Dec. 2011)

The father of a woman who is portrayed as the 'Ophelia of Hamlet' in an investigation following an abuse claim said this morning the description of his daughter was terribly hurtful. In1989 she first made a complaint that she had been abused for four years by Fr Ronat.

'It's very difficult to read and I find it very upsetting. My daughter was 14 or 15 when Fr Ronat started to abuse her not 16 or 17 as was suggested. It's just all lies. The church seems to think it is immune from telling the truth. That's the most upsetting part,' he added. (It was well established that Fr Duane arrived in their parish in Sept. 1986. Ailis was born in May 1970. She was over 16. The first of her visits to Fr Duane was after Christmas 1988. Her mother arranged the meeting and subsequent ones per phone. The reason her mother gave was that Ailis had performed very poorly in her Christmas tests. Ailis was 18.)

SECRECY AND ARROGANCE FRAME CHURCH RESPONSE TO THE CLOYNE
REPORT
(*Corkman*, 28 July 2011)

The Cloyne report clearly states that the Vicar General felt more emotionally drawn to the alleged abuser rather than the victim; 'Oh that is natural if you had a curate in hospital terminally ill, but emotionally you can't go in cold and not feel at all for this man, who is also suffering who is terminally ill, and who has a short time left with his family,' he said.

'Those words are surely cold comfort for children who suffered at the hands of priests,' [Ailis's father said].

CHAPTER 8

The first instance (Cloyne tribunal)
Defence on behalf of Daniel Duane (in reply to the pleadings of the promoter of justice)

Species facti

Fr Daniel Duane is a priest of the Diocese of Cloyne, born 16 March 1938 and now approaching his 75th birthday. He studied in Maynooth and was ordained there in June 1963. After a short temporary mission in Wales, he returned to his diocese, where he worked in Blarney for a year and a half. Then he lived in Mallow from 1967 to 1984, initially as chaplain to De La Salle preparatory college in Mallow from 1967 to 1971, with part-time curacy in the parish from late 1969.

In 1971 he was instructed by the diocese to qualify as a career guidance officer for St Colman's College, Fermoy. After studies in Dublin and Limerick, he qualified in 1973, and for the next thirteen years, until 1986, his full-time job was in career guidance at St Colman's College, Fermoy, with the task of interviewing each of the more than 500 boys studying there each year. This would mean that he was involved in several thousand individual career guidance meetings with teenage boys in those years, as well as counselling hundreds of young people of both sexes during weekend retreats and workshops.

For most of this time he resided in Mallow, commuting daily to St Colman's, Fermoy, for fifteen years, until room was made for him to live in St Colman's, where he resided from 1984 to 1986. His residence in Mallow was mainly in a house beside the Resurrection Church. Another priest, who was chaplain to the vocational school, also lived there from 1979 to 1983. Fr Mick Corkery lived in the house for the following year, 1984. The house became an open house for many seeking counselling or perhaps just social meeting. Four classmates, A. W., Naveen, Muirin, and Edana, were among those who availed themselves of the open-house atmosphere. All four subsequently lodged complaints against Fr Duane.

His early years in the ministry coincided with the euphoria following Vatican II, when all kinds of novelties became fashionable, including openness to new ideas, expectation of changes in church practices, face-to-face confessionals, the charismatic movement, 'tactile theology', which is a euphemism for hugging in the American style that was then becoming fashionable because of American TV, and so on. In hindsight, some of these were imprudent or dangerous. I recall writing an article in *The Furrow* on confessional rooms in which I presciently warned that some women might project their fantasies onto their confessors, to which allegations the best defence might be an inch of solid mahogany, as in the *crates* or grille required by canon law c. 909f. in confessionals, and I advised that before taking a saw to the traditional confessional, one should recall the old proverb 'never take down a fence until you know why it was put up.'

The accusations

Beginning in 1989, complaints began to be made against Fr Duane of inappropriate conduct which occurred many years earlier and which could be delicts under canons 2359 and 2368of the 1917 Code of Canon Law or the corresponding canons 1395 and 1387 of the 1983 code, depending on which was in force at the time of the crimes' alleged commission. Some of these alleged inappropriate acts are detailed in the Cloyne report, Chapter 9, which is devoted to Fr Duane under the pseudonym Fr Ronat and which, in spite of its imprecision and confusion, has been submitted as documentary evidence to the Cloyne tribunal in this case. I use it, along with the risk report, also imprecise and confused, and the evidence taken in the Cloyne tribunal itself, to set out the allegations made against Fr Duane relevant to the charges against him. These are listed in the *libellus* dated 30 July 2009 submitted to the tribunal by the promoter of justice. These were maintained unchanged by him in spite of my well-founded objection to most of them and were accepted unchanged by the tribunal in the *concordatio dubii* on 9 September 2009.

The first complaint was made in 1989 by 'Ailis' (Cloyne report §§9. 5–9. 36; risk report §§41–58). Ailis was born 28 May 1970, and her complaint in 1989 referred to 'kissing in the priests' house' when she was 17 or 18 (which would have been in 1987–8). Kissing a 17- to 18-year-old is not a delict under canon 1395 or any other canon. By 1995 when Ailis met the bishop, it was reported as 'sexual abuse' while she was between 15 and 19, and after she had died in November 2006 and her father had ramped up a media campaign against Fr Duane, he was describing it as 'rape' of his 14-year-old daughter.

The second complaint made to the diocese according to the Cloyne report was made in September 1996 by 'Bretta' (Cloyne report §§9. 37–9. 47; risk report §§66–81) in regard to alleged abuse of her son, Mathew. She was to give evidence in a session of the tribunal held in Dublin on 21 September 2010, but she did not turn up. Why she was called to give evidence at all is not clear as she or her son are not mentioned in the libellus of accusations against Fr Duane or in the promoter of justice's pleadings, and so this complaint is of no interest to the tribunal.

The third complainant mentioned in the Cloyne report is 'Caelan', who complained in December 1997 that she had been abused during confession at a retreat held sometime between 1979 and 1981. She is referred to as Caelan in the Cloyne report §§9. 51–9. 61 and does not figure in the risk report. Though the charge sheet presented to the tribunal by the promoter of justice charges Fr Duane with violation of canon 1387 of the 1983 code [anachronistically, this code not then being in existence], the pleadings of the promoter of justice do not mention her or press the charges.

The fourth complainant mentioned in the Cloyne report is 'Donelle' (Cloyne report §§9. 67–9. 97; risk report §§82–100), who said she first complained to the Kanturk parish priest around 1999–2000. She complained to the Gardai in October 2005 of sexual abuse between the ages of 15 and 20. She was born 13 June 1956, which would put the alleged abuse in 1971–6 during the time of the old code, which is not referenced in the promoter of justice's list of charges.

Donelle was called to give evidence to the tribunal on 16October 2009. She appeared accompanied by her friend Naveen, who was not expected on that occasion. They refused to give evidence until after the Cloyne report was published and created a confrontational scene for about three and a half hours. They both were interviewed at length two and a half years later by the tribunal on 18 April 2012.

The promoter of justice takes all his accusations in regard to Donelle from the risk report. Apart from one passing reference to her allegation that Fr Duane sexually abused her from when she was a child, all the specific accusations refer to events when she was over 16 and therefore are not delicts in the code, old or new.

The fifth complainant mentioned in the Cloyne report is Edana (Cloyne report §§9. 67, 9. 71, 9. 100–101; risk report §§101–104). Edana was born 4 October 1965. The promoter of justice takes her allegations against Fr Duane from her own evidence to the tribunal (as the Cloyne report and risk report do not have any specific detail). The action complained of is described by the promoter of justice as frotting, and the time of occurrence was claimed to be when she was in fourth year in school. This would not pinpoint her age at the time of the alleged actions as being under or over 16.

The sixth complainant mentioned in the Cloyne report is Fenella (Cloyne report §§9. 121–123; risk report §§105–116). She was born 24 May 1969 and was a novice nun for some time but left. She complained to the Diocese of Cloyne in 1999 that Fr Duane plied her with drink and anally raped her. She was 21 at the time of the event alleged. Clerical sodomy is a delict or crime, irrespective of age, in both codes, so this is a valid accusation. Whether it is provable remains to be argued.

The seventh complainant mentioned in the Cloyne report is Keita (Cloyne report §§9. 128–130; risk report §§117–125). She was born 4 May 1958, and in February 2009 she made a complaint to Gardai and to the diocese of unspecified 'sexual abuse' when she was 15, around 1973. Neither the Cloyne report nor the risk report gives any specific details of the alleged abuse. In regard to Keita, the promoter of justice depends on the experts of the risk report, who could not come to any conclusion but hypothesised that '*if* certain evidence *were to emerge* in the future[,] it *might* demonstrate that the respondent was engaging in behaviour which *would* create the opportunity to abuse Keita sexually'. The promoter of justice left this allegation to the wisdom of the judges. Surely such a quadruple futuribile is a scraping of the bottom of the canonical barrel!

The eighth complainant mentioned in the Cloyne report is Muirin (Cloyne report §9. 132; risk report §§138–139). She was outside the remit of the Cloyne Commission and is not dealt with by it, but she was interviewed by the Cloyne Diocese, and the risk assessor made use of the diocesan files. The only thing Fr Duane is accused of doing to Muirin according to the risk report is 'rubbing her face'. The promoter of justice does not include Muirin in his charge sheet, and so she is not of interest to the tribunal.

The ninth complainant mentioned in the Cloyne report is Naveen (Cloyne report §§9. 132–133; risk report §§133–137). She was born 1 January 1966 and is the one who accompanied her friend Donelle at the confrontational meeting with the then judges on 16 October 2009. Taking his information from the risk report, the promoter of justice's allegations against Fr Duane are of masturbation and fellatio from the age of 13 to the age of 16. If prior to the age of 16, these would be violations of canon 2395 of the 1917 code. It remains to be seen if they are proven.

The Cloyne report

The ecclesiastical proceedings against Fr Duane became entangled in late 2007 with state involvement through the Department of Health, the HSE (Health Service Executive, established in 2005), and the Government Commission of Investigation under Judge Yvonne Murphy (established in

March 2006 to investigate clerical child abuse cases in Dublin Archdiocese, and whose remit was extended in March 2009 to investigate Cloyne Diocese). It also became entangled with the involvement of the CEO, appointed by the bishops in July 2007 as CEO of the National Board for Safeguarding Children in the Catholic Church. The context of this involvement, which is quite complex, is briefly as follows:

The Ferns report on clerical child abuse in that diocese was published in October 2005, and the corresponding Dublin report was published in July 2009. These focused intense public and media attention on clerical child abuse.

In April 2008 the counselling service Faoiseamh sought advice from the church's National Board for Safeguarding Children in regard to the complaint made by Donelle against Fr Duane. (This was after the DPP rejected her allegation.)After several meetings or requests for meetings with the complainants; the parents of a deceased complainant, Ailis; the minister for health and children; the HSE section on children services; and the Cloyne Diocesan authorities, the CEO produced a draft report in May 2008 on Fr A and Fr Duane (pseudonym Fr B) cases. He sent this draft report to the diocese, which was not too pleased with it and responded trenchantly.

In July 2008, CEO sent his final report, along with the diocesan response to the earlier draft, to the Office of the Minister for Children, which did not consider that they had commissioned it and suggested that it should properly to be sent to the HSE. Indeed, the Office of the Minister for Children on 3 July 2008 asked the CEO to withdraw his report, shred it, and issue something softer to the HSE, which request the CEO angrily rejected. The Interdiocesan Case Management Advisory Committee were outraged by the Elliott report when they got it in July 2008 and responded even more trenchantly. They had their response published in the *Irish Times* in January 2009 after the Diocese of Cloyne had published the Elliott report on their website in December 2008.

Of course, in spite of the pseudonyms, Frs A and B could be readily identified locally. This led to a lot of media coverage over the next few years, with leaks supplied by the complainants clearly assuming the guilt of Fr B, and also clearly implying that the diocese was guilty of child endangerment and of a cover-up on behalf of the guilty clergy. Since Ailis died in November 2006, her father helped orchestrate the agitation against the accused Cloyne priests. Independently a group calling themselves Religious Abuse Truth (RAT), led by a Kevin Flanagan, agitated for the 'North Cork Ten' complainants, picketing courts, the DPP, and politicians, with placards and a Facebook amateur TV channel. These have been threatened with prosecution by the police for their activities, but their campaign has undoubtedly helped poison the atmosphere against the accused priest. All this agitation pressurised the politicians, including Seán Sherlock and Barry Andrews, the latter of whom since 2008 had become the minister of state for children, who decided to extend the remit of the Dublin Investigative Commission to the Diocese of Cloyne, with the same judge, Yvonne Murphy, in charge. This the government formally did on 31 March 2009. Judge Murphy's Cloyne report was finished in December 2010 and published in July 2011, with Chapter 9 concerning Fr Duane (alias Ronat) heavily redacted because of ongoing cases being taken against Fr Duane by the DPP in two separate cases at the behest of A. W. and Naveen in the Cork Criminal Court (the DPP had declined to take cases in regard to any of the other complainants). The full text of Chapter 9 was published in December 2011 after the two trials in the criminal court in Cork had been completed, acquitting Fr Duane of the charges in both cases brought against him by the DPP on 17 May 2011 (A. W. case) and on 25 November 2011 (Naveen case).

The risk assessment report

In January 2009 Cloyne Diocese decided to employ a specialist risk assessment company to provide risk assessment reports on certain accused priests, including Fr Duane. The risk assessor was recommended for this task by the principal social worker for North Cork HSE. The report on Fr Duane was admitted as evidence for the tribunal by the principal judge as notified by his letter to me dated 12 November 2012. This letter strongly emphasised that Fr Duane had freely signed a consent form agreeing to participate, in full knowledge that it was not a confidential process.

In fact Fr Duane participated reluctantly and in response to the bishop's carrot-and-stick approach in his letter of 10 February 2009: 'I write to let you know that it will be necessary for you to have a number of meetings with a Risk Assessor and his associate. … Your co-operation in this process is essential to the decision which I may make regarding your future ministry. Without your co-operation I will not be in a position to make any change in your current restrictions. … As your Bishop, I must insist that you co-operate in this process.' The sincerity of the bishop's carrot-and-stick approach may be judged from the fact that the carrot of the prospect of removal of restrictions is offered just eleven days after his delation of Fr Duane to the CDF on 30 January 2009 with a *votum* or recommendation that he be kicked out of the priesthood *ex officio et in poenam*, that is directly by the Pope and without trial and without right of appeal. Naturally, in 2009, oblivious of the bishop's votum, Fr Duane felt that he had no option but to undergo the assessment in the offered hope of removal of restrictions. Instead, he is now faced with the serious repercussions it has on his right of defence in this trial, a trial of which Fr Duane had no inkling in 2009, though the bishop surely had if his preferred solution of fast-track defrocking was not granted by the CDF.

On Fr Duane's behalf, on 5 December 2012 I strongly objected to the admission of the risk report as evidence, mainly on the ground that it was compiled without a real, free, and legally valid consent from Fr Duane, and particularly because it was in violation of the human right not to incriminate oneself. I reiterate these objections now for the attention of the tribunal. The tribunal, however, persisted in admitting the report, and the promoter of justice uses it very extensively in his pleadings.

In iure

Since this is my first presentation to the tribunal in a penal case, a few preliminary remarks on penal law will be appropriate. These remarks are in no way intended to be disrespectful to the tribunal. Rather, they are intended to express to the tribunal the human rights philosophy which underpins a truly just penal law system.

Our promoter of justice in this case, in his very illuminating address to the Canon Law Society[1] last year, quotes Pope John Paul II's first address to the Rota in 1979 as saying, 'The task of the Church and her historical merit to proclaim and defend in every place and in every time the fundamental rights of man does not exempt her, but rather obliges her to be a mirror of justice (*speculum iustitiæ*) before the world' and 'The great respect due to the rights of the human person, which have to be guarded with every care and concern, must lead the judge to the *exact* observance of procedural norms which constitute precisely the guarantees of the rights of the person.'

He also warns against any blurring or confusion of the roles of prosecutor and judge, quoting Gratian: 'Let no one presume to be at the same time accuser and judge or witness.'[2] And in his pleadings to this tribunal,[3] mindful of his own doctoral thesis,[4] he quotes Gratian again on the need for proper juridical procedure: 'Quod autem nullus sine iudiciario ordine damnari valeat, multis auctoritatibus probatur.' He also quotes Joannes Monachus on the presumption of innocence until proven guilty: 'Quilibet praesumitur innocens nisi probetur nocens.'

Mercy, not vengeance: the keynote

The penal law of the church keeps in mind the mercy of Christ as well as the repression of crime: 'Go now and sin no more.' At the very beginning of the 1917 code's treatment of the penalty law of the church, quoting from the Council of Trent, we are told the following:

> Bishops and other ordinaries should remember that they
> are shepherds and not smiters (*pastores non percussores*[5]),

---

[1] Canon Law Society of Great Britain and Ireland Annual Conference, 7–11 May 2012, pp. 20, 21, published in *Studia Canonica*, 2012, p. 343.

[2] Ibid. p. 20.

[3] Pleadings of the promoter of justice, §8.

[4] Leuven Peeters, *The Presumption of Innocence in Canonical Trials of Clerics Accused of Child Sexual Abuse*, 2010.

[5] *Percussor* in Latin usually has the strong meaning of 'murderer, assassin, bandit, thug'.

and that they must so rule over their subjects as not to domineer over them but to love them as sons and brothers; they should endeavour by exhortation and admonition to deter them from wrongdoing lest they be obliged to administer due punishment after faults have been committed. Yet if through human frailty their subjects do wrong, they must observe the precept of the Apostles, and reprove, entreat, rebuke them in all patience and doctrine; for sympathy is often more effective for correction than severity, exhortation better than threats of punishment, kindness better than insistence on authority. If in view of the seriousness of a crime there be need of punishment, then they must combine authority with leniency, judgment with mercy, severity with moderation, to the end that discipline, so salutary and essential to public order, be maintained without asperity, and that those who have been punished may amend their ways, or, if they refuse to do so, that others may be deterred from wrongdoing by the salutary example of their punishment.[6]

This same passage from the Council of Trent was confirmed as the basis of the current law as well, being quoted in the praenotanda to the drafts of revised law as it was being prepared prior to the 1983 code.

Equality of access to documentation

A basic right of defence in legal proceedings is 'equality of arms', which includes the right of access to documentation by prosecution and defence. Both sides have a limited right of discovery of documents whereby a judge can be asked to requisition certain documents which are common to both parties (canons 1544–1546). Cloyne Diocese supplied a huge amount of documentation, much of it defamatory to Fr Duane, to Judge Yvonne Murphy and the Cloyne Investigative Commission, as well as to the risk assessor, for their respective purposes. Fr Duane was advised by me as

---

[6] 1917 code, canon 2214 §2, quoting Council of Trent, Session XIII *de ref.*, cap. 1.

his advocate to apply to Cloyne Diocese under the Data Protection Acts 1988 and 2003 for all the files in the possession or under the control of the diocese relevant to him. He eventually got some documentation, some of it heavily redacted, that is with parts blacked out, but he was given no guarantee that he had gotten all the documentation of interest to him in regard to his case and his right to proper defence, without which the trial verdict would be irremediably invalid (canon 1620, 7°).

Naturally, with the diocese in control of what they chose to disclose, Fr Duane reasonably suspected that, apart from the heavy redaction of the documents released to him, certain relevant documents which he would like to have access to were simply not given to him. For example, knowledge of the payments made to the various complainants would be of great interest to him in assessing the motivation of the claimants. And documentation of how the vicar general, effectively the one in charge of child abuse allegations, handled his case would be of interest.

But a more serious problem is the fact that the diocese deliberately supplied deliberately forged documents. The Cloyne report proved this in regard to the Fr Caden case (Cloyne report, §21. 14ff.) and is especially scathing in regard to the bishop's duplicity (§21. 20).

The very same duplicity is true in regard to Fr Duane. Among the documents released to Fr Duane by the apostolic administrator under the data protection legislation was what purported to be the votum of the bishop when sending Fr Duane's case to the Congregation for the Doctrine of the Faith (CDF) on 30 January 2009, an absolutely vital piece of information for him. In the bishop's votum, as supplied to Fr Duane, it concludes with the sentence 'I recommend that this priest be encouraged to seek a dispensation from the obligations arising from Sacred Orders.' The votum in the very same delation to the CDF as published in the Cloyne report ends with the bishop asking that 'a derogation from prescription be granted so that a penal judicial process may be initiated, or that he may be dismissed from the clerical state ex officio et in poenam' (Cloyne report §9. 126).

Curia ius novit

This is the old adage that *curia ius novit* has the double meaning that the tribunal is presumed to know the law *and* is obliged to acknowledge and uphold it. Regrettably the Cloyne tribunal falls short in its fulfilment of this adage.

Ne iudex ultra petita

Even before the trial began, the promoter of justice in his libellus referenced laws not in existence at the time of the offences alleged, and he persisted in this error after it was pointed out to him. The tribunal ratified this in the joinder of the issue decreed on 9 September 2009. In accordance with canon 1513, they could have changed the statement of the point at issue to cover both old and new codes, but they did not do so and are now stuck with the consequences laid down in canon 1514, that the stated terms of the controversy cannot be validly changed without a new decree of the tribunal. *Ne iudex ultra petita*: the judge cannot go beyond what the tribunal has been asked to decide. If asked to convict Fr Duane of anything in accordance with a canon of the 1983 code, this can only be applicable to something which occurred on or after 27 November 1983, when the new code came into force. Anything which occurred before that would have to be charged as a violation of a canon of the 1917 code; otherwise there would be a violation of the principle of nonretroactivity contained in canon 9: 'Laws concern matters of the future, not those of the past.' This is a fundamental principle of all law, civil or canonical.

Prescription

This same principle of nonretroactivity is the main basis of my objection to the claim that the Congregation for the Doctrine of the Faith could validly 'derogate' from prescription. At the very first session of the tribunal I asked under what law was the trial being held and was told it was under the code, and not by delegation from the CDF as referenced in the old code, canon 1555, or the new code, canon 1402. Under the code law (old code canon

1702f. and new code canon 1362) criminal actions are prescribed after three years in solicitation cases and after five years in sexual abuse cases, so all criminal action was barred once these time limits had passed. I cited for the attention of the tribunal Fr Charles Renati's article in *The Jurist*, 2 (2007), 503–19, which I found persuasive.

The very concept of derogation from prescription is a violation of basic human rights law, and if this case eventually winds up in the European Court of Human Rights, I trust that the CDF and courts following it will be found guilty of violation of basic human rights philosophy. If the three- or five-year time limit has expired, prescription has already taken place, the possibility of action is extinguished, and it cannot be revived. No medicine will resuscitate a dead corpse.

As well, derogation from prescription violates the principle of nonretroactivity of law. There is no problem about framing a *new* law on prescription or in changing the time limits from five to ten or twenty years, or in changing the terminus a quo to the age of majority plus ten or twenty rather than the time of commission of the crime, but this must be law for the *future*, not the past. Where the legal system applicable to the case does have a law on prescription, and where the time limits have actually passed, that applicable law has done its job and extinguished the action, so that no one, not even the bishop or the CDF or the Pope, can revive the action. The horse is dead, and flogging it will not work.

When the US bishops in 1994 and the Irish bishops two years later got from Rome changed terms for prescription, no one took them to have retroactive effect, as is evident from the canonical commentaries on them at the time. In 1996 I had extensive correspondence with a fellow canonist on the exact import of the rescript which the Irish bishops had received, and neither of us ever conceived of its having retrospective effect; our discussion concerned the exact dates it became prospectively effective.

My argument on prescription was dismissed by the promoter of justice in his response dated 9 September 2009, arguing that, under canon 1555 of the old code and 1362 of the new code, offences reserved to the Holy

Office/CDF were and are not subject to prescription. Au contraire, the alleged offences with which this case is concerned were never *reserved* to the Holy Office/CDF, so his argument fails. I shall expect the court to address my argument at the beginning of their decision, as accepting it will preclude the need to go any further into the allegations against Fr Duane. He is entitled to the benefit of the law on prescription, which is, after all, the law of the church which the tribunal is bound to uphold.

Procedural defects

At the very first session of the tribunal I had to point out that the tribunal had violated canon 1508 in not supplying Fr Duane in advance with a charge sheet listing the charges against him, and also in asking a leading question inviting him to admit guilt in violation of canon 1728. Subsequently the tribunal was prepared to take evidence, and in fact it did take evidence, from several witnesses without informing the defence, thereby depriving the advocate of his right under canon 1559 to be present at the taking of evidence. Nor was any heed taken of canon 483 §2, which requires that the notary be a priest in cases involving the reputation of a priest. Nor was any heed taken of the *relectio* requirement of canon 1569, nor was the opportunity given to the deponents to make additions, deletions, corrections, or variations to the evidence given. When the *publicatio processus* and *conclusio in causa* (canons 1598–1599) were decreed, they were not properly notified to the accused defendant. Some of the acta (e. g. the notary's account of the session of 21 August 2009) and the documentation presented to the tribunal in the session of 16 October 2009 by Caelan were never supplied to the defence.

But the greatest problem I had with the trial was the actions of the principal judge who, in the absence of the promoter of justice at any of the evidence-taking sessions, took on himself the prosecutorial function which is proper to the promoter of justice and not to the judge. Certainly in penal cases, according to canon 1452 the judge can and sometimes must proceed exofficio instead of always awaiting the actions of the parties in the case, but this does not include combining the role of the accusing promoter of justice and judge in one person. As Gratian said: 'Let no one presume to be at the same time accuser and judge or witness.' Accordingly I was nonplussed to learn that when Donelle contacted the archbishop on Good Friday 2008 under the mistaken impression that he was the bishop's superior and could discipline him, she was referred to the principal judge to discuss her problem, thereby involving him in this case even before this trial had been initiated. When Caelan presented some documentation to the tribunal while giving her evidence, the principal judge indicated that the tribunal already had this documentation, thereby indicating that he had already in his possession documentation not properly introduced onto the table of the tribunal. And he clearly indicated during the tribunal sessions that he had been in contact in advance with witnesses, negotiating with them and persuading, even cajoling, them to attend.

This exercising of a controlling and prosecutorial function is not part of the judge's function and could impact on his duty of impartiality. It also gave rise to my suspicion that the principal judge was in possession of information not before the tribunal, deriving from his position as canonical advisor to the archbishop. It was this suspicion of mine that, in the session taking evidence from Fr Duane, so irritated the other two judges who thought that my suspicions were directed at them.

There is no separation of powers in the church: the diocesan bishop (or apostolic administrator in this case) combines legislative, executive, and judicial power in his one person (canon 391). Even when he exercises his primary judicial power through the judges whom he appoints (canon 1419), such judges are his judicial *vicars*, and they 'constitute one tribunal with the bishop' (canon 1420). It would be improper if the archbishop, who has a very clear personal interest in the prosecution of Fr Duane for more than one of the reasons mentioned in canon 1448, were to be seen as indicating his preference for the outcome of the case or providing the material towards achieving such a preferred outcome. Hence my client's concern about the archbishop's interview on *Morning Ireland* with Rachel English on 20 December 2011 (after the delayed chapter of the Cloyne report on Fr Duane was issued), which clearly assumed my client's guilt, and about the archbishop's assumption of responsibility for paying compensation (six-figure sums(!) by all accounts) to those who had lodged complaints against Fr Duane, although the state director of public prosecutions had on several occasions declined to initiate prosecutions on the basis of these complaints, and when eventually pushed by political pressure to allow two prosecutions to go ahead (presumably the ones he regarded as strongest and most likely to succeed), the state courts returned an acquittal in both cases on 17 May 2011 and 25 November 2011.

The possibility of the archbishop influencing the principal judge also explains my client's concern about the provision by the archbishop to him of the risk report on which the promoter of justice relies so heavily in his prosecution of my client. My client, Fr Duane, is entitled to rely on the total impartiality of the tribunal, which is bound to 'the *exact* observance of procedural norms which constitute precisely the guarantees of the rights of the person' as the promoter of justice quotes from John Paul II, adding the emphasis to *exact*.[7]

After the very first session of the tribunal in August 2009, I drafted a letter for Fr Duane's attention in which, apart from protesting the irregularities which had occurred in the session of 21 August, I proposed that we state in the letter to the tribunal that we awaited expectantly from the tribunal the total impartiality appropriate in a judicial college arbitrating between the partial cases presented by the prosecution and defence. Judges in any court should come with clean hands, *manipulite* as the Italians say, and an open mind. Canons 1447–1448 express the sensitivity of the code to the necessity of avoiding prejudice in court personnel, and canons 1449–1451 allow for lodgement of objections against court members suspect of bias. I suggested that we should express our expectation too that we would be afforded what in human rights jargon is called 'equality of arms', that is equal access of both sides to the same information and resources. I proposed that we also clarify that any material gathered by the bishop or his agents, the Garda, the HSE, the media, et al., is not before the court unless and until properly introduced at the evidence-taking stage of the trial. Even the bishop's preliminary investigation in accordance with canon 1717 §1 is supposed to be given to the promoter of justice in accordance with canon 1721 §1 to help him formulate his initial libellus or

---

[7] *Studia Canonica*, 2012, p. 343.

petition—not to the judge, not to the tribunal, not to the bishop's delegate for Child Abuse Affairs in the adjoining archdiocese.

In my draft I also proposed to note that it is absolutely forbidden for any judge to take account of material outside the acta of the case lawfully presented in court. Any information given to the judge which is intended to remain outside the acta of the case, whether from the parties, the advocates, or anyone else, is absolutely prohibited. *Omnino prohibentur partium vel advocatorum vel etiam aliorum informationes iudici data, quae maneant extra acta causae* (canon 1604 §1). [8]

After discussion with my client, we decided to put our trust in the tribunal and not to lodge any objection in accordance with canons 1447–1451, which would seem to challenge the impartiality of the tribunal. And so in the letter as sent to the tribunal we decided to omit from it those references in the above paragraphs which might seem to be accusatory or to imply the possibility of bias. Instead, we would await events to see whether the tribunal would or would not be fair and impartial. We still trust that the tribunal will be scrupulously fair and impartial and will, as is normal in the state courts, refuse to be intimidated or influenced by any outside interference and act strictly in accordance with the law of the church as contained in the code and in the principles of the rule of law, being truly a mirror justice, *speculum iustitiae*, as Pope John Paul II hoped.

Criteria for the assessment of evidence

I draw the attention of the tribunal to the binding rules for the assessment of evidence laid down by the Code of Canon Law. These are particularly important where, as generally in this case, the allegations made by the complainants against Fr Duane are uncorroborated.

---

[8] This is similar to *embracery*, the word English law uses to describe corruption of the course of justice by feeding information to jurors outside the court proceedings.

Uncorroborated allegations evidentially valueless

Where there are no witnesses to events being described, as they were solus cum sola, and it is the word of one person against another, the basic rule is very simple: canon 1526— 'The onus of proof rests upon the person who makes an allegation.' Uncorroborated allegations have zero value; they acquire value in proportion to the strength of the corroboration. This obviously makes it very difficult to provide legal proof of what happened when only two people were present together and the assertion of one is denied by the other. Further, even if the second person does not deny but just remains silent, the tribunal cannot draw any adverse inference from the silence— 'the accused person is not bound to admit to an offence' (canon 1728 §2). For this reason alone all the uncorroborated claims of abuse made by the claimants in this case cannot be accepted by the tribunal to find Fr Duane guilty of anything.

Even the risk assessor admits that 'it is impossible to categorically conclude that someone has committed a sexual offence if they persist in denying the allegation' (risk report §25). If the judges follow the promoter of justice's monition that 'judges must always translate the conclusions of the experts into categories of the juridical order' (pleadings §10 g), and if they correlate this with Pius XII's classic discourse on moral certainty (ibid. §5), it will be clear that the risk assessor's statement amounts to saying that moral certainty cannot be achieved where the accused persists in denying the allegation and there is no independent corroboration. Unfortunately he goes on to contradict his own principle throughout his assessment by finding Fr Duane guilty in practically every instance, although Fr Duane denied the accusations and there is no independent corroboration of the accusers' claims.

Nullum crimen, nulla poena, sine lege praevia

Nothing is a crime and nothing can be penalised unless it has been designated as a crime in legislation already in force at the time of its commission— 'laws concern matters of the future, not those of the past' (canon 9). 'Christ's faithful have the right that no canonical penalties be inflicted on them except in accordance with the law' (canon 221 §3). What is penalised in old canon 2359 and new canon 1395 is strictly limited to what is stated in these canons and cannot be extended to cover other kinds of sexual sins which are not explicitly mentioned. Not every sexual sin is a canonical crime!

The exact content of a crime must be proven

Whereas in canon 1395 (or canon 2359 of the old Code) a particular act is criminalised only when committed with a person under 16, there is no crime unless it is proven *both* that the victim was under 16 *and* that the specific criminalised act was committed.

Credibility of evidence

The basic criteria for whether evidence is legally credible is given in canon 1572:

> In weighing evidence, the judge … is to take into account:
>> the condition and uprightness of the witness;
>> whether the knowledge was acquired at first hand, particularly if it was something seen or heard personally, or whether it was opinion, rumour or hearsay;
>> whether the witness is constant and consistent, or varies, is uncertain or vacillating;
>> whether there is corroboration (*contestes*) of the testimony, and whether it is confirmed or not by other items of evidence.

Canon 1573 reads, 'The deposition of one witness cannot amount to full proof, unless the witness is a qualified one who gives evidence on matters carried out in an official capacity, or unless the circumstances of persons and things persuade otherwise.'

In this case evidence was taken by the tribunal from Caelan, Fenella, Edana, Donelle, and Naveen, and was taken from the accused, Fr Duane, and from one witness nominated by him.

Credibility of the risk report

It is noteworthy that the promoter of justice bases most of his arguments on the second-hand evidence of the risk assessor and his associate, who jointly wrote the report, which was intended to assess the risk of Fr Duane to further abuse children. This purports to be based on a professional analysis of the documentation supplied to him by the Diocese of Cloyne, plus interviews with Fr Duane, statements supplied to him by Bretta and Fenella, and a meeting jointly with Donelle and Edana to allow them to ask questions about the process being done by the assessor, subsequent to which Donelle passed on some documents to him.

In assessing the import of the risk report (November 2009), it should be remembered that though the assessor and his wife have impressive academic qualifications, they were hired for a particular task, that is to assess the risk of Fr Duane re-offending. This corresponds with the presupposition that he *had* actually offended in the ways alleged by his accusers, which they reasserted as fact in their many leaks to the media, who, in accordance with their agenda, swallowed them whole. It is also a presupposition which seems to have been shared by the bishop in his votum to the CDF and by the archbishop in his interview on *Morning Ireland*.

The risk report comes up with the desired verdict. While prefacing many of its conclusions with an 'if' clause, the clear intent is to accept that the 'if' clause referring to past offending is in fact verified and that Fr Duane presents a risk of future offending. The range of the report's perception of this future risk is all-encompassing: 'We believe it is likely that Fr Duane has a sexual interest in male and female children as well as adult women; however, this does not preclude a sexual interest in adult males' (risk report conclusion, §195). If such is the case, then how did the many thousands of boys at St Colman's to whom Fr Duane was counsellor and the whole male population of Cork escape? And since the most recent alleged abuse dates back to twenty-three years ago, how did the assessor's 'risk' so suddenly and thoroughly disappear at that point in time? Should a clean sheet for a continuous period of twenty-three years not count? In regard to future risk, should the assessor not take account of the decline of sexual interest with advancing age, the time *ubi defervescat luxuria*, when sexual interest has gone off the boil, as St Ambrose put it, though in a different context?

The attitude of lawyers, canon or civil, and indeed of historians too, is to listen to everyone and believe no one until allegations and claims are proven by independent corroboration. The risk report, the media, and the bishop and archbishop seem to have been unduly gullible in believing the traumatic stories of the complainants and attributed their psychiatric problems to the trauma of their abuse, discounting the possibility that their psychiatric problems were the cause of, or at least contributed to, perceptions (or fantasies) of having been abused. Certainly the acquittal of Fr Duane in two trials in the state criminal courts tends to show that the judges and juries there believed Fr Duane rather than his accusers. For those too who put their faith in Judge Yvonne Murphy's Cloyne report, it is worth noting that she emphasised that 'it was not the function of the Commission to establish whether or not child sexual abuse actually took place but rather to record the manner in which complaints were dealt with by Church and State authorities' (Cloyne report §1. 6). This is in marked contrast with the perception fostered by the media and generally accepted by the public that clerical child sexual abuse was proven rife all over Irish dioceses and covered up by the knowing bishops.

Refutation of the promoter of justice

With these preliminaries, let us now address the specific charges against Fr Duane in the libellus of the promoter of justice.

I.   General points applicable to all claimants

1.   All charges are barred by prescription.

In general, I submit that all the charges are barred by prescription. I do not accept that the CDF can derogate from prescription, for three reasons:

It would be retrospective legislation contrary to canon 9.

The effect of prescription will have already taken place after three or five years in accordance with the code law.

Immunity from prosecution and from penalties, acquired in accordance with prescription after three or five years, is an acquired right which remains intact in accordance with canon 4.

2. Nearly all of the charges are charged under laws not in existence at the time of their alleged commission and are *extra petita*.

Under the law cited in the libellus accepted by the tribunal (the 1983 code and *Sacramentorum sanctitatis tutela* and its 2003 amendments) and reiterated by the promoter of justice in his pleadings, only actions after 27 November 1983 are covered in what the tribunal has been asked to adjudicate on. *Ne iudex ultra petita*: the judge cannot go beyond what he was asked to decide on.

3. One of the acts criminalised in canon 2359 of the old code is *delictum contra sextum decalogi praeceptum cum minoribus infra aetatem sexdecim annorum*. In canon 1395 of the new code the wording is '*Clericus qui ... contra sextum Decalogi praeceptum deliquerit ... cum minore infra aetatem sedecim annorum.*'

These are the precise legal limits of the underage sexual abuse which is criminalised, and any charges made must be sustained under these precise terms, not ambiguous and imprecise phrases such as *abuse* or precise technical phrases such as *paedophilia* or *frottage* loosely or incorrectly used.

4. In no case where the alleged crime was age-related does the prosecution prove *both* that the alleged act was contrary to the relevant law *and* that the claimant was under 16 years of age.

Proof of both of these is necessary to sustain the charge.

5. There is no corroboration of any of the charges.

Every individual charge must be proven on its own merits. The concatenation of several charges has no corroborative effect. The sum or product of zeros is still zero. Apart from the evident collusion of some of the complainants in the protracted public and media campaign against Fr Duane, their adjustment and inflation of the complaints to maximise their chances of compensation is a feature of their claims and of their evidence.

II. Refutation of individual claims

Edana

In regard to Edana there is no canonical crime specified by the promoter of justice, nor does he attempt to offer any proof that Edana was under the age of 16 at the time she alleges she was abused. The risk report gives at third hand (Edana → Bishop→ Risk) the allegation of 'sexual abuse' at approximately 15 years of age, but again there is no corroboration of the alleged act or her age at the time. The Cloyne report mentions she claimed to have been 'abused' at age 15 but again offers no corroboration or proof.

On the contrary, Fr Duane denies he ever abused her, and he gives circumstantial evidence (cited in the risk report, §§117ff.) that she was already in her second year in college and about 20 years of age at the time of her first visit to his house, that there was no couch in the house, and that he did not practise hypnosis at the alleged time. Like the DPP who 'declined to prosecute on the basis that the alleged incident occurred 35 years earlier and a prosecution would be unsafe based on the available evidence' (Cloyne report, §9. 129), the tribunal must find that there is simply no canonical basis for Keita's charge, and Fr Duane must be acquitted on this count.

Edana

The charge levelled against Fr Duane by the promoter of justice in regard to Edana is frotting when she was in her fourth year in school and over the next few years. There is no proof offered that she was under 16 at the time of the alleged incident when she was in fourth year. She would have been certainly over 16 at the time of the alleged further incidents alleged.

Fr Duane denies that any such incidents of frottage occurred, and when rather aggressively questioned by the tribunal, he gave circumstantial evidence that Edana never visited him on a one-to-one basis until 1983 (her main visits were to another priest and not to Fr Duane). So, canonically, the alleged incidents of frottage asserted by Edana and vehemently denied by Fr Duane are unproven (the onus of proof rests upon the person who makes an allegation—canon 1526). So too the age of Edana at the time of the alleged incidents is unproven. And finally, in weighing the evidence in accordance with canon 1572, 1º and 4º, the tribunal might take account of the fact that Edana has, on her own evidence (21. 1), had three serious depressions and that, on Fr Duane's evidence, Edana and Ailis were in psychiatric care together (his evidence 54. 18, 55. 2).

So the tribunal must acquit Fr Duane in regard to Edana's claims on the grounds of her unreliability, lack of corroboration of her claims, lack of proof of her being under 16, and circumstantial evidence given by Fr Duane indicating the impossibility of her claims being true.

Naveen

The promoter of justice charges Fr Duane with fellatio and masturbation with Naveen from when she was age 13 until just before her 16th birthday on New Year's Day 1982. He takes his charges from the risk report and partly from Naveen's deposition to the tribunal. The complaint cited in the Cloyne report is just that 'she had been abused by Fr Ronat when she was about 16'.

Initially the DPP declined to take a case against Fr Duane on the basis of Naveen's allegations, but he was eventually pressured into doing so. On 25 November 2011 Fr Duane was unanimously and quickly acquitted by the jury on the evidence presented in court, which is essentially the same as that presented to this Cloyne Diocesan Tribunal.

This evidence was very detailed and seemingly plausible, but there is no corroboration presented by Naveen or by the promoter of justice. In face of the denial by Fr Duane that any of these events took place at all, and his giving of equally detailed and plausible circumstantial evidence which is completely contradictory to Naveen's evidence, the tribunal must rely on the canon which says that the onus of proof is on the person making the allegation. Naveen does not provide any such corroborative proof for the promoter of justice to support his case. This is exactly why the Cork Criminal Court found for Fr Duane on the ground that his memory of events was more reliable than hers. So the judges must find that Naveen's allegations are uncorroborated and unproven and therefore acquit Fr Duane on these charges. Three priests testified that she never mentioned sexual abuse by Fr Duane to them as she had claimed in her statement to the Gardai, and she denied she ever applied for compensation, when in fact it was proven by the defence that she had applied twice.

Donelle

In regard to Donelle, the promoter of justice takes all his material from the risk report, starting from Donelle's alleged disclosure to a priest in 2005 that 'she had been abused by Fr Duane from 1969 [when she would have been 13] to 1974'. The promoter of justice quotes extensively from Mentor to interpret this as an example of grooming.

With regard to Donelle when under 16 years of age, there is no corroboration of any such delicts, even though Fr Duane admits that Donelle may have had a crush on him and even stalked him. With no corroboration of any delict, the tribunal must again find in favour of acquittal in regard to the accusations of unspecified sexual abuse from 1969 to when Donelle reached 16. Fr Duane had clear alibis for the allegations she presented to the DPP, and the DPP returned a nolle prosequi with an explanation that there was no evidence of a crime.

Ailis

Ailis, who according to the Cloyne report was the first to make a complaint against Fr Duane, died in November 2006. The libellus of the promoter of justice charges Fr Duane with violation of canon 1395 of the new code with 'Ailis when she was aged about 17' and takes all his information on the alleged violation from the risk report. The details of the alleged violation are unclear and vary from source to source, but two things are quite clear: that Ailis was already over 16 when Fr Duane came to her parish in, and that none of the impugned actions of Fr Duane (holding hands, hugging, intimacy stopping short of sexual intercourse, cuddling, a comforting hand on the shoulder) come within the ambit of canon 1395, with the exception of her father's claim that Fr Duane 'raped her and another girl constantly for three years', for which there isn't a shred of evidence.

So for lack of corroboration of any of the allegations, and for clear evidence that Ailis was over 16, the tribunal must acquit Fr Duane of this charge too.

Fenella

The promoter of justice's charge here is that Fr Duane sodomised Fenella in 1990, which would clearly be contrary to canon 1395 of the new code and is not age-related. Fr Duane absolutely denies the charge, and Fenella has no corroboration to offer. So on the principle of canon 1526 §1, the charge is unproven and Fr Duane must be acquitted.

The promoter of justice seems to take Fenella's story as true, without any corroboration, and then quotes a paragraph from the risk report which also assumes that her account is more likely to be true than Fr Duane's. The judges' function is not to use the concept of grooming to provide an excuse for disbelieving Fr Duane and believing Fenella. Their function is to accept that there is absolutely no corroboration of Fenella's story, and so no proof of her allegation. Therefore they must acquit Fr Duane.

Caelan

The promoter of justice's libellus accuses Fr Duane of violating, on some date between 1979 and 1981, canon 1387 of the 1983 code and the norms of Article 3 of the *motuproprio 'Sacramentorum sanctitatis tutela'*, 30 March 2001, including the amendments of the Supreme Pontiff dated 7 and 14 February 2003, with Caelan during a retreat. In his pleadings he does not refer at all to this charge, but I feel I must comment on it because it is within the *petita* of the libellus.

The references to the law on solicitation in confession are anachronistic, as the alleged offence in 1979–81 predates the law referred to of 2001–2003.

The statement in the Cloyne report §9. 55 that 'Under canon law, solicitation in the confessional is treated in the same way as child sexual abuse regardless of the age of the person concerned' is arrant nonsense.

Touching Caelan's midriff and making reference to 'the heat of the Holy Spirit' descending upon her (Cloyne report §9. 51) is not by any stretch of the imagination a solicitation of a penitent to commit a sin against the sixth commandment of the Decalogue of canon 1387 of the new code, or the *sollicitatio ad turpia* referred to in the then current old code.

Conclusion

None of the charges levelled against Fr Duane is canonically proven, and the tribunal must, in accordance with the law, acquit Fr Duane of all the charges and must not impose any penalty.

It is a matter for the bishop to remove the restrictions on the ministry of Fr Duane based on false and unproven charges and to accept his offer of resignation from office in accordance with canon 538 §3 when he reaches his 75th birthday next March.

Mgr Maurice Dooley,
Advocate for Fr Daniel Duane
8 March 2013

The findings of the first Instance of the Cloyne Tribunal

Fr Duane was found guilty of sexually abusing Donelle and Naveen as minors, of sexually abusing Edana and Fenella as adults, and of soliciting Caelan in confession. The penalty was dismissal from the clerical state.

Rome

I was being monitored by the bishops' CLDs on behalf of the bishop. There were also two priests, who were my immediate aids. And I held monthly meetings to confirm my non engagement with people under 18 in my house or car. Mgr Dooley and I went to Rome for the appeal or second instance and stayed in the Pontifical Irish College. I had notified the chief ClD of my itinerary, as was usual when I left my ordinary domicile. Midway through our stay in the Irish College, the president called Mgr Dooley and me to his office for discussion. We knew it was serious, but we had no idea what the matter could be. It transpired that it was my omission to tell the president that I was barred from being near children under 18. There were under-18s in the college. It was obvious that somebody from Cloyne was in contact with him. The monsignor and I sensed the president's discomfort and agreed to find alternative accommodation right outside the Vatican. We discovered that there were children staying there as well. I was being supervised by Mgr Dooley. We both speculated there would be children on the plane home as well, and we felt that I was not violating my conditions in all three situations. At a subsequent meeting with the bishop, the CLD accused me of being flippant. I reminded him that in the Irish College the concern was that I was speaking to a mother and son (over 18) whom I knew.

In the CDF waiting room I kept thinking of the poor wretches who suffered in the dungeons beneath during the Italian Inquisition. I thought that things had changed since then with the new form of psychological persecution of *Waiting for Godot*, replacing the physical torture of the rack. All the material I read concerning the impasse between the CDF and the Pope was indicating that I would be just another 'blade of grass' to be trampled in the power struggle, and my predictions were later realised when Godot arrived from the said CDF in the guise of the final verdict of laicisation. The waiting goes on; maybe that was Samuel Beckett's simple message in *Waiting for Godot*? The Cloyne tribunal was established in August 2009. It took nine months to establish the CDF tribunal to try the appeal and a further year to reach the result. Meanwhile, most of my colleagues were pessimistic about the outcome, but I surmised that they didn't have all the evidence and kept good faith that justice would be served.

CHAPTER 9

Restitutio in integrum a Daniele Duane petita

Presiding judge in Duane case *coram* CDF
Palazzo della Congregazione per la Dottrina della Fede
Piazza del S. Uffizio, 11
00120 Città del Vaticano
Roma, Italy

Dear Presiding Judge,

Restitutio in integrum, part 1

1.   I, Daniel Duane, priest of the Diocese of Cloyne in Ireland, hereby apply for *restitutio in integrum* in regard to my case, decided in first instance in the Cloyne Diocesan Tribunal in a judgement dated 12 March 2013, and in the second instance in the tribunal of the Congregation for the Doctrine of the Faith in a sentence dated 19 December 2014 and delivered to me on 7 January 2015 at Bishop's House, Cobh, by the interim chargé d'affaires of the Dublin Nunciature.

2.   I do so in accordance with canon 1645 because I can clearly establish that the judgement was unjust. Injustice can be clearly established according to canon 1645 §2 if:

the judgement is so based on evidence which is subsequently shown to be false, that without this evidence the dispositive part of the judgement could not be sustained;

documents are subsequently discovered by which new facts demanding a contrary decision are undoubtedly proven; ... and

a provision of a law which was not merely procedural was evidently neglected.

3. I need not provide at this point the full justification of my claim that injustice can be clearly established, but I will give an outline of the argumentation.

Species facti

4. I was born 16 March 1938 and am now 77 years of age. I was ordained as a priest for the Diocese of Cloyne in 1963, and after a short temporary mission in Wales, I served for forty-two years in the Diocese of Cloyne until 2005, when I was forced to resign from my parish after complaints that I had allegedly, several decades earlier in the 1970s, sexually molested a number of teenage girls. At that time in 2005, I was suspended by my bishop from all public ministry.

5. After complex events, detailed in the first instance trial, I was summoned to an ecclesiastical penal trial, alleging violations of canon 1395 §2 (sexual abuse of minors under 16 and rape) and canon 1387 (solicitation in confession), all of which charges I deny.

6. The church trial began in August 2009 but was suspended shortly thereafter at the demand of some of the complainants, pending the publication of the report of a state investigation into the affairs of the Diocese of Cloyne and of the result of criminal court cases in which I was being prosecuted for child abuse by the Irish State. After I was acquitted twice by judge and jury in the state trials, and once the full Cloyne report was published in December 2011, the church trial resumed in March 2012.

7.   There were eight charges in the promoter of justice's libellus or petition, and the first instance Cloyne tribunal found me guilty of the charges in regard to four of the allegations of sexual abuse (canon 1395 §2) and the one allegation of solicitation in confession (canon 1387). The Cloyne tribunal did not deal with the accusations made by one of the persons mentioned in the promoter of justice's libellus, since she was deceased, and the charges made by two others whose names were mentioned in the libellus were dismissed with negative verdicts by the first instance Cloyne tribunal.

8.   The penalty imposed by the Cloyne tribunal for each of the five guilty verdicts was dismissal from the clerical state.

9.   I appealed to the Congregation for the Doctrine of the Faith (CDF), cumulating the appeal with a plaint of nullity, as required by canons 1629, 2°, and 1625, because of several obvious nullities in the Cloyne judgement. The procedural nullities of the Cloyne judgement were sanated by the CDF, and the second instance tribunal of the CDF, with you as presiding judge, confirmed three of the first instance guilty verdicts in regard to violations of canon 1395 §2 (in the cases of Edana, Naveen, and Donelle) but did not confirm the other guilty verdict of violation of canon 1395 §2 (in the case of Fenella) or the guilty verdict of violation of canon 1387 (solicitation in confession in the case of Caelan).

10. My petition for restitutio in integrum applies only to the affirmative verdicts relating to Donelle, Edana, and Naveen. My reasons for asking for restitutio in integrum would, however, also apply to the cases of Fenella and Caelan if that were necessary, as there is no corroboration in either case, and the accusations of Caelan do not fulfil the definition of the crime of solicitation in confession.

In iure

I.   *No corroboration*

11. The main reason why I argue for restitutio in integrum is that there was evident neglect of a provision of a law which was not merely procedural,

namely canon 1526, which reads: 'The onus of proof rests upon the person who makes an allegation.' This necessarily means that if the person making the allegation has no independent corroboration, the onus of proof is not discharged, even if this also necessarily means that the uncorroborated claim must fail. Or as the old adage has it, *unus testis, nullus testis*—one witness is no witness. This may result in a perpetrator sometimes getting off scot-free, but the alternative, that of believing uncorroborated claims, would give the advantage to dishonest claims and transfer the burden of proof to the accused, contrary to the basic human rights principle enunciated in canon 1526. Hence there can be no verdict of guilty unless there is independent corroboration of an accuser's claim.

12. The case against me was presented by the promoter of justice in the first instance but was obviously dependent on the evidence presented by Edana, Naveen, and Donelle. It is also obvious, in general, that where a crime is committed with no one present except the perpetrator and the victim, it is very difficult to provide independent corroboration. In fact the promoter of justice, who never attended any of the sessions of the court taking evidence, provided no independent witnesses at all and left it to the judges of the court, and particularly to the initiative of the presiding judge, to persuade witnesses to attend.

13. The promoter of justice in the first instance of this case, as expressed in §15 of his pleadings, was acutely conscious of the fact that 'Apart from the statements of these witnesses and the denials of Fr Duane, there is no independent evidence contemporary with the time of the alleged events. Any other evidence before the court relates to the reactions of various individuals when they were informed by the complainants of what had happened in the past.' He then tried to develop an argument from Benedict XIV's 1741 Constitution Sacramentum Poenitentiae on solicitation in confession, which, he said, allows that sometimes one witness will suffice, and the judges 'are permitted to proceed with the judgement of the case,

if they find that the circumstantial evidence is strong enough. [9]'It is the contention of the promotor of justice,' he continues, 'that the special risk assessment undertaken by the risk assessor and associate [the risk report] … provides enough circumstantial evidence for the judges to reach moral certitude in the case before them.'

14. This rather tendentious interpretation, contrary to the plain statement of canon 1526, is the reason why the promoter of justice in the first instance makes most of his presentation in the form of direct quotations from the risk report, which is a report on me, commissioned by the diocese from the risk assessor and his associate (forensic services), who specialise in risk assessment of persons accused of sexual abuse. I marked the direct quotations from the risk report in yellow highlighting, and this illustrated graphically how much the promoter of justice took from the risk report. In the promoter's pleadings in regard to Edana (§§29–32), Naveen (§§33–35), and Donelle (§§36–40), almost everything is direct quotation from the risk report (59 lines) except for brief statements listing the women's allegations (16 lines), recommendations to the judges to bear the concept of grooming in mind (15 lines), and a strange and irrelevant allegation of a similarity the promoter saw between a remark of mine and a remark of Oscar Wilde during his trial (8 lines).

15. This dependence on the risk report is remarkable in view of the fact that the authors of the report interviewed me but never interviewed any of the complainants and based their information on documents that two of them handed in to them. Furthermore, the Cloyne tribunal did not appoint the authors of the risk report, they never met them, and they did not inform them of the requirements of the code canons 1574–1581 on the use of experts, such as defining their terms of reference, their methodology, and how their conclusions were derived from their expert observation and professional expertise.

---

[9] This is a rather liberal interpretation of what Benedict XIV actually said in *Sacramentum Poenitentiae*: 'Dantes etiam, si opus sit, … facultatem … procedendi cum testibus etiam singularibus, dummodo praesumptiones, indicia, et alia adminicula concurrant.'

16. The conclusions arrived at by the authors of the risk report do not at all follow from the principles they state as their methodology. For example they state that it is impossible to make a definitive diagnosis of risk where the subject of the interview denies firmly that he committed any abuse (as I did), and yet they go on to conclude that I am a risk even now to all ages and sexes: 'We believe that Fr Duane has a sexual interest in male and female children and adult males. Anyone calling to Fr Duane's house is at risk of sexual assault. Despite his denial we believe he is guilty.' Qui nimis probat, nihil probat!

17. Although I and my advocate strongly objected to the admission of the risk report as supposedly expert evidence in the case, the Cloyne tribunal accepted it, and the judges in their judgement of the court depended to a considerable extent on it.

18. For this reason, I commissioned a recognised expert, Dr Patrick Randall, MA (clinical psychology), PsyD, Reg. Psychol., associate fellow of the Psychological Society of Ireland, consultant, clinical and forensic psychologist, and director of Forensic Psychological Services, to give me an assessment on the reliability or otherwise of the risk report. His conclusions[10] were that 'the assessment conducted by the risk assessor was methodologically unsound and consequently there was little prospect of gleaning an objective risk assessment. It is recommended that a thorough risk assessment be completed with Mr Duane. It is also recommended that any decisions informed by the report of the risk assessor be reviewed, given the unreliability of the methods utilised.'

19. I would hold that Dr Randall's conclusions completely undermine the basis on which the first instance promoter of justice argued his case and also undermine the basis on which the first instance judges reached their decisions to find me guilty of the accusations made by the complainants who gave evidence to the Cloyne tribunal. Accordingly the injustice of the first instance judgement is clearly established in accordance with the criteria laid down in canon 1645, n. 1° and n. 2°, and my petition for restitutio in integrum should be granted.

---

[10] His full report is appended to this letter.

20. **Corroboration versus credibility.** If any claim by the prosecution (promoter of justice) or a witness is to be accepted by the court as legally proven, there is need for independent corroboration of what is claimed. The first instance judges make no attempt to base their decision on any *corroboration* but, instead, concentrate on asserting the *credibility* of the witnesses. This is the wrong criterion for assessing evidence: those who lack credibility may sometimes tell the truth, and those who possess credibility may sometimes tell lies or may be mistaken, so credibility is no proof that an assertion is true. That is why the law says that the onus of proof rests on the person who makes an allegation, so that the word of one person will not prove the allegation, and that some independent corroboration, either from another witness or from circumstances, is necessary.

21. As regards credibility, even if it is an essential quality in a witness, it is hard to see how anyone could describe Donelle as a credible witness when she was brazen enough to fantasise in an ecclesiastical courtroom before four priests about her preferred mode of death for me—that I be thrown into a bath of acid, that I be nailed on a cross and planked outside a church, and that I be castrated, adding that she couldn't think of the worst death for 'that man' (i.e. me).

22. **Corroboration versus collaboration.** The second instance sentence of the CDF tribunal does not deal with the necessity of *corroboration* either but with the presence or absence of *collaboration*, which word is mentioned several times in regard to the evidence of the claimants. This is hard to make sense of unless it is a typographical error, as neither I nor my advocate based any argument on the presence or absence of collaboration between the witnesses. In fact there are plenty of indications of collaboration or collusion between the witnesses, though my advocate did not dwell on them in presenting my defence. Collusion was particularly evident in the cases of Edana and Naveen, who were classmates in school, and in the case of Naveen, who turned up uninvited at the session at which Donelle was scheduled to give evidence on 16 October 2009. The two of them insisted that the notary and my advocate leave the courtroom, and then they harangued the three judges for three and a half hours in what the judges recorded as a meeting which was 'emotional, angry, intense, difficult, erratic, and very confrontational'.

II. *The unreliability of 'recovered memory'*

23. A second reason for seeking a restitutio in integrum is that the first instance judgement neglected to see the reason why the various people who accused me of abusing them several decades earlier when they were allegedly under 16, suddenly, after counselling for their various psychiatric problems, came up with their claims of abuse. The theory is advanced that child abuse is so traumatic that memory of it is repressed or 'blocked', but that the blockage can be removed in counselling and the memory 'recovered' many years later.

24. The facts are that the several people who accused me had no difficulty in maintaining their friendly relationships with me up to about 2005. Then suddenly, in the atmosphere of a media storm of some well-publicised cases of actual abuse, and while undergoing counselling for problems unrelated to me, they claimed to have recovered remembrance of abuse. This theory of 'recovered memory' was popular for a while, not only in popular media accounts of alleged abuse but also even in apparently scientific circles. The theory has been debunked by expert psychiatrists as a general explanation of the sudden change from friendly relationship to active hostility based on claimed abuse, and in many court cases 'recovered memory' has been proven to be very unreliable and often shown to be the result of implantation of suggestions by the counsellors. For example, a person being counselled in regard to depression might be told that she has 'sad' eyes and asked if perhaps there is a reason to be found for this in childhood abuse. A suggestible person could easily be led to imagine there were such incidents and to genuinely believe they had occurred.

25. Two common features of all my accusers is that they had normal, friendly relationships with me for decades before they made any accusations and that they all discovered their accusations in the context of psychiatric counselling, some of them even being hospitalised in the same mental hospital at the same time. A feature common to the evidence taken in the Cloyne tribunal from the three women with whom this petition is concerned, Edana, Naveen, and Donelle, is that each of them spoke of having blocked out unwelcome incidents from their minds, and each of

them claimed they recalled these memories in the course of counselling or psychological investigation aimed at discovering the cause of their unexplained psychological problems such as depression, sleeplessness, and inability to make or sustain normal relationships with men. The same claims appear too in extrajudicial statements made to the police or to the church authorities, documents which were not presented to the ecclesiastical tribunal but which were part of the police or church investigations.

26. I am exploring with a renowned and acknowledged expert in the theory of 'blocked memory' and 'recovered memory' whether this might explain the sudden and puzzling reversal of normal social friendship to active and virulent hostility of some of my accusers. This expert has not yet come back to me with her report, but when she does, I would hope to be able to provide proof from this renowned expert that the implanting of ideas of child abuse in the minds of these suggestible women by their counsellors or psychologists or psychiatrists could be the real reason for the accusations levelled at me by these disturbed women who projected their imaginative fantasies onto me. Nor would I discount the possibility that some of them may have suffered abuse at the hands of another person and then transferred the accusation of guilt onto me.

27. For these two main reasons, namely the evident neglect of the fundamental principle that the onus of proof rests on the prosecution, which needs to provide independent corroboration of the claims of child abuse contrary to canon 1395 §2, and the showing up of the claims as being falsely based on 'recovered memories', I submit that I should be granted a restitutio in integrum so that the case might be properly tried ab initio by an independent tribunal.

Psychological Report and Assessment of Risk
Assessor and Associate Report on Fr Duane

Strictly Confidential
Psychological Report

The material contained in this letter is confidential. It is for the use of only those persons for whom it was prepared. This letter should not be made available to anyone else without the written permission of the undersigned. This letter was prepared for Mr Daniel Duane. This letter needs to be read in its entirety, and excerpts cannot be extracted and used in other reports.

1. Demographic details

Name: Daniel Duane

Date of birth: 16 March 1938

Reason for referral: Review of risk assessment

Documents reviewed:

Tribunal of the Diocese of Cloyne Protocol: P 52/2009–27961. Transcript of Evidence of Fenella, 19 April 2012.

Tribunal of the Diocese of Cloyne Protocol: P 52/2009–27961. Transcript of Evidence of Edana, 19 April 2012.

Tribunal of the Diocese of Cloyne Protocol: P 52/2009–27961. Transcript of Evidence of Donelle, 20 April 2012.

Tribunal of the Diocese of Cloyne Protocol: P 52/2009–27961. Transcript of Evidence of Naveen, 20 April 2012.

Tribunal of the Diocese of Cloyne Protocol: P 52/2009–27961. Transcript of Evidence of Fr Daniel Duane, 25 July 2012.

Risk Assessors' Specialist Risk Assessment of Fr Daniel Duane, 17 November 2009.

2. Background to referral

Mr Duane was self-referred to this service for expert advice regarding his upcoming trial before a canonical court. Mr Duane is appealing charges relating to historical sex offence allegations before the canonical court. He requested that the risk assessment conducted by risk assessor and associate be reviewed by the undersigned to determine whether it was conducted in an appropriate manner and whether the results reported by the risk assessor and associate could be viewed as valid and reliable.

It is beyond the scope of this assessment to comment on the level of risk posed by Mr Duane, as we have not conducted a risk assessment. It is also not possible for us to comment on the veracity of the statements made by the alleged victims as we have not conducted any assessment work with them.

Mr Duane (previously Fr Duane prior to laicisation) claims that he did not sexually abuse the alleged victims, and he views the risk assessment.

3. Assessment of risk conducted by risk assessor and associate

We did not see Mr Duane in a clinical capacity, nor did we conduct a risk assessment with him. We also did not interview any of the witnesses who gave evidence at the tribunal of the Diocese of Cloyne or assess them in any way. However, in preparing this letter, the undersigned had sight of the transcripts of evidence from Fenella, Edana, Donelle, Naveen, and Daniel Duane from the tribunal of the Diocese of Cloyne, and also the risk assessor's specialist risk assessment on Fr Duane.

It has been widely recognised that currently the most accurate methods of assessing risk of sexually offending are based on four principles. These are

(1) obtaining a detailed functional analysis of the offence process in order to determine how the offenders' problems contributed to their offending, (2) applying a suitable actuarial risk assessment, that is one that is bound in empirical research, to assess the global level of risk, (3) identifying stable dynamic risk factors that make potential treatment targets, and (4) monitoring acute dynamic risk factors that indicate the immediate risk of reoffending. [11]

Risk assessments purport to be an objective assessment of the likelihood of someone committing a specified offence within a specific time frame. A number of methods are usually employed to ensure that an objective, repeatable assessment is completed that can be relied upon.

It is beyond the scope of a risk assessment to determine which party has told the 'truth' or whether a version of events is more or less believable than another version of events. There are a number of risk assessment instruments that provide reliable indications of risk. It is normal for a number of instruments to be used in any one case. These should cover both static (unchangeable) variables and dynamic (changeable) variables. In addition it is common practice to use psychometric instruments to provide objective indicators of offence-related variables.

Theories that explore the aetiology of sexual offending are helpful only insofar as they identify areas that merit further empirical exploration and verification to determine the utility of the theory.

In the case of the report compiled by the risk assessor and his associate, they do not specify their methodology, but it is evident from the report that they reviewed statements made by the alleged victims, which they put to the accused priest, and noted his responses. They then appeared to have extrapolated behaviour and attitudes that they attribute to the accused.

Following this they applied a theory developed by one of the authors of the report which has not been validated by peer review, and which has little

---

[11] A. R. Beech, D. D. Fisher, and D. Thornton, 'Risk Assessment of Sex Offenders', *Professional Psychology: Research and Practice*, 34/4 (2003), 339–52.

prospect of discriminating offenders from non-offenders, to determine whether there were similarities in the accused's behaviour to a group of offenders.

There is no evidence of the risk assessors having used actuarial risk instruments or structured risk instruments to determine risk. There is no evidence of their having used any psychometric methods to determine the presence or absence of offence-related variables.

4. Conclusions and recommendations

The assessment conducted by the risk assessors was methodologically unsound, and consequently there was little prospect of gleaning an objective risk assessment.

It is recommended that a thorough risk assessment be completed with Mr Duane. It is also recommended that any decisions informed by the report of the risk assessor and his associate be reviewed, given the unreliability of the methods utilised.

It is recommended that Mr Duane complete a Fitness for Ministry Assessment should questions be raised about his professional conduct.

Dr Patrick Randall, MA (clinical psychology), PsyD, Reg. Psychol., Associate Fellow of the Psychological Society of Ireland
Consultant and Clinical and Forensic Psychologist
Director

Restitutio in integrum, **part 2**

Review of evidence overlooked and ignored by the first instance (and unchallenged by the second instance) in the light of the discrediting of the Edana risk assessment and the evidence of 'false memory syndrome' in the claimants' depositions

1.   Donelle, Edana, and Naveen stated that they were sexually abused by Fr Duane in the 1980s and that their minds 'blocked' or 'suppressed' the memory of the sexual abuse, but they 'recovered' memories of the alleged abuse decades later, around 2005, while in therapy. The evidence presented by these three claimants to the Cloyne Diocesan Tribunal needs to be reviewed in the context of modern expert views by Dr Elizabeth Loftus and Dr Patricia Casey on 'false memory syndrome'.

2.   As indicated in my lodgement of a request, dated 2 April 2015, for restitutio in integrum, the reliance placed by the Cloyne tribunal on the risk assessment report is completely discredited and undermined by the expert opinion of Dr Pat Randall, an expert forensic psychologist and risk assessor, who testifies that the report is methodologically unsound and 'unreliable'. (All copies of the said risk assessment are to be located by the bishop and withdrawn from circulation because of their serious defamatory content.)

3.   I now address the second major source of injustice in the sentence of the first instance sentence, namely that the judgement is based on a very uncritical acceptance of the evidence taken by the Cloyne tribunal from witnesses or claimants which can be shown to be false and that, without this evidence, the dispositive part of the judgement could not be sustained.

4.   All three claimants whose claims were accepted by the Cloyne tribunal and confirmed by the CDF tribunal stated that they were sexually abused by Fr Duane in the 1970s or1980s and that they 'blocked' or 'suppressed' the memory of the sexual abuse, but they 'recovered' memories of the alleged abuse decades later, around 2005, while in therapy.

5.   On the contrary, during the intervening quarter of a century before the claimed 'memory recovery', they behaved as persons totally unaware

of any alleged abuse, as confirmed by their maintenance of a cordial and friendly relationship with Fr Duane during this period. Both experts, Dr Casey and Dr Loftus, claim this sequence of events is typical of 'false memory syndrome'.

6. The supposedly 'recovered memories' are therefore not an acceptable proof of the existence of any such abuse of which Fr Duane was claimed to be guilty.

7. Dr Casey and Dr Loftus also claim there is no evidence that the human memory can or does block out any traumatic events and that there is no evidence to prove that childhood sexual abuse is an exception to the rule. These 'recovered memories' are termed 'false memories' and have very little or no value in court. As a result of this modern interpretation, most jurisdictions of the Western world regard this type of evidence as 'unreliable'. In fact some states of America regard it as 'junk science' or hearsay. In Ireland, as far back as 2005, the Irish State Appeal Courts acquitted Nora Wall, a former nun who had been convicted in the lower court of rape, because the only evidence against her was 'recovered or false evidence'.

8. As indicated in the attached Appendices 2 and 3 (Chapter 5 on *Memory* from a book by Casey, Craven, and Brady, 2010, called *Psychiatry and the Law*, and 'Recent Advances on False Memory Research', by Elizabeth Loftus and Cara Laney, in *South African Journal of Psychology*(2013), the assessment of the validity of so-called 'recovered memory' is a much debated topic, and the majority view is that 'recovered memory' is as often as not 'false memory' and quite unreliable as proof in law cases, especially when there is question of alleged recovery, decades later, of memory of sexual abuse in childhood.

9. The experts also claim that 'false memory' can be identified by certain qualities in the evidence being assessed, referred to as *contamination*, *condensation*, and *embellishment*. These qualities can be easily discerned in the depositions and other statements of all three claimants. Factual errors and uncertainty about details and dates can also be identified.

I. Review of Naveen's evidence

10. A. W., Naveen (born 1 January 1966), Edana (born 4 October 1965), and Muirin, all of whom made allegations against Fr Duane, were classmates in the same school. They sat their Intermediate Certificate examination in 1981 and their Leaving Certificate examination in 1983. Naveen, Edana, and Muirin used to call as a group, not to Fr Duane, but to another priest with whom Fr Duane shared a house. It was alleged that they did so by invitation, after a retreat allegedly given by Fr Duane and another priest.

11. In fact, it was accepted to the satisfaction of the court in both circuit criminal trials of Fr Duane that:

Fr Duane did not participate in this retreat;
the probable date of the retreat was 1981;
Fr Duane wouldn't have known any of the group calling on the other priest before that, and even then, it took considerable time, because of his duties in St Colman's College, before he met them; and
none of them were calling on their own while his fellow priest and their joint housekeeper were resident in the parish up to September 1983, when they both left.

12. The unlikelihood of their visiting the house individually, rather than as a group, was corroborated by Edana, who stated that she didn't call in the year of her Leaving Certificate, which was 1983 (Edana deposition, 16. 4).

13. Naveen called with others for about two years or more before calling on her own. She testified: 'We [the group] would call to the house every couple of weeks. ... It was very seldom Duane and the other priest would be in the house at the same time. ... Dan Duane began to encourage us to call individually. ... I was 13 years old' (first Garda statement). That would be 1979, two years before the retreat (therefore an anachronism).

14. She said she knew Fr Duane before the retreat (Cloyne first instance sentence, §168). She wouldn't have known him before the retreat as he had

nothing to do with parish affairs. She changed her statement to: 'she didn't know how it came about that she started calling on her own' (second Garda statement). These are *direct contradictions.*

15. In her deposition she claimed Fr Duane invited her to come alone to discuss her domestic problems. (This is an instance of embellishment.) The other priest left in September1983. Naveen made no reference to the housekeeper. According to her account, Fr Duane was always alone when she called. It's his recollection that they didn't call before 1983. She declared in her statement to the Gardai that she started calling in 1979. ... Fr Duane didn't meet her until after 1981 or 1982 and only in a group session.

16. In her statement to the diocesan delegate for child abuse allegations, Naveen claimed to be 16 when she started calling (she was 16 in 1982). The other priest only arrived in summer of 1979 (the retreat was in 1981), and the group were calling a good while before Fr Duane met them and for a good while after he met them. The main topic of conversation was the Intermediate Certificate. There were ten or twelve in the group. As Fr Duane was only lodging in the house, he would not be there very often, so it took some time to get to meet them. Fr Duane said: 'We shared a resident housekeeper, and we agreed that, since there were two priests sharing the one house, the housekeeper would answer the door and phone 24/7' (except for her day off on Monday, when she would travel with Fr Duane to her home in Fermoy. He would collect her again in the evening). She left in 1983. Fr Duane shared the house for another year with Fr Mick Corkery.

17. Naveen says: 'It was summer of 1980. The first incident with Fr Duane happened ... not long after starting my periods' (first Garda statement). This would have been *prior* to the retreat in 1981. ... 'I got home from Duane's house on that occasion. I cannot be certain, but I have a sense he might have given me a drive home' (first Garda statement). She claimed how difficult it was 'to get home to get across the town in her soiled dress' (second Garda statement, p. 3).

18.

> Naveen's recollection of circumstantial evidence was criticised by the judge in the civil trial. She gave different versions of dates and events as in the above evidence.
>
> She also referred to a Kathleen, who could not be traced.
>
> She was 'unaware that she spoke to RD, her ex-boyfriend, about Duane'. RD corroborated Fr Duane's evidence.
>
> She insists that she stopped calling when she reached 16 years of age. (She claimed to have discussed *The Thornbirds*, a TV miniseries, first shown in Ireland in 1984. She was 18 in 1984.)
>
> She denies that she was friendly with Fr Duane up to 1992, when she called on him at his house.
>
> She couldn't say whether she had intercourse with Fr Duane.
>
> She was in psychiatric care for an unrelated issue and never mentioned the alleged abuse.
>
> She blames hypnosis for her inability to remember. She says she blocked the abuse out of her mind, and yet she claims to have suffered from nightmares for twenty years.
>
> The other priest may not recollect her calling in a group, but she nominates five, including Edana (first Garda statement).

20. Fr Duane moved to St Colman's in 1984, but he maintained contact with Naveen through postcards and Christmas cards, and he met her a good few times. They were on friendly terms up to the time she got married.

21. In her statement to the Gardai, Naveen claimed to have mentioned the alleged abuse to three priests, but all three denied this under oath in the civil court trial. In the civil trial, as the priests gave their evidence, she kept saying 'that is not true' until the judge intervened. ... Again she denied she instructed her solicitor to sue for compensation until the judge intervened. The judges in the first instance appear to have rationalised and ignored the three priests' evidence. Naveen 'wanted' or 'tried' to tell them, but she didn't.

22. She declared that 'all priests are "scum"' and said that she wanted her solicitor to put Fr Duane 'behind bars', that is in prison.

23. She said that she called on Fr Duane in Buttevant. He has no recollection of her calling, but her ex-boyfriend did call. He wanted to know what was wrong with Naveen and why was she calling on him. He corroborated that to the Gardai. That was her reason for calling on Fr Duane before she got married (*c.* 1991), to apologise for RD's visit and interrogation. Fr Duane assured her that it wasn't her fault and that it hadn't damaged their friendship. On her last visit (she drove her own car, a grey-coloured hatchback, to his house, even though he had to meet her and show her the way because it was dark), she talked about marriage and disclosed that she had a problem: she could not bear anybody touching her lower abdomen, and the thought of a child in there would drive her mad. It immediately prompted him to advise her to discuss this thoroughly with her future husband. He wished her well and parted with the usual hug and good wishes.

24. Also she talked about *The Thornbirds*, a TV miniseries, in 1983: *The Thornbirds* was filmed in the United States in 1983, but it wasn't shown in Ireland until 1984. This supports Fr Duane's evidence that Naveen didn't call on her own until after 1983. Donelle also compared herself to the young girl in *The Thornbirds*.

25. Naveen also states: 'As he [Fr Duane] was doing it [i.e. abusing her] people were coming to the door' (first Garda statement). In fact, the window was large and transparent so that people could see what was going on in the room from the outside. So, how could she be lying on the couch and being allegedly abused and know that people were coming to the door? Where was the housekeeper?

26. She also said, 'We talked about a book called *Forbidden Love.*' Fr Duane never heard of it.

27. Naveen never talked about marriage or children, yet in her statement to the Gardai she said that 'he [Fr Duane] wanted to give me a child'.

28. **Hypnosis.** Ailis's father was the first to promote hypnosis in 2008, in a newspaper article (*Sunday Tribune*, 22 Apr. 2008). Apart from Keita and Naveen, there was no mention of it in any of the complainants' statements prior to this. Donelle's followed on his statement. (This is

a typical example of 'contamination' of evidence and symptomatic of false memory syndrome.)Donelle made her allegation in 2005 and never mentioned hypnosis, but since then she has made reference to being under a spell. She claimed she mentioned it to the bishop in 2006, but he denied it (Cloyne report). None of Naveen's group experienced hypnosis.

29. Neither Naveen nor Edana ever made appointments. Fr Duane never encouraged them to call. They never seemed nervous or afraid. The only reason they stopped calling was their lack of transport to Fermoy when Fr Duane went to live there.

30. Naveen told the diocesan delegate for child abuse allegations that she couldn't remember because of hypnosis. She always thought she was 16 when the abuse started, but now she realises she was 13. She also claimed in her statement to him: 'I cannot remember because of the use of hypnosis.' Her therapist stated that she mentioned sexual abuse by two priests but never went into any detail over thirty-five therapy sessions within one year. It emerged at the civil trial that she attended a psychiatrist about an unrelated issue some time before she made the allegation and never referred to the alleged abuse or to hypnosis.

31. She also alleged that Fr Duane said he noticed her at Legion of Mary meetings. Fr Duane had nothing to do with the Red Cross since 1971, and he had never been to Legion meetings, as he had nothing to do with the parish. His job was in Fermoy, in St Colman's, 9 a.m. –4 p.m. on all school days. He organised school retreats but never gave them as they conflicted with his school hours.

32. **Contamination of evidence.** 'I also know I wasn't there when I was 17' (Naveen, 11. 8–9). She didn't start calling until she was 17 or 18, and she called in 1984 (when *The Thornbirds* TV series was first shown in Ireland).

33.

> Naveen didn't come to Buttevant, which she claims, and she did come to Fr Duane's house in Kanturk, which she denies.
>
> Naveen claims that she had oral sex with Fr Duane in his car, and he has no recollection of her ever being in his car: 'I remember the

drives home, my head being pushed down in the car' (Naveen, 11. 15–18). This shows traces of contamination with Donelle's account: 'I remember being in his car and him waving out the window to people. … My head was on his penis across the car with his hand down on top of my head' (Donelle, 21. 17–22). These incidents are fabricated and never happened.

34.

There are traces of embellishment too in references to choking feelings (globus hystericus) by Donelle, 'All the things I can't eat … tomato' (Donelle, 21. 26–22. 3), and by Naveen, 'golf balls in my throat' (Naveen, Cloyne report, 27. 10).

35.

Naveen would never call in the summer because, she says, 'he [Fr Duane] always went to the States' (Naveen, 12. 6–7), repeating what Donelle (20.17.18) and Fenella stated. 'However,' she says, 'I believe I was 14 years of age and that it was summertime of 1980 … because of a silly white dress and I wore and sandals' (first Garda statement, p. 2).

36.

Donelle mentioned 'blood on a napkin' (Donelle's deposition, 16. 25). Naveen similarly speaks of Fr Duane allegedly saying, 'This blood is sacred' (Naveen, 14. 23). This does not appear in any of her earlier statements and is another contaminated embellishment.

37.

'God would approve' appeared in Naveen's evidence at the trial for the first time (termed 'embellishment' by Fr Duane's barrister). She added more embellishments, for example 'using the Bible and wearing a stole' ('ribbon'). 'He would stand up and put his hand on the Bible the same as he would have done when he abused me' (Naveen, 16. 15–17). This is the first time this piece of alleged and bizarre evidence appears.

38.

> She also claims that 'the abuse took place over a two-year period'. But she claims 'over three years' to the tribunal (Naveen, 10. 15).

39. Naveen states that 'when driven home, it was like he was finished with you; bye, bye, bye, hurried' (Naveen, 13. 5–7). Fr Duane has no recollection of ever driving her home or of her being in his car. Donelle has a similar embellishment: 'The worst part of it all was the total dismissal. I often wondered why my leg wasn't broken' (Donelle, 39. 1–8).

40. Naveen claimed, 'He had even given me something stolen' (the book *Unconditional Love*). Fr Duane has no recollection of ever seeing that book. The executive librarian with Cork County Library and Arts Services testified, 'This book would be available from Post Primary School Library in the early eighties, and no records now remain. I cannot state where this book *Unconditional Love* ended up.' The allegation that Fr Duane stole the book is untrue.

41. Naveen's 'recovered memory' was probably triggered by Edana, who contacted her and told her she was abused by Fr Duane (Naveen, Garda statement). Naveen was amazed and made her allegation just months later.

II. Review of Edana's evidence

42. In the first instance the judges could not reach moral certainty (Sentence, §§164, 167) on what age Edana was when she was allegedly abused by Fr Duane. Their verdict was therefore abuse of a vulnerable *adult*. If so, the allegations by Edana were barred by prescription, and the decision of the second instance should have been not to confirm the decision of the first instance tribunal, *pari ratione* with their decision (pp. 12–13) not to confirm the decision of the first instance tribunal in regard to the Fenella and Caelan allegations, as they decided to interpret strictly the CDF's 'derogation from prescription for actions concerning the delict of sexual abuse of *minors*' (letter, 5 May 2009, Prot. N. 52/2009 – 27961, emphasis added). The ordinary rules of prescription in canon 1362 therefore apply.

43. Edana came to Fr Duane's house (which he shared with another priest) with a group including Naveen and A. W. She commenced to call on her own only after the other priest left in September 1983. She never made an appointment, and she was never invited. She maintains it was always on a Saturday night. Fr Duane was seldom around on a Saturday night as he usually went out socialising, mostly to the golf club. He didn't drink alcohol, but he liked a game of cards in the members' lounge.

44. Edana alleges she was 'assaulted and beaten, wrongfully detained and falsely imprisoned, and subjected to sexualised behaviour by Fr Duane on her casual visits' (claim form). These are the usual phrases put in by lawyers to bolster up their claims for damages.

---

45. Edana alleges that all these visits took place on Saturday nights when the other priest would be at meetings. He detested meetings, but the priest who replaced him was usually out on a Saturday night at meetings. She states that during these visits, she and Fr Duane 'drank cups of tea and talked' (Garda statement, 1). She mentioned being in the kitchen and in the corridor. 'We were both laughing' (Garda statement, 1). That would indicate that there was no housekeeper present, that is that it was later than September 1983 (Edana, 8. 17–26, 9. 3–4).

46. Edana had no real friends, and she was very unhappy. Fr Duane left in August 1984, and she had no means of transport to Fermoy. However, they communicated by postcards and Christmas cards.

47. She came backstage after a Holy Show concert in Connolly Hall, Cork, to meet Fr Duane, and he gave her a lift back to her lodgings in Wilton in Cork city. That was Christmas 1984, four months after Fr Duane left the parish. She called on him a few years later to his house in Kanturk and didn't seem nervous. He enquired if she had met any nice men, and she immediately appeared uneasy—talking about relationships was to her 'dirty talk'. He didn't sit alongside her. He never sat near her; the nearest would have been when he gave her a lift in the car. Her peers were well aware that Edana did not like talk about relationships or any contact with men.

48. Fr Duane and Edana exchanged Christmas cards for a few years after that as he kept reminding her to collect her sunglasses. He went to her parents' funerals and talked to her. Ailis's father described her as 'Ailis's school-hood friend', and she also shared psychiatric care with Ailis. It is strangely coincidental that shortly after Ailis died, Edana went to the Gardai. She also contacted Naveen and told her she had gone to the Gardai. Naveen and her friend Muirin then went to the Gardai. Muirin's allegation was that he touched her on the cheek with his hand in front of a witness. The Gardai assured Fr Duane that there was no sexual allegation; nevertheless, he was sued by Muirin's lawyers for 'wanton frequent sexual abuse'. She received monetary reward like all the others. Fr Duane showed a photograph of Edana wearing jeans in his house dated summer of 1984. They both made allegations that they had been sexually abused while wearing dresses. Unfortunately, the housekeeper died some years ago and is therefore unable to provide evidence to refute the claims of these women.

50. The risk assessor and associate were in receipt of all the above-mentioned evidence. He again seems to have overlooked their constant amicable relationship with Fr Duane for such a long period of time after the alleged incidents. This behaviour is not consistent with being victims of sexual abuse. The DPP recognised it. It was evident in the second civil trial in Cork Criminal Court that Naveen unsuccessfully denied that relationship. She totally avoided mentioning it to the Gardai. Edana partially denied it when she said that she and Fr Duane met casually in Kanturk. Fr Duane's recollection is that in fact she called on him at his house. Her behaviour would hardly indicate fear around somebody who is alleged to have sexually abused her.

51. In sum, Edana, Naveen, and Donelle were unaware of any abuse and behaved accordingly before 'false memories' were triggered in therapy. They subsequently rationalised their friendly relationship with Fr Duane, trying to explain away their coming back for 'more abuse' by being hypnotised or under a 'spell' and unable to stop calling.

52. **Age variation.** According to the first instance sentence, §152, 'Edana says she was around 14–15 years when she began calling.' The retreat was

held in 1981 during her Intermediate Certificate year. It is unlikely that it was before the real certificate examinations, because of the earlier trial examinations ('mocks'), so it is more likely to have been in the autumn of 1981. They called in groups after the retreat for a good while before Fr Duane met them.

53. 'Then I suppose later on I would have called on an individual basis.' Edana is not very definite about how long after. Even if she called, she would have been 16 years of age in October 1981, which is only one month after the retreat, and that is highly improbable as already established. Fr Duane's evidence is more definite and credible.

54. None of the group called individually until the other priest left in autumn of 1983. They *started* calling on him, not on Fr Duane. The absence of the housekeeper (after she left in September 1983) is strong corroboration of Fr Duane's account.

55. If Edana was allegedly sexually abused and allegedly 'shocked, unable to react, paralysed with fear, and numbed' (first tribunal sentence, §167), *then why did she keep calling back*? It must have been because she was unaware of any abuse. She would have continued calling thereafter, only for the fact that Fr Duane left and she had no method of transport. This is another example of false memory.

56. **Counselling.** Edana had serious domestic problems with her father and her brother. She started counselling in 1995 because 'she was very unhappy and depressed'. The reason for going for counselling was for this unhappiness and depression, and not to discuss alleged sexual abuse, since she wasn't aware of any. After five or six years in counselling, she claims she became conscious or aware of the alleged sexual abuse. It has to be repeated that the expert evidence of Dr Loftus and Dr Casey is that there is no evidence that traumatic events can be blocked from the human memory, and thus recovery is not possible. The alleged sexual abuse was not responsible for her depression and unhappiness (Edana, 11. 21–23). In her 'claim form' she claims the alleged sexual abuse was the cause of all her problems. She resumed counselling in 2004 and says that therapy was 'all about the abuse'.

57. According to the first instance sentence, §162, Edana had a crush on the other priest, and it would be very unlikely that she would call on Fr Duane while he was still resident with him. This corroborates Fr Duane's version of events, that she didn't begin to call until the other priest had left in September 1983. She claims she called in 1981–2.

58. After 1983, with the other priest and housekeeper gone, Edana wouldn't be taking any risk of meeting him. She admitted meeting Fr Duane at a concert in 1984, and she denied it in her deposition (claim form) (Edana, 19. 20).

59. Edana testified that 'I wasn't visiting the house in my Leaving Certificate year [1983]' (Edana, 16. 5–6). Fr Duane presented a photograph of her taken in 1984 in his house. She said too that 'between leaving school and meeting Dan Duane in Kanturk there was no contact at all' (Edana, 19. 18–20). But she omitted to mention her presence at the Holy Show (concert in Cork in 1984) and the two times when he reminded her to collect her glasses. 'I met him on two occasions shortly after, and he has hinted I should call for them' (Garda statement,1).

60. The other priest observed that she had a gender issue. Her attire was masculine, and she had a huge issue with her father. 'I don't know if she met him [Fr Duane] on his own.' In her first Garda statement, she admitted to having a crush on the other priest. She was calling on him before she called on Fr Duane. This would indicate that she didn't call on Fr Duane until after the other priest had left the parish, that is after September 1983. This corroborates Fr Duane's version of events. The judge in the civil trial commended Fr Duane's recollection of events and said that 'he trusted his memory'.

61. The Cloyne first instance tribunal (§166) thinks otherwise: 'Despite Fr Duane's efforts to *deliberately muddle* and *confuse dates* and *events*, in addition to *undermining* the *credibility* of the witness and her motivation, the judges have arrived at moral certainty about the credibility of the incidents of sexual abuse.' So the tribunal accuses Fr Duane of giving

evidence that was *deliberately* misleading, whereas in fact Fr Duane was recollecting events and dates of what had occurred, not inventing.

62. The other priest expressed *surprise* at allegations of inappropriate behaviour.

63. **Alleged blocking of memories.** Edana claimed she blocked the incidents of abuse from her consciousness. 'I suppose I just pretended it wasn't happening' (Edana, 7. 17–18). 'I like to say I didn't even tell myself it had happened' (Edana, 7. 27–28). 'Like when this happened to me I buried it, I denied it had happened to myself. I didn't contemplate it afterwards' (Edana, 10. 10–13).

III. Review of Donelle's evidence

64. Donelle was in a friendly, cordial relationship with Fr Duane just months before she made the allegation; that is, up to 2005 she was not aware of any alleged sexual abuse. She completely trusted Fr Duane, seeking from him counselling with all her problems, in private, behind closed doors. When she failed in persuading him to succumb to her advances, she changed dramatically. She sent him a text later stating that of all her problems, the biggest and worst was his rejection of her.

65. Ultimately, when the high court case she took against the bishop and Fr Duane, seeking compensation, collapsed, she, together with Ailis's father, started a public campaign of hatred and false allegations against Fr Duane. They used the print media, social media, TV, and radio. Her psychiatric report, ordered by lawyers for One in Four (an advocacy group agitating for alleged sexual abuse victims), revealed her inability to clearly recall past events, thus undermining her competence as a credible witness and collapsing her case. She posed under different pseudonyms and embraced the mantle of a 'woman scorned'. Her evidence to the DPP (director of public prosecutions), one of the most experienced investigators in the state, was sent back with a nolle prosequi and an explanation that there was 'no evidence of sexual, criminal behaviour'.

66. **Age.** Fr Duane agrees that Donelle called on him at his house when she was 14, circa 1970. He barred her from calling when he discovered she had a 'crush' on him. Her diary corroborates this 'crush', and her calling with money for the Red Cross and other petty excuses. She describes him as in 'a funny mood ... not funny', that is, not pleased with her visits. Except for her first visit with a Mass card, which was brief, she was never alone with him. There was no physical or emotional contact with her. She claims her diary ends before any alleged abuse (Donelle, 41. 36), but there is no corroboration offered. Fr Duane was out of the parish for 1971, 1972, and most of 1973. He supplied documentary evidence to support this claim (diplomas and diocesan records). Donelle continued to call on his mother during those years when Fr Duane was not there. He allowed her back after the death of her father in June 1974, by which time she was 18. She claims her visits 'could be a few times a week' (Donelle, 28. 21) but again provides no corroboration. Fr Duane claims she visited about once a fortnight. The priest who shared the house with him said she visited about 'once every three weeks', which corroborates Fr Duane's evidence.

67. Fr Duane presented the same evidence to the first instance tribunal, giving multiple alibis of his being in the USA on vacation, in Dublin on a full-time course, and in Limerick on a part-time course at the times of Donelle's alleged abuse. Not only was there no alleged abuse, but also there wasn't even opportunity for it to take place. Fr Duane's evidence was clear and constant from the outset. Donelle's evidence, on the contrary, was wavering and uncertain.

68. She offered as evidence a diary or scrapbook which neither the presiding judge in the first instance deposition nor the bishop scrutinised, and which had 'no details of sexual abuse'. However, it did support Fr Duane's view that she had a 'crush' on him, and that he warned her not to be calling. She wrote in the diary: 'I called to Fr Duane today with Red Cross money. He was in a funny mood ... not a funny mood.' He was displeased. She knew she was being discouraged, despite the view of the judges in the first instance that he was not discouraging her enough. Yet those same judges failed to stop her from ranting and threatening Fr Duane and even the judges themselves in her deposition.

69. Donelle's impact statement and highly descriptive and embellished account of alleged sexual abuse appear at first to be authentic. However, she admits to having had a sexual relationship for years with a married man, which she claims was a 'horrific relationship' (Donelle, 30. 20). She says, 'He was just pure temper, a complete nutcase of a man. It was difficult getting away from him.' She also says, 'I feel I have been a target for abuse all my life. Every association I have had with men since, they have all been older, one worse than the other as regards abuse' (Donelle, 9. 20–1). Her impact statement and sexual abuse allegations against Fr Duane are seriously diminished by that evidence. Her admission of multiple instances of sexual abuse by other men, in contrast with her friendly, cordial relationship with Fr Duane up to the time she made the allegation, casts serious doubt on her claim. Furthermore, Fr Duane corroborated this cordial relationship with artefacts, letters, CDs, and text messages, e. g., 'I could not bear you not being in my life' and 'We were not an ugly union.'

70. Fr Duane never solicited her to call; indeed, he barred her from calling. Where is the evidence that grooming occurred? Is it not possible, even probable, she is projecting or transferring all the abuse she ever suffered with other men onto Fr Duane? This is not unlikely in view of false memory, which is often allied to such transference.

71. **Donelle's money motive.** A priest's evidence, which predated the Garda evidence, was significant re her making the allegation of abuse. 'She talked mostly about money. All she wanted was money. Her whole emphasis was on money.' This is contrary to what she claims herself, and also what the judges accepted, that her daughter's age was the reason for making the allegation. The presiding judge claims that she discussed her alleged sexual abuse with a priest. She did mention 'horrible things', but they did not *discuss* them. He merely assumed she was referring to abuse of some sort.

72. The judges also claim she discussed her alleged abuse a few times before she made the allegation to the bishop. There is no specific evidence for this. What is specific is that she went to the bishop for the first time in 2005–2006. As a result the bishop requested a priest to contact her,

and he advised her to go to the vicar general. She also contacted a lawyer, who sued Fr Duane for the 'horrible things' he allegedly perpetrated on her as a teenager. There were no specifics. The priest's evidence is contemporaneous with the first allegation to the bishop and should not be considered as corroboration.

73. **Donelle's credibility.** The first instance judges dwelt on *credibility* as a criterion for proof rather than on evidence. In our first submission requesting restitutio in integrum, we presented some examples of her *incredibility* rather than her credibility. Continuing on, we present more evidence on the lack of credibility of her evidence. There were at least twenty-seven fabrications in Donelle's deposition. The following is a sample of some more of these untruths. She claimed Fr Duane abused his own relation; that he had a vasectomy; and that he called on her at her house and held her son in his arms. (Fr Cogan baptised the child (it's recorded in the parish register), so Fr Cogan would have visited her house. Fr Duane is willing to undergo medical tests.)She claims that he played cards with her father, that he brought priests to their house, that he officiated at her father's funeral. (All these claims are untrue—Fr Duane had no duties in her parish.)She claimed he took her to a doctor in Cork after her misadventure with her first sexual encounter. (Her deposition, 38. 18, is the first time she mentions this; it is not in any of her earlier statements. Fr Duane mentioned it first in his statement to the Gardai and also nominated her accomplice.)She also claimed she wrote a threatening letter to him, which is not true. She never referred to the other correspondence. She referred to her cousin Fr J as a bishop (deposition, 6. 13), which is not true. She portrays Fr Duane as a drinker. In fact, he was a Pioneer (teetotaller) until the early 1980s, and though he never wore the Pioneer pin after that, he certainly didn't drink a lot. Contrary to her claim, Fr Duane doesn't have 'false hair or a false tan'. For somebody who claims to have called on him several times a week, that is a serious blunder. She claimed in an article in the *Irish Examiner* (14 July 2011) that 'on seeing a similar car to his she would be rendered speechless, unable to move an arm or breathe'. A few years previously she was completely comfortable in his house with all the doors locked.

74. She made several allegations to the CEO (NBSC) in 2008 about Fr Duane. These were proven false by independent witnesses:

She said he was officiating at weddings—not true.

She said he was on the altar at funerals—not true.

She said she phoned his parish priest (PP) in 1990 making a complaint about Fr Duane. The PP denies he received any such call. The bishop corroborates the PP's evidence.

She claimed the bishop mentioned hypnosis. He denied it.

She claimed the vicar general said the allegations were first raised in the early 1980s. He denies he said it.

Her claim that Fr Duane visited other complainants with another priest is not true.

She claimed the diocese covered up in her case. (The Cloyne report 9. 106, 88, 86, 87, 112, 103 found no cover-up in her case.)

75. Contrast this persistent lying with the first instance sentence in §105 where the presiding judge implies that Fr Duane is not a credible witness, citing just *one instance* where he answered, 'No comment. Not guilty' to an unlawful leading question where he was protected from answering the question by canon 1728 §2, which says that the accused person is not bound to admit to an offence. (This was the third time his advocate intervened to suggest that he answer just 'Canon 1728 §2' when the judge asked leading questions inviting admission of guilt. It occurred in the very first session of the tribunal, the *contestatio litis*, which had to be declared invalid.)Fr Duane's response was interpreted as not telling the truth, when at least he ought to have been granted a not guilty plea in accordance with the law.

76. In contrast, in the first instance sentence, §126, the judges were impressed with the credibility (!) of Donelle and acknowledged how traumatised she was by the alleged abuse, ignoring her abusive past with other men and her cordial relationship with Fr Duane up to the time she made the allegation. It appears from her long list of fabrications that she is incapable of discerning truth from fantasy, traces of *pseudologia fantastica* or pathological lying (Casey, Craven, Brady, 5, #4).

77. Donelle's deposition is best described in her own words: 'I am all over the place now, but I am so angry' (Donelle, 24. 22). It is permeated with irrational jargon and embellishments completely lacking evidence, interspersed with bouts of vitriol, hatred, death wishes of a barbaric nature, and threats of a serious nature to the judges if they did not deliver her desired verdict, a guilty verdict. The judges were silent, which indicates consent. In the interests of due process, one would expect an intervention. They allowed her to run like an unbroken horse with free rein, either afraid or unwilling to intervene.

78. The judges also experienced the haranguing by Donelle and Naveen in the three-and-a-half-hour aborted session of 16 October 2009 which was described by the judges as 'emotional, angry, intense, difficult, erratic, and very confrontational', and these same judges nonchalantly accuse Fr Duane of failing to stop her from calling to his house! The apostolic administrator failed, the DPP failed, and the judges failed. One obvious omission by the judges in Donelle's deposition was to seek her views on her friendly relationship with Fr Duane up to the time she made the allegation.

79. On the other hand, Fr Duane's deposition was laden with evidence and was constantly challenged by the judges. This may be a subtle imbalance, but it is still an inequity. At the end of the session, his advocate adverted to same: 'I must say I was astonished at your asking questions in relation to canon 1728, paragraph 2, which invited Dan to accept responsibility for certain things' (Dan Duane deposition, 103. 29–104. 1)!

80. **The risk report.** The first instance judges placed great emphasis on the risk assessment with its now proven flawed assertions as circumstantial evidence to support their verdict that Donelle was abused as a minor. In fact it is Donelle's recollection that is fundamentally flawed (false memory), as noted in her psychiatric report, and her recall is blighted by her irrational hatred of Fr Duane. 'My hatred for him I cannot describe' (Donelle, 9. 24). 'I hate him, I hate him' (Donelle, 16. 27). 'How I haven't killed him I don't know' (Donelle, 22. 10). 'I am so angry with the legal system of this country, I am so angry with the church' (Donelle, 17. 19). 'I'm all over the place, I'm so angry.' Compare that with her assertion 'I

could not bear you not being in my life' (Cloyne tribunal sentence §114). Her evidence has all the hallmarks of false memory.

81. All the claimants' evidence to the tribunal is riddled with embellishments compared to their Garda statements. For example, there is no mention of fellatio in their Garda statements, whereas their depositions are strewn with it. Fr Duane has always maintained that it never happened, and he trusts his memory.

82. **False memory syndrome.** Blocked or repressed memory has been neither accepted by mainstream psychology nor unequivocally proven to exist. According to the leading expert in this field, Elizabeth Loftus, 'There is no credible scientific support for the notion of repressed/recovered memories' (Laney, Loftus, p. 138,#3).

83. In July 2012 the Minnesota Supreme Court ruled that repressed memory is not acceptable as evidence and is equivalent to superstition, hearsay, or junk science.

84. Nora Wall, a former Irish nun, was wrongfully convicted of rape in June 1999. She was the first woman in the history of the Irish State to be convicted of rape and the only person in the history of the state to be convicted on repressed memory evidence. One witness, Regina Walsh (repressed memory), had a psychiatric history, and the other witness, Patricia Phelan, subsequently admitted to having lied. In December 2005, the Court of Criminal Appeal in Ireland certified that Nora Wall had been the victim of a miscarriage of justice.

85. Elizabeth Loftus also says, 'Traumatic memories are not necessarily accurate memories' ('Creating False Memories', *Scientific American*, 227/3 (2005); and *The Myth of Repressed Memory*, by Elizabeth Loftus and Katherine Ketcham,1996). She claims that repressed memory faces problems of altered memory. In one experiment a teenage boy was able to conjure up a memory of an event that never happened. If a normal person can do it, then how much more likely it would be for susceptible people with emotional and traumatic experiences to conjure up altered memories.

86. In one study, 85 per cent of therapists believed the recovered evidence to be authentic through use of symptomatology. Most recovered memories are triggered while subjects are in therapy, and Loftus believes that when subjects present symptoms of depression and unhappiness, therapists believe that it has connections with child abuse, physical or sexual. And when the therapist suggests early childhood abuse as a possible cause, then it may trigger a recovered memory or plant a false one in the subject's consciousness. Loftus also observed that sufferers of depression and unhappiness are desperate to find a cause or reason for their illness, and an innocent suggestion could plant a 'false memory'.

87. When 'recovered memory' first was used as evidence in 1991, *Newsweek* magazine was fascinated with the concept and described it as 'forgetting to remember'. Psychiatrist Bessel van der Kolk in 1995 theorised that aspects of traumatic experience appear to get stuck in the mind, and when traces are remembered and put into a personal narrative, they are subject to be 'condensed, contaminated, and embellished' ('Dissociation and the Fragmentary Nature of Traumatic Memories', *Psychiatrist*(1995)).

88. Elizabeth Loftus (of University of California and formerly of Washington University) is in the forefront of research in repressed or 'false' memory. Most theorists believe there is no scientific evidence to support recovered memory. The views and research of Dr Loftus and Dr Cara Laney (Reed College, USA) are included with this appeal (Loftus and Laney, p. 138, #3).

89. The summary concludes that 'human memory can be extremely malleable … that traumatic events are normally remembered all too well, and that there is no good evidence that the particular trauma of sexual abuse should have its own separate memory system'.
'False memories apparently had real consequences (like true memories) for those who developed them' (Loftus and Laney, p. 141,#1).

90. Dr Casey, Dr Craven, and Dr Brady conclude that often 'there are accusations of child sexual abuse directed at those who have committed no such crime. Those working with survivors of traumatic events noted

the existence of amnesia and the subsequent recovery of these memories during treatment for some unrelated disorder, and noted that they could be planted by suggestion by therapists to vulnerable subjects giving rise to what we call "false memory syndrome"' (Casey, Craven, and Brady, pp. 3 and 4).

91. **False memory and the law.** The result of all this research and findings is that most jurisdictions in Western society regard 'recovered memory or false memory evidence' as unreliable. We have already alluded to the Nora Wall case in Ireland and the various states in the USA. The Law Reform Commission of Ireland is extremely sceptical in regard to 'false memory' and demands strong corroborative evidence in its stead.

92. It is time that canon law takes cognizance of all this research and progress in the Civil Code and adopts it in its code.

93. **Edana.** According to the first instance sentence §154, Edana could not explain why she did not protest or say 'stop' … 'kind of unbelievable as it might seem'. She buried it. 'So even though I wasn't consciously aware of the abuse, I think it had done its damage' (Edana, 21. 16–17). There is no need for any psychoanalyst to interpret this. Common sense would indicate that what she was really saying was that though she was not conscious of the alleged abuse, it was the cause of all her problems. Is this an example of cognitive distortion?

94. Elsewhere, her evidence reflects the characteristic traits of 'recovered memory': condensed, contaminated, and embellished. She claims that the alleged abuse was the cause of her depression. 'I know it's not direct evidence, but it is how I feel and how my life has been.'

95. **Naveen.** In the Cloyne report (ch. 27. 10) Naveen said: 'I remember an evening when I first began to relay the events that had happened to me with a friend, the feeling of revulsion that swept over me, the constant need to put my hand over my mouth in case I'd get sick. The feeling there were golf balls stuck in my throat, and we both laughed at the irony and we both cried with the pain. I kept rubbing my fingers to my hand as if to try to remove the stickiness. I felt sick in simply discussing it. I remember

holding my stomach to suppress the need to throw up. I remember feeling haunted by music in the background, the sound of his voice directly in my ear, even [though] neither of those things was actually happening. I remember the smell of incense, the Bible, the open confessions, the removal of his collar when he wanted to touch me more intimately. Nightmares, waking up with a sense of him standing by my bed and my head at his hips. Feverish nightmares, glimpses at events that had taken place but never enough to get a full picture. Separate instances. They all mulch into one, one long brain-turning, nauseating roll of events. My head being pushed down, my body being invaded, the weight of his body on me was so big, so overpowering. In my mind I have wanted to run so many times, but I can't. I am trapped because wherever I go the nightmares haunt me.'

96.   This is a beautifully written piece, but a reality check doesn't tally. For example, the author spent thirty-five sessions with her therapist without mentioning any of the above details. She couldn't remember because of 'hypnosis'. She blocked it out and yet still claims to have had nightmares. Again she refers to incense and open confession and the Bible, mistakenly implying that Fr Duane was part of her parish when he was just merely a lodger in the house.

97.   Naveen also says, according to the Cloyne report (ch. 27. 16), 'My teenage years became obsessed with a feeling there was something evil in me. I used to think if people really knew me they wouldn't approve. I believed no man would ever be interested in me for my mind because I think too much. A man would only see There is no mention of 'nightmares'.

98.   Naveen (couldn't recall her pseudonym in her deposition to the tribunal) said in her first Garda statement that Fr Ronat (Fr Duane) abused her at 16 (9. 133) and that a priest made inappropriate remarks in confession. She didn't name the priest, but it was intended to point a finger in Fr Duane's direction. This did not emerge in the subsequent trial because she had by now realised that Fr Duane didn't hear confessions in her parish.

99.   **Risk report.** Naveen didn't give evidence to the risk assessment. All the above evidence was presented to its personnel. They dwelt on the

discrepancy between dates, i.e., the end of 1983 and the beginning of 1984 (identifying the pebble and ignoring the rock). The claimants allege that they were 'children' when they called on Fr Duane. Naveen kept harping on this theme right through the civil trial. The evidence indicates otherwise. The judge, in his summary to the jury, cautioned them to be oblivious of emotion and stick to the evidence. In line with the risk assessment's assessor's theory of cognitive distortion, the claimants were purporting to be children, without corroboration of their age, appearing to be seen as being specially groomed for alleged sexual abuse. The assessor believed them. The promoter of justice illustrates a point from the assessor's analysis. 'There was no actual contact whatsoever because I was not anyway inclined, tempted' (Dan Duane deposition, 23. 12). He compared this to Oscar Wilde's response in assumed similar circumstances in his trial: 'He was a particularly plain boy—unfortunately ugly.' Wilde was on trial for homosexuality, which was then a crime. So, portraying sexual interest in men and, much worse, in underage males was taken to be indicative of criminal intent. But what is the relevance of this? Fr Duane was on trial for alleged frotting of an alleged female minor. The promoter of justice assumed Edana was a minor. Fr Duane's evidence indicates otherwise. So, Fr Duane was on trial for alleged frotting an adult female. Attraction to a heterosexual adult is not indicative of criminal intent.

100. In fact, Fr Duane was illustrating that the lack of attraction in the alleged incident (masturbation) is bizarre and stretches credibility to the limit. A priest corroborates the lack of attraction, and even she describes herself: 'I was ugly, and he'd have no time for me' (Edana, first Garda statement).

101. It is our opinion that the belief the assessor displayed in Edana's account is ill-founded and unconvincing. The basic ingredient for credibility, namely, evidence, was missing. Attitudes and assumptions are not substitutes for evidence.

102. Another obvious example of the assessor's flawed logic is his basic premise, that is he assumed that most of the callers to Fr Duane's house were underage girls. The opposite was the case, and the few who were

calling were coming to see another priest. Fr Duane was seeing underage boys in St Colman's every day. The assessor builds a case from this distorted assumption of Fr Duane grooming the vulnerable. Fr Duane claims that he did not solicit or invite people to his house, and the only alleged, unfounded evidence given against him was supplied by Donelle, Ailis, and Keita. The DPP did not believe them. The assessor did.

103. **Circumstantial aids to trigger 'false memory'.** Because all four claimants claimed they recovered memories of abuse, it is important to describe the atmosphere that pervaded during the recovery mode. The public campaign wielded against Fr Duane in the media after the publication of the Elliot report in December 2008 would be highly suggestive and act as the trigger to recovery of (false) memories. Keita and Fenella refer specifically to the publicity (Ailis's parents radio interview with Marian Finucane) and made allegations together with Fenella, Naveen, and Edana (Fenella, 19. 10–24), who were friendly with Ailis's parents, as was Donelle. She and Edana were in therapy for four or five years and could have been influenced by symptomatology. Donelle makes reference to it when she tells of the elderly woman who suggested that she had 'the most beautiful brown eyes, but they are the saddest eyes I have ever seen in my life—what happened to you at all' (Donelle, 31. 18–20)? This is a good example of how symptomatology can influence a subject. Donelle took notice of it and began to believe it. 'Talk to somebody about it.'

104. Symptomatology is the study and classification of symptoms. Some forms of depression and unhappiness can be symptoms of 'early child [hood] abuse'. The therapist could 'put the idea into the head by suggestion'. Donelle believed Ailis's father's account of Ailis's multiple rape and sexual abuse at 14 allegedly perpetrated by Fr Duane. (Fr Duane was stationed 25 kilometres away when Ailis was 14 and didn't meet her until she was 18.) Ailis's father believed Donelle's allegation of being raped at 13. Before the Cloyne report was published, all the claimants were supposedly raped as children. (This was claimed by the agitation group who called themselves the 'North Cork Ten'.)The Cloyne report exposed them. Fenella expresses regret. The alleged rape of Ailis and friend was false. Donelle's allegation of rape and sexual abuse was found to have 'no evidence'. They then pinned

their hope on Naveen. Naveen asks Fr Duane in a text after the trial: why everybody (claimants) was afraid of him. They began to doubt their own allegations. They were depending on the multiplicity of allegations as proof.

105. Fr Duane's recollection of dates and their corroboration hasn't been challenged. The reason put forward by all of the accusers (apart from Caelan) is that Fr Duane had this extraordinary power over them. Edana kept coming back to be allegedly abused, and she couldn't explain it; Ailis's father says, 'For some reason I cannot explain, she couldn't get away from him'; Donelle claims that Fr Duane had 'power' over everyone, including the vicar general, the bishop, and even the judge in the civil case, and that wherever Fr Duane went, she was compelled to follow. Fenella was so 'vulnerable', she kept calling back, despite the alleged abuse and the fact that she didn't like him, even though she attended a preferred counsellor before she'd called the first time, because of this power he allegedly had over her. As a judge in a popular TV show would say: 'It's time to get *real*.'

106. Would any of these excuses be acceptable to a jury or any judicial forum? Fr Duane's evidence on the age of the claimants is far more credible than their uncorroborated version. So too is his evidence of their friendly contact with him right up to the time they made the allegations. His recollection of the 'numerous historic' events of the cases is impeccable. All these indicate that there is no reasonable doubt that they were over 16 at the relevant times and that sexual abuse simply did not occur.

IV. Summing up

107. **Lack of due process.** Had we known what we have learned recently in relation to monies paid and letters of apology sent to the complainants before the tribunal proceeded, we would not have taken part in the process. This is compounded by the fact that the presiding judge who was appointed by the apostolic administrator, who paid the monies and signed the letters of apology, was privy to this information as his diocesan child advocate and did not come without prejudice. Realistically, this is 'presumption of guilt' on the tribunal's part.

108. When the apostolic administrator announced the resumption of the tribunal on *Morning Ireland* (a public radio programme), he apologised to the 'victims' of Fr Ronat (Fr Duane) after the latter had been just acquitted and proven innocent in the Cork Circuit criminal court. He then told the nation that Fr Ronat would be the focus of the tribunal and invited his 'victims' to participate. Due process had been denied again.

109. **Grooming.** Grooming, which was presented by the promoter of justice as a very important factor in the criminality of child abuse, entails the deliberate pursuit and engagement with subjects for the purpose of future abuse. There is no evidence that grooming occurred in allegations against Fr Duane. Both Naveen and Edana called in groups to see another priest, not Fr Duane, up until 1983. Fr Duane happened to be in the same house. He did not invite them to call individually. They didn't start to call on him until after September 1983; he never encouraged them to call back. They called unsolicited and mostly in 1984, and they were all adults by then.

110. There is no evidence or corroboration to support their allegations, and their credibility is very much on the lower end of the scale. All three were in therapy with unrelated problems when the alleged 'recovered memory', or in reality 'false memory', occurred, triggered by the therapist or by the environment of clerical abuse hysteria. The risk assessment should never have been admitted as acceptable evidence in the court and should no longer be the acta, so all the flawed conclusions of the assessor cannot prop up the uncorroborated assertions of the complainants as some kind of circumstantial corroboration. And now that their recollections, supposedly recovered from blocked memories, are properly designated as false memories, there isn't a shred of evidence left in the case against Fr Daniel Duane

CHAPTER 10

INTO THE DEPTHS OF THE ABYSS

My friends and those close to me would no doubt describe me as a positive person, outgoing and optimistic without a bother in the world. I always believed that in every human being there is a slight contradiction; in every comedian there is a very serious side struggling to emerge; in every philosopher there is a comic side eager to please. We humans are not all we appear to be. It is difficult to self-analyse, but one should always try, because all knowledge begins with self-knowledge. If you don't know yourself, how can you know and understand somebody else? If the person needs to know God, then the priest needs to know the person. I would describe myself as light-hearted and deadly serious, deeply committed to what I do without showing it, fiercely loyal, honest in word and deed, deeply emotional, and tactile.

I have always taken words seriously and I get inwardly annoyed at empty promises from others. Why don't people mean what they say and fulfil a promise? Why don't they stick to their promises? When dealing with young people, I am extremely conscious of not making promises I cannot fulfil. When you disappoint somebody once, it lingers forever in their minds and erodes trust, the most precious bond of a human relationship. Words become useless if they are not sincere in interaction with others.

Now you can understand how difficult it is to be serious and comical in priestly ministry.

Truth is special to me, because if I deny it, it still remains the truth, and the denial adds a heavy burden to bear. When we were young, succumbing to the temptation to deny our transgressions was always easier than to own up to them, but I learned with time and experience that it was better to face the truth and have peace of mind. Peace of mind is essential for equilibrium and well-being. I consider myself as fair and just, and when confronted with injustice, I meet it head-on.

All I wanted in my school days was to be treated fairly, and I think that is the expectation of school pupils today; it is the expectation of everybody. I'm very lucky that I didn't drink alcohol; I never had hangovers and mood swings.

I cannot say the same about temper. I had a vicious temper as a youngster. One man who worked for us described me as 'a wicked little fecker'. It was possibly due to the fact that I was the youngest boy of five sons and the most vulnerable target for the bigger ones when horsing around, but my accuracy with stones and the catapult was a deterrent to offset assault at close quarters, and my speed of retreat to safety kept the bigger ones at bay. As I grew older and bigger, I got leaner and meaner, and there was no need for the catapult on the new level playing pitch. The temper never left, but like the wind and the sailing boat, I used it to positive effect rather than fight it. In hurling, when there was dirty play, I'd respond with more vigorous fair play, which would frighten the daylights out of the culprit, not knowing when I would really retaliate, making him a nervous wreck.

My two older brothers, who won two Cork County Intermediate Hurling medals with Shanballymore in 1948–9, told me that on the day of the final, their centre back was young and was being targeted by a 'rogue' opponent who had a reputation for dirty play. The centre back got the first ball and drove it downfield more in dread than in confidence; his dirty opponent began to 'sledge' him by warning him of his bad temper and dirty play. The centre back ran wildly out to the wing and sent the ball down the field again. Then he calmly returned to his dirty opponent and confidentially, in a whisper, told him that he was out of the Lee Road only for the day and not to tell anyone. The Lee Road was then known as the mental asylum in Cork. His opponent believed him and kept well away from him, resulting in him being substituted. The young centre back played a 'blinder', and his team won the match.

This tactic worked for me. I got a cowardly blow in the genital area in a college match, and afterwards the culprit uttered a hollow apology. I, in my agony, replied, 'No, boy, but you will be if you come within ten yards of me!' He didn't, and was replaced. When I'm alone now, I lose patience with myself for dropping things and making silly mistakes. I might take it out on the kettle or a saucepan.

Going back to when I was 8 or 9, I hit a big old metal kettle with the poker because it wouldn't boil and broke the knob of the lid. To my eternal shame, that old kettle is still there as testimony to my silliness. Nowadays it escapes with just a simple warning.

With a hot temper and a deep-seated ethos of fair play, I found that retribution was inevitable when I was the victim. Woe to the unfortunate culprit who was at the receiving end of a blistering, sarcastic tongue and imaginative and creative retaliator. Blacklisting was usual and lasting. All of that tempered as I matured, and now I bear no grudges or harbour any hatred against anyone, even my false accusers. It wasn't easy to bring this about, but I don't take credit for the conversion; the Christian command to 'turn the other cheek' was the initial stimulus, but plain selfishness was the main ingredient. Hatred is the most negative and self-destructive emotion of the human psyche, the worst cancer of the emotions. No matter how much one is provoked, hatred is not the healthy response; no matter how much one hates, it achieves nothing in alleviating the problem. The agent of hatred has achieved the goal when he or she receives hatred in return. When faced with non-reaction, the subject of the hatred has wasted vital emotional energy and is consumed by emotional turmoil. The first forgiveness is the most difficult, but the surge of emotional well-being that follows is like releasing a prisoner from the chains of captivity. Forgiveness is the most satisfactory and most rewarding of our emotions, liberating all the others, and especially the capacity to love.

The Holy Show, which I was privileged to compere, was a light-hearted concert of priests singing and raising funds for charities, and usually I would end with a little quip of advice: 'Love your enemies; you'll drive them mad!' and 'Live every day as if it were your last, and one day you will be right!' The final sentence of any homily would be 'It takes a braver person to shake the hand than shake the head.'

Family feuds in Ireland endure for generations. As one story goes, the father of one of these feuding families, on his deathbed, in order get absolution and the last rites from the priest, told his family that he had forgiven the other feuding family, but that if they did the same, he would turn in his grave. Forgiveness is essential for salvation; the judgement you will give is the judgement you will get; 'Forgive us our trespasses, as we forgive those who trespass against us.' I take consolation from those words, but I don't take credit for the forgiveness of others. Forgiveness makes me feel free of the bond of hatred, which is extremely liberating.

St John, the Beloved Disciple, is very forthright about our duty to love our neighbour, 'If you refuse to love, you are dead; to hate your brother is to be a murderer, and murderers, as you know, do not have eternal life in them'(1 John 3:14–18). Jesus tells us to 'love our enemies ... be compassionate ... do not judge ... do not condemn ... grant pardon ... give, because the amount you measure out is the amount you will be given back' (Luke6:27–38). We will be our own prosecution on Judgement Day. If we have nothing to offer, we will have nothing to gain.

There is an old story that confirms this: the only gift a miser gave in his whole life was a shilling to a beggar to get rid of him. When the miser appeared before Peter, he just barely qualified for a reward, so Peter told him he would lower the shilling on a string and pull him out of purgatory into heaven. As he was pulling him up, other misers latched onto him to get a piggyback into heaven. He kicked them off, saying, 'Get off me. That's my shilling.' And as he said it, the string broke. Even in death he couldn't part with the shilling.

My health was on the decline from 1989. My doctors were unsure of the cause, and after I'd made several visits to hospital and undergone multiple tests, no diagnosis was reached. I wasn't losing weight, but the constant fatigue and flu like symptoms persisted, making the most menial tasks seem burdensome. I was worried also about the extra workload on my colleagues, but they were understanding. Of course there were sceptics, including one consultant who was of the opinion that it was all up in my head, but my own doctor was very supportive and open-minded. Eventually, we concluded that it was ME or CFS (constant fatigue syndrome).

I went on a special regimen to improve my immune system and used hydrotherapy (a cold bath every morning and regular cold showers) to help increase the blood flow. I found it difficult but helpful; nevertheless, the fatigue and flu symptoms would return every year. I dreaded these bouts of inertia and the horrible symptoms that accompanied them. I was too tired to get up and too tired to sleep or rest properly. A trip to the bathroom was a huge demand, and I literally collapsed into bed on return. Pat, my faithful housekeeper, was both nurse and cook. I could spend three weeks in bed before experiencing any improvement. I couldn't say Mass or read the office, but I did manage the recital of the rosary.

The first allegation of sexual abuse hit me like a lump hammer in 1995. I wondered what it could be, because I knew I had done nothing inappropriate. When I met with the vicar general and heard the contents of the allegation, I was more puzzled than ever about where the sexual assault existed. Ailis had been to my house for advice, but what I was hearing was a complete misrepresentation of the events as I recalled them. She claimed to have called for career guidance. I gave career guidance advice to the students of the local secondary school. It was agreed that they would call in pairs to my house across the street from the school. She called with her friend. When she called on me on her own, it was 1988 and was prearranged by her mother by phone, who was worried about her Christmas results. Ailis called four or five times, and all her visits were arranged by her mother. During these visits she dwelt on her father's physical abuse and on being molested at 12 years of age by a man. There was no wine as she claimed; there were a few beer bottles in the fridge. One night she took a bottle of beer from the fridge, and I took it away from her.

In her recollection she had wine, was sexually abused on the couch which didn't exist, and was calling for career guidance at my invitation. Her mother could corroborate my evidence with regard to the appointments by phone, but she didn't, which puzzles me. I have a very clear recollection of her first phone call.

The controversy about Ailis's age is mind-boggling. Ailis gave three different ages, one to the bishop, another to the psychologist, and yet another to Archdeacon Twohig. She was in my house at age 17 but not on her own. She was over 16 when I arrived in the parish. There are many more contradictions which will be dealt with in detail under each claimant's allegation. I left the vicar general's house totally baffled, but I had managed a smile when he said she claimed that I followed her to America. It's frustrating when others' recollections don't match one's own version, but independent witnesses will corroborate that her other recollections were inaccurate.

I scarcely had recovered from the first shock when Bretta and Matthew surfaced with a complaint. At least I knew what it might contain, and the fact that Matthew had assured me that he was not abused by me, yet I was still curious about what was the complaint. Again there was a conflict of recollection, but it was clear that there was no sexual abuse. The vicar general was more interested in protecting her from being accused of a false allegation than in crediting the alleged sexual abuse.

In December 1997 Caelan wrote to the bishop claiming that I abused her in confession. She had already made a statement to the Gardai. My first reactions were of surprise and alarm. *Will there ever be an end to the sequence of mysterious and spurious surprises?* I thought. The vicar general believed Caelan's claim until the Garda file was returned with a nolle prosequi and with my account of her statement, which clearly indicated that there was no clear evidence of either sexual or physical abuse, but the other tenuous claim arose, that it might constitute 'solicitation in confession', which was a serious offence in canon law. However, my canon lawyer explained that in order for this canonical crime to be committed, there must be clear evidence that I invited Caelan to commit a sin. This clearly didn't exist, but the allegation rumbled on.

I was feeling helpless and frustrated and decided to clear the 'state of limbo' imposed on me by the bishop. He wrote to me forbidding me to have any interaction with children. The reality that I was a suspected child molester began to both puzzle and terrify me. There was no credible case of alleged child abuse against me.

I requested documentation from my files in order to issue a civil challenge to the legitimacy of my treatment by the diocese. I was flatly refused because of the confidential nature of these documents and was told that 'in no way in the world' would I be given them. A few short years later the whole world saw most of these documents published in the Cloyne report, and still I can't see those documents in full to this day. The State and Church have full access to these documents, and I don't. Kipling's idiom sums it up: 'When elephants fight, only the humble grass is trampled.' This will emerge more and more as my narrative progresses, culminating in the former Taoiseach's infamous speech on the publication of the Cloyne report. The blade of grass would be transformed into a sacrificial lamb to appease tension between Church and State.

This state of limbo was compounded by keeping me at bay by offering me a parish which they knew I would refuse because of its remoteness. I was offered a second remote parish and refused, but when I requested a parish in a suitable location, this was refused because it was too near my alleged victims. The reality still exists that I am not considered exonerated and will have to carry this baggage forever. It's time to take corrective action.

My legal team were presenting the available options, and the bishop and vicar general were worried according to the Cloyne report. Donelle was calling on me regularly at this point until I rejected her amorous advances.

In her last phone call she told me that a 'priest friend' of hers had asked her for a 'huge favour' and teased me with what it might be. I have no doubt that she was given confidential information about the alleged sexual allegations against me, that she assumed that they were true, and that in retaliation she made an allegation against me for allegedly treating her as 'only the Thursday girl'. She immediately donned the mantle of 'the woman scorned' and behaved accordingly.

The vicar general rang me and wrote to me that an allegation of sexual assault of a child had been made against me to a solicitor in Cork by Donelle. At this stage she was only looking for money. She erupted in fury when I refused through my solicitor and denied any ill treatment of her as a child. The vicar general rang me when she decided to make a statement to the Gardai during a counselling session, which I thought was very peculiar. I was ill at the time, but I assured him that I had no case to answer. Between my illness and the worry caused by this latest totally uncorroborated and unprecedented allegation, I was sinking into the depths of profundity—and worse was to come. The stress caused by the latest allegation scuppered any hope of a speedy recovery to full health and the prospect of returning to normal ministry, so in desperation I retired to avoid distress to my family, friends, and parishioners.

My body and mind were depleted even though I knew that I wasn't guilty of the crimes alleged against me, but who will believe me now? I was in a very lonely place, as my worst fears were being realised, and my world was collapsing all around me. And I did not know whom to trust anymore. My faith, even though severely tested, was my constant pillar of hope, and the celebration of the Eucharist was my source of sanity. Gradually I recovered and awaited to present my defence to the Gardai.

I was still living in Kanturk, and I figured a move to another house, one outside the parish, would free the way for my replacement. The vicar general had importuned me the previous year to retire, to accommodate my replacement. I heard about my present residence being vacant, so I inspected it and was pleased with the location and condition of the building. I moved there in August 2006, unaware of the consternation that would ensue. I was charged with moving without permission, because of the monitoring of my movements in regard to child protection.

Ailis's father was the source of an article in the *Irish Examiner* specifying my proximity to Ballyhass National School. What was omitted at the time was that I was living in closer proximity to the schools in Kanturk. The bishop sent me a letter ordering me to vacate the house immediately, which I gave to my lawyer, and I heard no more. The local PP became my new 'minder', and another PP became my mentor. We held regular meetings in my house over morning tea, and the minutes were sent to the child liaison delegate.

I was called by a Garda detective for an interview in November 2006. I heard the allegation against me and answered his questions. The file was returned in February 2006 with a nolle prosequi and a footnote stating that 'there was no evidence of criminal, sexual behaviour'. I was relieved and buoyed by the DPP's assessment of my evidence and the lack of evidence provided by Donelle. I thought the church would follow the state, but alas, I was deluded. The status quo persisted. Ailis made a statement to the Gardai, but I was never interviewed. It was sent to the DPP after she died and was returned with a nolle prosequi.

Ailis's 'schoolhood friend' Edana made her allegation shortly after Ailis's death and claimed sexual abuse. I was completely flummoxed as I'd never touched her, not even with a hug or handshake. She claimed frotting, or rubbing against her genital area, as a child while fully clothed. The DPP returned the file with a nolle prosequi and insufficient evidence to prosecute. I knew by now that people who frequented my house had been solicited by Ailis's father to bring allegations against me. There was worse to come.

The Cloyne report recounts the activity of Donelle and Ailis's father. After her civil action collapsed in 2008, Donelle met with Ailis's parents, according to the account her mother gave to Marian Finucane (on *The Marian Finucane Show* on the radio); together they formed an alliance to bypass the Cloyne and Garda findings and report directly to the CEO of the National Board for Safeguarding Children, established by the Irish Hierarchy, complaining about their sexual abuse by me. Her parents claimed that Ailis was regularly raped by me at 14 to 16 years of age. Donelle claimed she was raped at 13 to 17 by me.

The CEO demanded a meeting with the bishop to inspect the files, and he was refused at first, but after much publicity in articles in the *Sunday Tribune* written by Justine McCarthy using information provided by Donelle and Ailis's father, they met. The CEO prepared a report without being asked by the HSE or Barry Andrews, minister for children, and wanted it published. He sought indemnity from Barry Andrews and was refused. An impasse between the HSE, Barry Andrews, and the bishop ensued regarding the publication of the controversial report. The joint Limerick and Cloyne Child Protection Committee, comprised of well-qualified personnel, wrote to the CEO threatening litigation if he published the report. The Hierarchy advised mediation. Nevertheless, the bishop ignored the advice and published it on the diocesan website. Later he claimed that I could be identified by many even though my name wasn't revealed. He sent a votum to the Vatican seeking to have me summarily dismissed from the priesthood and, at the same time, cajoled me to undergo a risk assessment, implicitly promising me a return to ministry.

Meanwhile, the alliance of Donelle and Ailis's parents was actively providing the media with false allegations to blacken my reputation. This campaign will be dealt with in a future chapter. They were so successful that the diocese was highlighted in daily news bulletins which discussed the awful child sexual abuse of Father B. The Minister for Children, Barry Andrews, ordered Cloyne to be examined by the Murphy Commission, which spawned the Cloyne report, costing the State millions of euros.

As a result of the Elliot report, six allegations arrived in as many months: Fenella, a friend of Ailis, who had heard the latter's parents on *The Marian Finucane Show*, Muirin, Naveen, A. W., and two anonymous callers. Father Michael Mernagh marched from the Pro-Cathedral in Dublin to the cathedral in Cobh in the midst of widespread publicity to highlight the amount of clerical child abuse in Cloyne. All the cases in the public arena, apart from one, were allegations against me. The bishop retired temporarily to let the Cloyne enquiry proceed. During all this mayhem, my health was bearing up with the help of my doctor and friends.

I didn't want to burden my family with my problems. Again the celebration of the Eucharist helped me to literally ride the storm of false and defamatory publicity. I could live with myself and hoped for a resolution; surely, these once good friends did not believe their own allegations and would retract them sooner or later. The worst part was waiting for the post. Not a week would pass without a letter of trouble of some kind arriving, be it a fresh allegation, a precept from the bishop, or a registered letter from lawyers demanding compensation. The accusers all demanded compensation only weeks after making the allegation to the diocese.

The constant barrage of alleged allegations would have driven me to total despair only for another source of support, the G-factor presence throughout this period of darkness. The G-factor is grace, which is difficult to describe accurately in theological terms, never mind in ordinary language. It's a gentle push to act and behave in a more than human way, a spiritual crutch in handling difficulties. Jesus said to his apostles: 'I give you a peace the world cannot give.' I never contemplated suicide, and I believe that this was due not to my mental strength but to the G-factor, the prayers of my friends whom I met, and those who wrote sending Mass cards and benedictions. During the trials I could sense almost a feeling of levitation and inner peace not of this world. It reminded me of the sailor whose prayers in the calm helped him to sail in the storm. I received so many messages of goodwill and wishes from people who believed I was innocent, but there were many too who did not believe and passed me with cold shoulders. I understood their confusion from all the publicity and my deafening silence or inability to respond.

In 2007 Donelle issued litigation through Pearse Mehigan & Co., lawyers acting for the One in Four advocacy group, and the rest followed. It drained my coffers to send my legal team to the High Court in Dublin to present my defence. But the case never went ahead. Whether the lawyers were deterred by the substance of my defence or by Donelle's inability to recall certain areas of her past, the case collapsed in 2008. None of the others pursued their litigation, so there was no pressure on the bishop to issue monetary compensation. Nevertheless, he did initiate it in 2009.

Meanwhile, after the bishop stepped aside, the archbishop was appointed apostolic administrator of Cloyne and decided to pay considerable compensation to all the claimants. Naveen even received compensation after her criminal claim in the circuit criminal court failed. The complainants also received letters of apology for the abuse which I allegedly perpetrated on them. All the compensation was paid before the Cloyne tribunal concluded, and the principal judge, who was appointed by the archbishop, was privy to these settlements. This would be highly contentious in civil law.

I eagerly looked forward to weekends, knowing there would be no post, but that didn't last too long as the saga continued in the Sunday papers. Regular columns appeared in the *Sunday Tribune* and *Sunday Times* from information provided by Donelle and written by Justine McCarthy. Donelle, Ailis's father, and Fenella provided information for articles in the *Irish Examiner* written by Claire O'Sullivan. Trish O'Dea claimed that she was the first to write about the 'Cloyne Sex Scandal' in the *Corkman* (early 2008), and her sources were also Donelle and Ailis's father. Regular bulletins were published in the three aforementioned papers outlining the awful child abuse that existed in Cloyne and mentioning Father B as the perpetrator. My lawyers could do very little because I was legally gagged from commenting on an ongoing enquiry, while my trial by media was gaining momentum. They remained anonymous, while I was easily identified. It wasn't pleasant reading accounts of crimes which I was allegedly guilty of, with my hands tied behind my back, but in the back of my mind I hoped and prayed that I would be vindicated one day.

The complainants united into a group and called themselves the North Cork Ten. A handful of survivors (seven women and one man) accused me of priestly rape and torture of them as children and confronted the DPP for his failure to prosecute Fr B, the notorious child rapist. They were assisted by members of RAT (Religious Abuse Truth, a website for victims of abuse), fronted by Kevin Flanagan, Dave O'Brien, and Gerry O'Donovan, and by ITCCS (International Tribunal into Crimes of Church and State). They came to Cork and touted the public for monetary support for the North Cork Ten. They had a mock TV station reporting on Fr B's crimes. It struck me at the time that the multiple use of *rape* by all ten claimants illustrated their ignorance of the awful effects of rape on the victim. The rape victims I counselled dreaded the mention of the word, it had such an appalling effect on their life. The mention of it in news bulletins would revive the horror they wanted so desperately to eradicate from their lives. They dreaded any reference to the word, and yet here were alleged victims mentioning it without seemingly any duress. It didn't seem like typical behaviour of tortured and raped victims.

During the election campaign after the collapse of Fianna Fáil government in 2010, it was predicted in the opinion polls that Fine Gael and Labour would win with a huge majority. The North Cork Ten picketed the DPP's office and the Dáil; they met with Pat Rabbitte and Seán Sherlock outside the Dáil and presented their case for a prosecution of Fr B, also presenting their letters of apology from the archbishop. Mr Rabbitte, who was shadow minister for justice in the incoming government, expressed concern at the lack of action of the DPP and said they had a case. At this stage nine of the files had been returned from the DPP, leaving one yet to be examined. The *Irish Examiner* (21 Jan. 11) wrote: 'At least eight files on clerical abuse in Cloyne, which were sent to the DPP and returned without prosecution, are to be resent as one large file. The files all relate to abuse alleged to be carried out to the notorious Father B., who systematically assaulted and raped girls in North Cork.'

Eventually two cases of sexual assault were put forward for prosecution. I was notified by my lawyer, Kieran McCarthy, who was contacted by a Garda detective at 5. 30 p.m., saying I was to attend Mallow Garda Station the following morning at 9. 30 a.m. The detective explained the procedure; I was arrested outside the station and escorted to the courthouse, where I was charged with sexual abuse. There was mayhem outside the courthouse when I emerged, and the only stroke of luck was the rain. I had my golf umbrella with me to protect me from complete exposure and wandered back to my car with the paparazzi behind me in what seemed like a surreal trance. *Who am I? Is this really happening? Will I be thrown to the lions of the media for food? What's next?* I got to the car and sat motionless and traumatised for what seemed like a lifetime, until I regained some form of composure and quickly realised that I must tell my family before they heard or saw the news. I gradually regained some form of normality and told all my family; they were extremely upset but completely behind me. I was in my nephew's house when the news came on; I'd been captured on film beneath my umbrella. When that news began to register, one of the kids who was watching it in another room rushed in shouting, 'Guess what? Father Dan will be famous. He's on the telly.' It was a little ray of sunshine in what was a dark and dismal day.

The next court appearance (7 April 2011) was the presentation of the book of evidence and setting the date for the first trial. My family agreed that they would walk by me to and from the court. When we arrived at the courthouse, Naveen was outside with Donelle and the North Cork Ten, with Flanagan and Co. waiting. They were taken aback with the show of my support. Nevertheless, Donelle verbally assaulted Elsie, one of my supporters, and shouted, 'L— will be next.' Trish O'Dea was in the press area, and when my case came for hearing, I was cited for sexual assault, which to me was serious, but to the North Cork Ten it was petty in contrast with all their allegations of child rape.

There was an eerie silence of disbelief. We left the courtroom in unison, and on my way out I could see a serious altercation between the North Cork Ten and RAT. The media were a little muted as well, because they were expectant of serious child sex abuse. RAT was being used or abused by Flanagan and Co., who had been duped by Donelle and Co. and ceased supporting them.

The trial commenced on 16 May 2011. The claimant was A. W., who alleged that I put my arm around her and touched her breast area outside her clothes. This occurred after she broke down. I didn't recognise her or remember her calling, and I didn't recall any inappropriate behaviour. In her Garda statement she said she ran out of my house, but the front door had a double lock and she was terrified. In court she said that the door was locked with a chain restraint. The priests who shared the house with me testified that there was no chain or double lock on the door—it was a simple Yale lock. The kernel of the case was the long delay in reporting the alleged abuse. It was pointed out by my barrister, Jim O'Mahony, that it was obligatory in A. W.'s profession to report sexual abuse, and yet she'd waited for thirty years to report it. Another salient point in her Garda statement was that she claimed she didn't report it for monetary reward, but a week before the court hearing her solicitors sued me and the diocese for compensation.

The judge directed the jury to reach a not guilty verdict and in doing so cited several reasons besides the delay in reporting, reasons which were overlooked in the media in the long term. He was criticised by the Rape Crisis Centre for referring to the time factor. The late reporting was prejudicial to my defence in that the housekeeper, a potential witness, had died and the prosecution had set out the period of the alleged abuse too broadly:1 September 1980 to 1 April 1982. The judge doubted A. W.'s evidence with regard to extra study time. She didn't have contemporaneous corroboration of her allegations; she claimed she told a friend, but the friend had no recollection. I sat in the dock, whereas the North Cork Ten were in the public gallery during the trial.

As I was sitting in the dock, which was close to the press area, I could see the press reporters staring at me, this alleged monster child abuser, who was a work of their own creation, and watching my reaction to the evidence as it unfolded. They were another jury, with false evidence of all kinds of horrible abuse they had been given, and they looked bewildered with the charge against me being of the lowest category of sexual abuse. The DPP, presumably, put forward the two strongest cases of the ten allegations sent to him, and this was supposed to be the strongest case. The reporting of the trial was accurate but muted, and the hysteria of the previous years dissipated like steam in fresh air.

The North Cork Ten were present during the trial, and when the judge, Seán Ó Donnabháin, was in the middle of his summary of the evidence,

Donelle marched out of the courtroom in military style, displaying her displeasure at the verdict. She was followed later by Naveen, the appellant in the next case, who stopped and addressed the judge with: 'This court is a farce.' The judge ordered her immediate arrest for contempt of court. The people present got the notion, which I'd already experienced, that due process was not high on the agenda of the North Cork Ten.

I was greatly relieved at the verdict, but I was already confident, after hearing the claimant's evidence, that there was no substance to the allegation. I was sorry for the appellant because I believe she'd been duped and pressured by the North Cork Ten, which included three of her classmates, to make the allegation. Letters of congratulation from all over Ireland, and some from England, Wales, and the United States, kept arriving for weeks after the trial.

Naveen was the complainant in the second trial, which ended 25 November 2011 with a unanimous verdict of not guilty.

There was a respite from stress for a short period until the Cloyne tribunal, which commenced in 2009 and resumed on 18 April 2012. This tribunal was established by the apostolic administrator of Cloyne in 2009. He appointed his child protection delegate of his diocese and Cloyne as principal judge, and he selected the other two judges, the promoter of justice, and the notary. Mgr Maurice Dooley was appointed as my advocate at my request.

I was interviewed by the tribunal in the Cloyne Community Centre with regard to the joinder of the issue on 21 August 2009. Following objections lodged by my advocate, that session was declared null due to legal infringements, and the next meeting took place on 9 September. My accusers were invited to give their depositions to the tribunal, which now held its sessions in the Nano Nagle Centre, Killavullen.

Donelle arrived for her deposition with Naveen on 16 October 2009. They insisted that my advocate and notary leave the courtroom. After having done so, my advocate and the notary could hear from a distance the verbal altercation between the two women and the judges which ensued for over three hours from the courtroom. This was described by the judges as 'emotional, angry, intense, difficult, erratic, and confrontational'. I imagined that this behaviour would not be tolerated in the civil courts or in any other forum.

My advocate and the notary were shocked at the disrespect shown by the complainants and the tolerance or capitulation of the judges. Further involvement with the tribunal was halted by the claimants until after the publication of the Cloyne report in July 2010.

The Cloyne investigation set up by the Irish government was still in progress, but I had not been interviewed yet because of my medical problems. The first draft was sent to every witness who participated and to my lawyer, Kieran McCarthy, who was appalled at the content and demanded that I be interviewed. I had been invited to be interviewed by the tribunal when it was taking statements of evidence in Cork, but I could not attend because I was called on the day I was to have my hip replacement, and by the time I was out of hospital, the Cloyne investigation had moved to Dublin. I was ordered by my medical advisor not to travel long journeys for at least six weeks, with the result that I was never interviewed at that time. Later the tribunal arranged for an interview in Dublin, and I was accompanied by Kieran. The interview lasted three hours with a break in the middle.

We could sense the uneasiness in the tribunal as I delivered my defence, producing evidence that I had already given in my interviews with the vicar general and which the tribunal may not have seen, such as the date of my first meeting with Ailis, the appointment made by her mother by phone at the end of 1988, and the fact that she was over 18. The draft version of Chapter 9 was mostly about the controversy concerning her age when she first called on me on her own. I produced documents and letters to support my evidence. I was cross-examined by about my nonattendance at the earlier sessions, and I explained my medical condition. Nevertheless, I was severely upbraided by counsel, for the Commission, for not disregarding my medical advice. There was difficulty also with my saying a private Mass in a house; it was obvious that the tribunal didn't grasp the difference between Mass in private and Mass in public. I produced the letter the bishop sent me, and in it there was no mention of Mass in my house only. The Commission confused this letter with a letter which the vicar general showed me post factum and accused me of violating an instruction which in fact I hadn't seen. It really amazed me that the Commission with such professional personnel could make such elementary errors.

All the allegations made by Donelle to the CEO were false. I gave the relevant corroboration needed to the tribunal. If my evidence was to be fully applied, the whole of Chapter 9 would have to be altered, but with the government and claimants urging expedited publication, this wasn't likely. Later in the High Court, when my legal team sought sight of my deposition, they were refused on the grounds that it was the sole property of the tribunal.

I will print all the evidence I gave to the tribunal, and the reader can compare it with what is printed in Chapter 9. I had sent three factual errors I discovered in the draft report to the tribunal to address, and it refused to amend them. The first one dealt with Ailis's age when she called for the first time. She was over 18; the tribunal printed that she was 19. The second was the vicar general's letter to me, which I gave to the tribunal, advising me not to appear at confirmation in Ailis's parish because of her parent's belligerence. It assumed erroneously that it was Kanturk, my parish, confusing it with another letter, and wrongfully used it as corroboration for another agenda. (I have already dealt with the third error on a previous page.)

Resumption of the Cloyne Church Tribunal

After the publication of the Cloyne report in July 2011 (with large deletions dealing with me) and the supplement with the complete text of Chapter 9in December 2011, the Cloyne Ecclesiastical Tribunal sought to persuade the complainants to cooperate with a resumption of the stalled trial. Eventually on 19 April 2012, Fenella and Edana gave their depositions, followed the following day by the depositions of Donelle and Naveen. Caelan had given her deposition in 2009 before the interruption caused by Donelle and Naveen's outburst. On 30 June the tribunal took brief evidence from two of my priest colleagues, and in a weak effort to get corroboration for Edana's evidence, they took evidence from Edana's sister. Later, on 25 July, I was aggressively interrogated by the tribunal for over three hours. Finally, as a token gesture to me, a witness on my behalf was heard on 6 October.

In accordance with canon law, the next stage for the prosecution and defence was to submit their arguments to the court. My advocate submitted detailed legal arguments for the consideration of the tribunal, the most essential one being that the claims of my accusers had zero evidential value unless and until they provided independent corroboration to the tribunal of their claims that I had sexually abused them. No such corroboration was provided for the claims of any of the five complainants. In the cases of the complaint by Edana, the evidence given by her sister was only repetition of what Edana was claimed to have told her in 1998, of my masturbation in Edana's presence around 1983. This was only hearsay, and neither independent nor corroboration. In regard to the other four complainants, no corroborating witness at all was even called by the tribunal.

The decision of the tribunal gave no reasons or rebuttal of the argument and instead concentrated on asserting the credibility of the complainants. On this basis, which is not a valid one, they found me guilty without addressing my real defence. There were many other flaws in the tribunal's verdict, so much so that the verdict was declared invalid by my advocate when being sent forward on appeal to the Congregation for Doctrine of the Faith (CDF) in Rome, and it had to be *sanated* from serious errors by the CDF.

My advocate and I both informed the bishop and the child protection delegate for Cloyne of the errors. They had promised the complainants that they would publish the result of the secret trial at a press conference, and I admonished the CPD that the bishop was risking my name being identified to the press by the claimants, who had the ear of the press already. (I kept notes of this phone call.) They ignored my concern, and I was later identified by the claimants in the press.

Press release

The beginning: 1989

Ailis. Mother and daughter made an allegation to a priest that Fr Ronat and daughter were *kissing* in his house.

In 1995 both parents and daughter ramped up the allegations to *sexual assault* perpetrated on their daughter (as a child). Ailis, their daughter, gave three different ages to diocesan personnel, (a) 15–19, (b) 17–18, and (c) 16–18.

Ailis made a statement to the Gardai in 2005. Fr Ronat was never interviewed by the Gardai.

In 2008, after Ailis had died, her father further ramped up the allegations to *multiple rape* perpetrated by Fr Ronat on his daughter and another girl (unidentified) when they were 14, saying that this abuse continued for three years. Fr Ronat presented documentary evidence to the diocesan authorities of only arriving in their parish inSeptember1986, when his daughter was over 16 (date of birth: May 1970), and proceeded with further documentary evidence of meeting her alone for the first time when she was 18. Her father had forgotten or deliberately avoided mentioning that his daughter attended a different school in 1988 and 1989.

Ailis claimed that she 'called for career guidance and to discuss a personal problem' and said she was sexually abused by Fr Ronat for three years. It was well established that pupils looking for career guidance came in pairs to Fr Ronat's house. This arrangement was agreeable to the school and Fr Ronat. Her first and subsequent visits were arranged by her mother per phone in 1988. The reason her mother supplied was that her performance was poor in the Christmas tests in 1988. Fr Ronat left the parish in 1989. She called about six times in all.

After the alleged abuse, Ailis contacted Fr Ronat in the USA and met him. It was there that Fr Ronat realised that she had a 'crush' on him, and he refused to hold her hand as she requested. There were no more visits after that. Meanwhile her mother had come across love letters, and she had such a fright that she burned them. The love letters were allegedly from Fr Ronat to Ailis. Fr Ronat is absolutely sure that he never wrote letters to Ailis.

Having experienced a horrific relationship and a disastrous marriage, Ailis later wrote to Fr Ronat from London, seeking to 'get back to where we were', behaviour not consistent with someone who claims to have been sexually abused.

Fr Ronat discovered, only recently, that Ailis told Fenella that she was 'in love' with him. This 'infatuation', detected by Archdeacon Twohig in the first interview, had been summarily dismissed by the Cloyne Commission and almost ridiculed. Archdeacon Twohig was a skilled investigator and qualified in civil and canon law. In her Garda statement Ailis described him as aloof and barely tolerant of her presence. The Commission criticised his attitude; he behaved in a better way than their personnel did in my interview. After all, it was an investigative interview, not a counselling session. The infatuation is significant in interpreting her subsequent behaviour. She came forward because, she maintained, Fr Ronat was 'sexually abusing both young and mature people calling to his house'. There was no evidence to support this, and at this time there were many callers to his house. Perhaps jealousy was a possible motive. The only other allegation from Ailis's area was made by Fenella, a former novice nun, which was proven to be totally unfounded. Ailis made a statement to the Gardai in 2005.

Fr Ronat was not interviewed by the Gardai and did not see the statement.

The Garda file was sent to the DPP after Ailis died (November 2006) and returned with nolle prosequi in February 2007. Nevertheless, her father claimed she was alive at the time and that she was 'devastated' by the decision not to prosecute.

Donelle

In 2005 Donelle made allegations of 'child sexual abuse' perpetrated on her (as a child) by Fr Ronat, 'including full sexual intercourse'. To the Gardai she claimed to be 15 years old; to the tribunal, 15; to the CEO, 13; to Faoiseamh, 13; and to the High Court, 13.

The Garda file was sent to the DPP in 2006 and returned with nolle prosequi in 2007, citing the reason 'no evidence of criminal sexual behaviour'. Two counts of sexual abuse were listed for 21 June and July 1971. Donelle had a diary which ended abruptly in July 1971. It transpired in her deposition that it contained no evidence of her alleged sexual abuse, while at the same time it corroborated Fr Ronat's evidence of her infatuation with him. The bishop had claimed that her diary 'was clear evidence of sexual abuse of a minor' and applied to Rome to have Fr Ronat defrocked without trial, despite Fr Ronat presenting documentary evidence of being in the USA on both dates, and also presenting documentary evidence for 1971, 1972, and 1973 for further citations of alleged sexual abuse. The High Court claim lapsed in 2008, and then the public campaign was launched.

Phase two

The public campaign of vilification began in April 2008

Sunday Tribune, 20 Apr. 2008

An article by Justine McCarthy, based on information from Ailis's father, outlined serious child sex abuse by Fr Ronat of Cloyne Diocese. All the material included in the article had been previously given to the CEO by Ailis's father and Donelle. In the same paper, another article outlined the (alleged) serious omissions not being addressed by then bishop. The Cloyne report recounts the sequence of events. The main themes of the Elliot report concerns were:

> that diocesan personnel had never informed the Gardai or the HSE of Ailis's allegation, as was agreed earlier by the church guidelines, despite the fact that it was recorded in the files and elsewhere, e. g. in her father's interview on *The Marian Finucane Show*, that the family specifically demanded that the Gardai should not be informed and that Donelle had expressly requested no publicity (there was no civil law on mandatory reporting at that time), and the 'inadequate supervision of Fr Ronat'. Donelle made several serious allegations (nine) about his behaviour to him, and all were proven

groundless. Some of these allegations were that he was officiating at weddings and funerals, that he was visiting complainants and saying Mass in houses, and that the diocese was covering up. Together with another case (that of Fr A), according to the Cloyne report, this was the origin of the Elliot report, even though he, CEO, wasn't specifically requested to do so by any authority. It appears he accepted the allegations as fact, and hence he was refused indemnity to publish it. He was warned by the bishop, the vicar general, and their advisory committee not to publish it for legal reasons. The bishop consulted with his fellow bishops as to what was best to do with it, and without awaiting their counsel on 'mediation', and against the advice of his committee, he went ahead and published it. The bishop readily agreed that Fr B was easily identified by many people, including Ailis's father, and from that false platform both Ailis's father and Donelle began a public vendetta in the media for the conviction and defrocking of Fr Ronat. Articles appeared in the *Irish Examiner* (twice weekly), the *Sunday Times* (weekly), and the *Corkman* (weekly). The parents of Ailis spoke on radio and TV (*Morning Ireland, The Marian Finucane Show*, and RTÉ 1 News), and another claimant, Fenella, who heard their radio interview and allegations, herself made an allegation of 'anal rape' and fed the media with more falsehoods. And finally, all the claimants used social media under the name of 'the North Cork Ten' (who all claimed to have been raped as children by Fr Ronat). Due to this press tsunami, Fr Michael Mernagh marched from Dublin to Cobh amid huge publicity before Christmas 2008. Nothing had been published about the other cases in Cloyne at this time. Fr B was the main focus of all this publicity.

Fenella

Fenella, an ex-postulant from the parish convent, made an allegation of anal rape against Fr Ronat after seventeen years. She again gave different dates. She claimed Fr Ronat collected her in a blue Toyota and took her to his house. She gave three different accounts of menus of a meal he gave her. She then claimed he intoxicated her with a bottle of Famous Grouse whiskey and violently raped her.

Fr Ronat had a Peugeot car at that time; he never collected her; he never kept Famous Grouse whiskey; and he never made meals in his house for visitors. She maintained this occurred in 1990. As a result she attempted suicide in 1990, although she's not sure, saying it could have been 1991. Fr Ronat proved that she was calling on him in a cordial, social manner until Easter 1992. There were several witnesses to corroborate his evidence.

Justine McCarthy penned an article in the *Sunday Times*, sourced by Fenella, outlining her alleged abuse.

It defies credibility that if Fenella was violently raped, she would not have remembered the circumstantial evidence, that is the date and circumstances, and likewise that she could not recall the date of her attempted suicide. What is more bizarre is that she was able to recall with remarkable precision the day and time of her alleged collection. (She claimed it was on a Tuesday in July 1990 at 3.30 pm outside the convent school.) Furthermore, her subsequent behaviour and friendliness with her alleged abuser is completely contrary to the norm.

As a consequence of their mendacious allegations, Barry Andrews, Minister for Children, referred the 'Cloyne scandal' to the Murphy Commission, resulting in the Cloyne report (costing the taxpayer over 4 million euros).

They picketed the DPP's office and the Dáil and met Sean Sherlock and Pat Rabbitte (who seemed to think they had a strong case). They called on the Cork County prosecutor, who in turn importuned the DPP. Donelle wrote to the DPP and the archbishop on several occasions in menacing terms. Indeed she pranced out of the first civil trial in defiant fashion, followed by Naveen (the plaintiff in the second trial), who interrupted the judge as he was instructing the jury to find Fr Ronat innocent, shouting, 'This court is a farce!' The judge ordered her immediate arrest.

Donelle issued three threats to the church tribunal judges that if they wouldn't do something about him (i.e. if they didn't find Fr Ronat guilty), 'someone will'; 'I won't be responsible for my actions. I really won't'; and 'I don't know what I will do. I really don't.' She also wanted to 'kill him' and reiterated the threat several times. 'He is a monster, a beast. He should be crucified and ... castrated. ... I can't think of the worst death for that man.' Up to 2005, only a few years before this, she confessed to 'chilling out in his house' in a few minutes, quicker than the week it took her to relax at her own home. She called regularly to discuss her domestic and economic problems. All her visits were secret because of fear of her partner. She wanted all doors locked so that nobody, and especially her partner, would know she was visiting him (Fr Ronat). She was able to talk about debts she had incurred before meeting her partner. She could never talk to her partner or her siblings about these. She trusted Fr Ronat completely. She talked about her the exhibitions of her pupils; she brought Fr Ronat CDs of her favourite music (Jerry Fish) and favourite videos, *Quills*, being one of them. In her diary she had written about Fr Ronat: 'He is a lovely man.' When her case was rejected by the DPP, she contacted Fr Ronat again (who was forbidden by Cloyne Diocese from contacting her or any of the complainants). This time it was a text intended to evoke a response: 'Finding it difficult to sleep. Do you sleep well? I was in B— ... the river was so high ... so dirty and so fast. I felt so drawn to it ... almost teased by it. I'm still frightened by the slyness of it, its ugly gasping sounds. ... I hate full-flooded rivers, their compelling power, horrible, the sneaky beckoning power that could carry you away, away, away'(2. 47. 42, 23 January 2008). This was either a cry from the heart or an enticement to Fr Ronat to break his supervision conditions, that is not to contact a complainant. All this friendly and trusting behaviour is not typical of somebody who claims to have been 'savaged' as a child, enduring 'horrific abuse'. All her allegations were not corroborated, whereas all of Fr Ronat's evidence is corroborated.

False memory syndrome

Donelle, like the others, claimed to have 'blocked memory' or 'repressed memory', otherwise known as 'recovered memory'. The one outstanding case in Irish law regarding 'recovered memory' is that of Nora Wall, who was the first woman in the state to be convicted of rape and the only person to be convicted on 'recovered memory' evidence. Her conviction was later quashed by the Court of Criminal Appeal of Ireland in December 2005. It certified that she had been the victim of a miscarriage of justice because the only witness was dependent on 'recovered memory'.

Recovered memory evidence when it first appeared in the US courts was accepted as normal evidence. *Newsweek* in 1991 described it as 'forgetting to remember'. Nowadays, mainstream psychiatry doubts its unequivocal existence and can't find any credible scientific or clinical evidence to support it. Professor Elizabeth Loftus of California University and Professor Patricia Casey of University College of Dublin are the leading psychiatrists in this area. The Supreme Court of Minnesota, USA, in 2012, described it as 'junk science' or hearsay. Repressed memory is usually associated with early childhood traumas, whereas all the complainants were over 17when the alleged abuse was supposed to have occurred.

Most of the complainants explained the long delay in reporting by saying they suffered from 'blocked memory'. Donelle (in the 1970s) and Naveen (in the 1980s) claimed they were sexually abused by Fr Ronat and that they 'blocked out' the traumatic experiences until 'recovering' their memories of it while in therapy for unrelated problems.

Both Dr Casey and Dr Loftus, and the majority of psychiatrists, maintain that this is not possible. They say 'there is no scientific evidence to support this theory' that was popular in the 1990s and is no longer in vogue. There is no evidence that the human memory can or does block out any traumatic events, and there is no evidence to show that childhood sexual abuse is an exception to the rule. What really happens is that when a client is in therapy, the therapist may suggest possible childhood experiences, including sexual abuse, and the client, desperate for a solution to his or her depression or mental malaise, may clutch the implant and create a 'false memory' of sexual abuse by misinterpreting innocent situations from the past. Subjects with 'false memory syndrome' really believe they were abused and can display symptoms like real victims. Dr Casey states: 'Often there are allegations of child sexual abuse directed at those who have committed no such crime.'

False memory and the law

Both claimants believe they blocked the alleged sexual abuse out of their memories and recovered it later during therapy in 2005. On the contrary, during the intervening quarter of a century, they behaved as persons totally unaware of the alleged abuse, as confirmed by their maintenance of a friendly cordial relationship with their alleged abuser, Fr Ronat, during this entire period. The supposedly 'recovered memories' are therefore not an acceptable proof of the existence of any such abuse of which Fr Ronat was claimed to be guilty. Most jurisdictions of the Western world regard false memory (recovered memory) evidence as unreliable. Some states in America regard it as junk science with little or no value in court. The Irish State, as far back as 2005, reversed the conviction of Nora Wall of rape and declared it a miscarriage of justice, because the only evidence against her was recovered or false evidence.

Fr Ronat's complainants explained the constant returning to be 'abused' as being 'under a spell' and unable to resist. The reason why they received special attention was that they claimed to be children. Fr Ronat demonstrated that none of the complainants were children (under 17) when they began to call on him on an individual basis. There was a housekeeper in the house 24/7 up to and including in 1983. They would have encountered the housekeeper, as she answered all doorbells for the two priests. The housekeeper left in September1983. The complainants never referred to the housekeeper and maintained that Fr Ronat was always on his own when they called. They would have been over 17 (according to dates of birth in 1983). In canon law, a minor is a person under 21 (according to the old code of canon law, it is prior to 1983) or under 18 (new code, since 1983), but the crime of clerical sexual abuse concerned only minors under 16 until the age limit was changed to 18 in 2001.

Phase three

The payout

The Diocese of Cloyne in 2009 issued letters of apology and paid hundreds of thousands of euros to at least seven claimants against Fr Ronat without his knowledge or consent before any trial or tribunal decision (to Donelle and Fenella, and later to Ailis's parents, and to Naveen after her civil trial and before the ecclesiastical trial). The bishop sent a votum (recommendation) to the CDF to have Fr Ronat defrocked without trial. In 2009 the CDF replied by authorising his successor, the then apostolic administrator, to form a canonical tribunal in the Diocese of Cloyne. He chose his child protection delegate as principal judge, who would have been privy to the payments and apologies given to the complainants. The tribunal was halted for a long period at one stage to allow the criminal trial of Fr Ronat to proceed in which he was found innocent of sexually abusing Naveen. Immediately after the acquittal of Fr Ronat, the archbishop gave Naveen monetary compensation and an apology for Fr Ronat's actions, and weeks later, in December 2011, he announced the tribunal's resumption on *Morning Ireland* (a programme having 700,000 listeners) and stressed that it would mainly focus on Fr Ronat's 'victims'. 'I want to apologise to the victims of Fr Ronat. ... Justice was delayed, and justice delayed is justice denied to the victims. ... Also a canonical penal process ... again I would invite and encourage the victims to participate in that. ... Fr Ronat will be the focus of that, and the people who were abused by him will be the witnesses.' Fr Ronat's legal team responded to what seemed to be a case of 'open prejudice', a denial of his right to the presumption of innocence, and demanded a suspension of the tribunal. They also advised Fr Ronat not to participate. His legal team received no reply to their concern. The tribunal resumed and invited Fr Ronat to participate. Hobson's choice! To be or not to be. After much deliberation, and having already experienced prejudice, Fr Ronat, believing his innocence would be vindicated, decided to participate. His advocate assured him that canonical procedure would prevail because the allegations had no corroboration and he had a strong, corroborated defence. If he hadn't participated, he would have been found guilty in absentia.

Despite the lack of corroboration of any of the allegations, Fr Ronat was inexplicably found guilty of all charges in the church tribunal. He then appealed to Rome. His advocate, Mgr Maurice Dooley, discovered numerous invalidating instances in the tribunal's judgement, all of which were sanated by the CDF. The judgement was given to the complainants by the principal judge and the DLP (diocesan liaison person), the latter having been forewarned by Fr Ronat that, if it were published, he would be identified by the complainants in the media. (Father Ronat informed the diocesan delegate in a phone conversation.) Two newspapers breached the confidential conditions of the Cloyne report by identifying Fr Ronat.

Neglect of the law and modern science

The lack of contemporaneous corroboration in the allegations was admitted by the promoter of justice (DPP in canon law). He included a risk assessment (privately commissioned by the bishop who had importuned Fr Ronat to participate in same to ensure his future in the diocese) as possible circumstantial evidence to assist the judges. This risk assessment appeared highly suspicious and prejudiced to the layperson's eye. Fr Ronat engaged the services of Dr Patrick Randall, MA (clinical psychology), PsyD, Reg. Psychol., associate fellow of the Psychological Society of Ireland, and forensic psychologist, to review it. He found it to be 'methodically unsound'. 'It is also recommended than any decisions informed by the report of the risk assessment be reviewed given the unreliability of the methods utilised.' He also asserts, 'It is also beyond the remit of a risk assessment to determine which party has told the "truth" or whether a version of events is more or less believable than another version of events.' The risk assessment made these judgements (acting as judge and jury) and in all instances sided with the complainants. The tribunal disregarded the salient theme of Dr Randall's findings; they also disregarded the views of modern psychiatry on false memory syndrome.

The DPP returned Donelle's file with a nolle prosequi because 'there was no evidence of criminal behaviour'. There is a huge chasm between the civil zero evidence and the canonical 'moral certitude' (or 'beyond reasonable doubt') of abuse, which raises serious questions about the equity of the tribunal.

The Cloyne report states there were eleven allegations of sexual abuse made against Fr Ronat. It failed to identify the nature and content of all of these; they included anonymous, trivial, and borderline cases. Five cases presented to the tribunal. In the first instance, the Irish ecclesiastical trial, Fr Ronat was found guilty on all five. In the appeal to the CDF he was found guilty of three, and one of these was ruled out by age, but they failed to redress it. In effect there are only two remaining allegations. As already explained, one of these was tried in the civil court, and Fr Ronat was acquitted. The other was dismissed by the DPP as having no evidence. Of the remaining allegations, one consisted of alleged 'solicitation' and alleged sexual abuse in confession. The DPP had dismissed both of these counts as being without evidence. Another allegation was touching the claimant 'on the face with the hand' in front of a witness. This particular claimant sued Fr Ronat and the diocese for compensation 'for multiple acts of sexual abuse'. Another claimant made an allegation of simulated sexual abuse (termed 'frotting') and received compensation from the diocese. Another claimant made an allegation of sexual abuse against Fr Ronat when she was 'only 15'. It transpired that she drove her parents' car to Fr Ronat's house, and at the time she was 19 and on heavy medication for postnatal depression. Donelle was involved in her coming forward. There was no evidence of sexual abuse; she was friendly with Fr Ronat for up to weeks before she made the allegation. She received compensation. Another allegation was made by the mother of a boy; she claimed her son was sexually abused by Fr Ronat. The boy made no allegation. She had made this allegation to a priest in Cork, and he referred her to Cloyne. A file was eventually sent to the DPP after the Cloyne report.

After 2009 six allegations of sexual abuse were made against Fr Ronat as a result of the public campaign by Donelle and Ailis's father, the former of whom claimed in the *Irish Examiner* (10 Jan. 2009) that every time she went out for a walk or was driving around town and a certain model car in a particular colour whizzed past, she freezes—unable to lift an arm or breathe—and is rendered speechless. Relationships have posed difficulties for her, she claimed. 'For me the bond of trust was broken so young that it became practically impossible for me to trust anyone.' (Years before that, and weeks before she made the allegation, she was in a trusting, cordial, friendly relationship with her alleged abuser, seeking comfort and advice. She claimed a flashback to when she was 16:'On seeing his car I would run towards it and leave my friend. ... She [her friend] hated him [Fr B] for that.') Her mother told Fr B that she (Sinead) could see his car from her room and would know he was at home.

'The father of a woman who alleges she was sexually abused as a teenager by Fr B has said he is aware of at least 10 more victims of the same priest ... and of one of the five I know they know of another five' (*Irish Examiner*, 24 Dec. 2008). 'His daughter, he claims (deceased 2007), was 14 when the abuse began, [and he] claims [she] was raped over a three-year period ... [and] is urging others to come forward. "Molesting a child, an innocent body, is to molest a mind forevermore. I know about this first hand."' His daughter (date of birth May 1970) was molested at 12, and neither he nor his wife provided her with counselling. Fr B arrived in the parish in late September 1986. She didn't call on him until December1988, and it was then she raised the earlier molestation (1982) and her domestic problems.

They sourced another article in the *Corkman* (23 Dec. 2008):'Justice has to be done and be seen to be done; I'm not talking about revenge—I'm talking about justice and that's what any victim of any crime wants and deserves.' Those were the words of the father of Ailis after the publication of the Elliot report. 'However, it has been an extremely difficult week ... and their pain is matched by a female victim. ... The woman who contacted the *Corkman* in 2005 has been pushing for 'Priest B's' prosecution ever since.' They pushed for the prosecution of Fr B by writing to the DPP, picketing his office, picketing the Dáil, entreating Pat Rabbitte, Sean Sherlock and the state solicitor, using social media, seeking the assistance of RAT, and forming the North Cork Ten. Flanagan (member of a support group) held protests in Cork and sought funds for them. This group had a TV slot on the RAT website quoting the false information on Fr B, resulting in a social network frenzy labelling him a serial paedophile.

The third claimant, Edana (born 4 November 1965)

The judges of the first instance could not reach moral certitude on Edana's age. If so, she was deemed over 16 and therefore not included in the derogation from prescription granted to the tribunal by the CDF. I cannot understand this decision in conjunction with the second instance decision, where the judges interpreted that two other cases were not within the derogation from prescription (because the claimants were over 16) and gave 'negative' decisions in both cases. (There was emphasis on latitude given by canon law to judges, but this latitude is tempered by other principles of law.)

CHAPTER 11

Referral to the Supreme Pontiff as specified in canon 1417

Daniel Duane
Cecilstown
Mallow
Co. Cork, P51 E704
Republic of Ireland

15 December 2015

Your Holiness,

Firstly, my apologies for imposing on your precious time as Supreme Pontiff of the Church, and secondly, it is with humility and desperation that I seek your intercession in accordance with canon 1417 in my quest for justice. Only recently, 29 October 2015, I was found guilty of sexual delicts by the CDF with three minors, and I was dismissed from the priesthood by the CDF.

My advocate, Mgr Maurice Dooley, a highly respected and experienced canon lawyer who previously represented the Holy See in the Council of Europe Committees, and I are extremely concerned about the equity of the judgement for not granting total reinstatement for the following reasons:

Notwithstanding the merits of the case, I trust my conscience and memory and can vouch for my innocence, but it is necessary to highlight our deep concerns on the apparent injustice of the decision based on the rule of canon law (or natural law).

> The neglect of the right to the 'presumption of innocence'
> The neglect of some basic principles of canon law
> The nonexistence of corroboration for the alleged delicts
> The doubt of 'moral certitude' on
>> the age of the claimants and
>> the commission of the alleged delicts
> The actual total conflict with the civil law findings
> The actual neglect of
>> modern psychology and
>> modern psychiatry.

For these reasons, Your Holiness, I am appealing for your intercession. I know from my conscience and recollection that I am not guilty of these allegations which date back to 1970s and 1980s.

I wish you continued health and every blessing in your extraordinary travels and work as Vicar of Christ.

Your humble servant,

Dan Duane

Conflict of civil and canonical conclusions

Previous to the first instance trial, I was found innocent by the Circuit Criminal Court (criminal court in Cork, Republic of Ireland, November 2011) of the charges of sexual abuse made against me by Naveen, and the DPP (director of public prosecutions for the Republic of Ireland) did not proceed with the second claimant's (Donelle) allegation of sexual abuse, citing the reason that, 'there was no evidence of criminal, sexual behaviour'.

I was found innocent by the criminal law of the Republic of Ireland on all allegations.

My immediate and extended family know and believe that I am innocent, as do most of the priests in the Diocese of Cloyne, together with the majority of people I served in my forty-two years of active ministry.

My advocate, Mgr Maurice Dooley, will give you a brief history of the allegations:

Genesis of the Cloyne report

Donelle made an allegation of sexual abuse (of a minor) to the Gardai (Irish police) and to the bishop (then bishop of Cloyne) against Fr Duane in November 2005.

In February 2006, Fr Duane was immediately withdrawn from public ministry without a preliminary enquiry by the bishop. He stated in the Cloyne report (the report of a judicial commission of enquiry under Judge Yvonne Murphy, established by the Irish government to investigate the handling of sexual abuse allegations of minors against priests of the Archdiocese of Dublin, and later extended to Cloyne Diocese) that her allegation was clearly 'sexual abuse of a minor', since he concluded she had a diary. Later it transpired that there were no dates or details in her diary of alleged sexual abuse. She maintained in her deposition to the Cloyne tribunal of the first instance that she ceased recording events in her diary before the alleged sexual abuse occurred. The diary appeared to be a scrapbook and wasn't examined by either the judges or the bishop.

Her allegation was rejected by the DPP. She also sued Fr Duane and the Diocese of Cloyne for monetary compensation, but her lawyers never pursued the case, and it finally lapsed in June 2008.

She then, together with the father of Ailis (who previously had made an allegation against Fr Duane of 'kissing', and who was now deceased), went to the CEO of the National Board for Safeguarding Children (an organisation set up by the Irish Hierarchy as a watchdog for monitoring clerical sex abuse of children) and put their allegations to him, both claiming that she and Ailis were continually 'raped as children by Fr Duane over a three-year period'. They also, under pseudonyms, went to the Irish media (newspapers, radio, and TV) on a campaign of vilification against Fr Duane. This led to the Elliot report and the Cloyne report.

There is no mention of 'rape' or 'torture' in the Cloyne report as alleged by the former Irish prime minister in his infamous speech against the Vatican.

Fr Duane had clear alibis for both allegations.

My advocate, Mgr Maurice Dooley, will now explain his deep dissatisfaction with the canonical procedure involving my trials.

Denial of the presumption of innocence

Donelle, despite the collapse of her legal quest for monetary compensation, received some and an apology for Fr Duane's alleged abuse from the archbishop (who was appointed apostolic administrator of the Diocese of Cloyne after the resignation of the bishop in March 2009). The bishop had already sent the allegations to the CDF with the votum that Fr Duane should be summarily dismissed from the priesthood. The CDF replied by instructing him to establish a canonical tribunal to examine the case against Fr Duane.

This tribunal was ultimately established by the apostolic administrator. He appointed his child protection advocate as principal judge, and he in turn selected the other judges and the promoter of justice. As principal judge and as child protection advocate, he would have been privy to the compensation and apology issued to Donelle.

As a canon lawyer, I deem this as a denial of the presumption of innocence.

The presumption of his innocence was again compromised on the resumption of the ecclesiastical tribunal (which had been halted while a criminal trial of Fr Duane was proceeding, and in which he was found innocent of sexually abusing Naveen). Immediately after the trial, the archbishop gave Naveen monetary compensation and an apology for Fr Duane's abuse.

Commenting on the Cloyne report, after the publication of its chapter on Fr Duane's case, the archbishop publicly stated: 'They [the claimants] were denied the justice they deserved.' The Cloyne report denied there was any cover-up or injustice in the Donelle and Naveen cases.

The principal judge told Donelle that the Diocese of Cloyne 'did everything by the book' in her case. He also stated in a letter to me that this case (Fr Duane) was 'part of the calamitous scandal that emerged from Cloyne Diocese leading to the resignation of a bishop, and the mismanagement of this case contributed to the most serious crisis in relationship between the State and the Holy See since the foundation of the State'. He provided this as one of the reasons why he wrote to the papal nuncio. The archbishop announced the resumption of the tribunal on public radio and invited Fr Ronat's (Fr Duane's) 'victims' to participate, repeating that the trial would be all about Fr Duane's 'victims'. He stated: 'I want to apologise. Heartfelt apologies to the victims of Fr Ronat [a pseudonym for Fr Duane]. Justice was delayed, and justice delayed is justice denied to the victims.' Fr Duane's civil lawyers objected strongly in a letter to the archbishop to what they described as blatant prejudice and advised Fr Duane not to participate in the tribunal. Had we known then about the compensation and apology issued to Donelle and Naveen, we would not have participated. This was done unbeknown to us and was a blatant violation of the presumption of innocence. Furthermore it could have influenced the mental disposition of the judges of the tribunal which he established.

Despite his legal advice, Fr Duane had no choice but to participate in the tribunal.

Lack of corroboration

It was obvious to me at the depositions of the complainants against Fr Duane that the principal judge was biased in his interrogation of the claimants and Fr Duane. While he allowed the claimants to wander off in long phases of uncorroborated and vitriolic attacks, he treated Fr Duane in a very hostile and adversarial manner, frequently questioning his evidence in a dismissive manner. On three occasions I was forced to intervene, advising Fr Duane not to answer leading questions which would admit guilt and telling him instead to invoke canon 1728, which says that 'an accused person is never bound to admit guilt'.

I couldn't find any corroboration in their depositions.

The promoter of justice agreed in his pleadings that there was no contemporaneous corroboration of the complainants' allegations, but he advised the inclusion of a risk assessment delivered on Fr Duane as possible circumstantial evidence. Fr Duane and I objected strongly to the admission of this risk assessment because of its suspect and flawed content and the limited information on which the conclusions were based. The tribunal accepted and applied it, ignoring the requirements of the code canons 1574–1581.

The risk assessment was privately commissioned by the bishop. I objected to its biased origin and content. The presiding judge insisted that since it was commissioned by the bishop, the assessor would not have Fr Duane's 'best interests at heart'. Our suspicions were justified by an independent analysis undertaken by Dr Patrick Randall, a forensic psychologist of Forensic Psychology Services in Dún Laoire, County Dublin. After a thorough examination, he found it completely unreliable, lacking any methodology, and unscientific. He also claims 'that it is beyond the scope of a risk assessment to determine which party has told the "truth" or whether a version of events is more or less believable than another version of events'. The assessors did this and in all instances stated their preference for the version of events claimed by the plaintiffs. We supplied a copy of Dr Randall's analysis of the risk assessment and the theses of Dr Casey and Dr Loftus in our plea for restitutio in integrum.

Naveen (born 1 January 1966) claimed in her evidence to the civil court that she told three priests and a woman named KT about the alleged abuse. KT could not be found, and the three priests stated under oath that they had no recollection of her telling them. In her deposition to the ecclesiastical tribunal, Naveen told the judges that she *intended* to tell the priests, and the judges accepted this as corroboration.

Lack of corroboration on complainants' age

Naveen (born 1 January 1966) claimed to the Gardai that she was 14 when the alleged abuse began. She claimed to the child protection advocate for Cloyne that she was 16, and then later she changed it to 13, and again she said that she couldn't remember because of hypnosis. The confusion was created by her calling initially with others on a priest with whom Fr Duane shared the house in 1981. They had a housekeeper who was resident with them all day, every day. She always answered the phone and door. Fr Duane was then working in Fermoy, some twenty-two miles away, in St Colman's College, to where he commuted every day. He would have met Naveen only in a group being counselled by another priest, and only on a very few occasions. The priest and the housekeeper left in September 1983. The group split up and its members began to call singly only after that. Naveen never mentioned meeting the housekeeper, and she claimed Fr Duane was always on his own, indicating it was only after September 1983 that she met Fr Duane on his own. She kept calling until 1984, when Fr Duane left. She would have been 17 or 18 when she first called on her own. It is certain she didn't call before 1981 as she claimed. Fr Duane wouldn't have known her then. The criminal court accepted 1983 as the more probable date when she first began to meet Fr Duane on his own because of the evidence presented. It is difficult for us to believe that the ecclesiastical judges reached 'moral certitude' that she was a minor under 16 at the time she was allegedly molested.

Donelle (born 13 June 1956) started to call with Mass cards as a schoolgirl. Fr Duane noticed her as having more than usual interest in meeting him or a teenage crush (which she claimed herself in her diary records), and he discouraged her from calling on silly errands. Finally he had to bar her from calling while he was there, but she befriended his mother, who was living with him at the time, and on that pretext she resumed calling. In April 1971 Fr Duane left to pursue further studies in a university in Dublin (150 miles from Mallow) and Limerick. He went to visit his family in the United States during the summer breaks in 1971 and 1972. He was mainly based in Dublin. The combined courses ended in 1973, at which time he took up the new post as counsellor to 500 boys in St Colman's College,

Fermoy. During those years he would not have met Donelle. Her father died suddenly in 1974, and from then on she would call. She was 18 years of age and attending a third-level academy in Cork. She claimed she was sexually abused by Fr Duane in June 1971 and July 1971. He was in the United States on vacation on both dates. In those years there wasn't even opportunity for the alleged abuse to occur.

I noticed that during her deposition, Donelle presented her psychiatric report to the principal judge, but he didn't inspect it, choosing to move on. Nevertheless, she alluded to her 'inability to recall past events clearly' and said that there were blank spots in her life with regard to photographs. I deemed this as significant when relating it later to false memory syndrome. I thought it was remiss of the principal judge not to inspect her psychiatric report. It is difficult to comprehend how the judges arrived at moral certitude on her age.

Lack of corroboration of proof of sexual abuse

Both Naveen and Donelle were on friendly terms with Fr Duane immediately prior to making the allegations. They showed no fear; they trusted him completely and shared their problems and worries with him; they didn't display fear or anxiety in his presence; they regarded him as their trusted counsellor, even sharing gifts and visits; and they showed no signs of having been abused. Then suddenly, they changed dramatically and, as if they'd had a personality transplant, ranted and spewed the most horrible vitriol at him in an inexplicable turn of events. Their friendly relationship with Fr Duane confused me as it is not behaviour consistent with victims of abuse.

It's when Fr Duane engaged the advice of Dr Patricia Casey on false memory syndrome that I realised it was typical behaviour of those suffering with false memory syndrome. Both Naveen and Donelle claimed to have 'blocked' the alleged abuse from their minds, an action which Dr Casey and Dr Elizabeth Loftus, both expert psychiatrists on this phenomenon, claim is not possible. Naveen and Donelle also allege that they recovered their memories of the abuse years later during therapy, another action the psychiatrists claim is not possible. They really began to believe that they had been sexually abused and behaved accordingly.

Much has been written on this subject of false memory syndrome. The majority of psychiatrists support Dr Casey and Dr Loftus on this and claim that there is no scientific evidence to support that the mind can block out memories or experiences of traumatic events, including sexual abuse, and that 'recovering memories' does not occur. The memories that occur are caused by suggestion or planted by therapists in counselling situations; hence, the term 'false memory' replaces the term 'recovered memory'. The evidence from witnesses suffering from 'false memory' is very unreliable. The reality is that most jurisdictions of the world disregard it as hard evidence and treat it as unreliable.

It is difficult to perceive that with this evidence and lack of corroboration, the judges reached moral certitude.

Neglect of the law

It is expected of judges of all codes of law to be competent in identifying and summarising all the evidence presented to them for adjudication in a manner which is equitable to all parties.

In Fr Duane's recent case for restitutio in integrum, we identified some vital omissions in the judges' evaluation. They never considered the vacillation in the claimants' evidence, and there were multiple discrepancies which were identified and which were both damaging to their credibility. They never alluded to the lack of the right to presumption of innocence. These are grave omissions. They treated Dr Randall's critique as unprofessional and not as a document alluding to its 'private commission'. They quoted extensively from it to support their view of its limitation, neglecting to note its salient theme, that 'it is beyond the scope of a risk assessment to determine which party has told the "truth", or whether a version of events is more or less believable than another version of events'. In all instances of the tribunal we demonstrated where the risk assessor actually did this and in all cases favoured the claimants' version, thus rendering the assessment biased and unscientific. Dr Randall identified a number of instances of the assessors' lack of methodology, but this was the salient point which the judges disregarded. It rendered the privately commissioned risk assessment that they depended on so much for corroboration 'unreliable and deeply flawed'.

The judges gave scant treatment to Dr Casey's and Dr Loftus's psychiatric expertise on false memory syndrome, dismissing it as irrelevant. They appear to be at odds in the face of modern psychiatry and seem out of touch with its impact on the law and yet willing to accept without reservation the 'unreliable and unscientific' findings of a risk assessment which raises serious concerns regarding the equity of Dan Duane's judgement.

Your Holiness,

My faith and, indeed, that of my family and friends, both clerical and lay, is badly shattered by what I have encountered from the church in my quest for justice. What was so frustrating for my family was the secrecy and non-transparency. My experience of the civil forum was so different. Not only did I obtain justice, but also it was seen to be done. In that criminal trial it took a mere fifty five minutes for the jury to declare my innocence.

I am 77 years old and retired. It has been five years since my trial began, and I still seek justice. Three of my siblings died in the last three years, and not being allowed even to concelebrate, never mind celebrate, Mass at their funerals was the most difficult experience for me and my three surviving siblings to have endured. That is why I appeal to you in this Jubilee Year to grant my desire for justice, so that I can continue to celebrate the Eucharist with family and friends until the Lord calls me.

Once again wishing you every grace in this blessed season,

Your humble servant,
Dan Duane

CHAPTER 12

RESULT OF THE APPEAL

I was notified by the Ordinary to attend the notification of the appeal findings at his residence in Cobh. The papal nuncio was represented by the interim chargé d'affaires, who read the results. I was found guilty of three of the claimants' allegations, Donelle's, Naveen's, and Edana's, and not guilty of two others, Caelan's and Fenella's. The judges could not reach moral certainty on Edana's age, yet they still found me guilty, which baffled Mgr Dooley and me. The Ordinary pleaded ignorance of the legalities and proceeded with the business of signing the notification papers. He was forbidden by pontifical secrecy to disclose the identities of the two complainants whose allegations were dismissed by the appeal, which resulted in inaccurate information being released to the press. Mgr Dooley and I were shocked and dismayed by the findings of the judges, and the more often we read the judgement, the more astonished we became at the seemingly unjust application of canon law. This is the final straw as there is no more we can do. As is expressed by the age-old dictum, '*Roma locuta est; causa finita est*' (Rome has spoken; the case is finished). We knew that the risk assessment was seriously flawed by the biased and unprofessional treatment of the limited material at the disposal of the assessors. I sought the best psychological advice available in Ireland and was directed to Dr Patrick Randall, MA (clinical psychology), Reg. Psychol., associate fellow of the Psychological Society of Ireland, consultant, and clinical and forensic psychologist in Dún Laoire County,

Dublin; he undertook to review the risk assessment to determine whether it was conducted in an appropriate manner and whether the results reported by the risk assessor could be viewed as valid and reliable. He reviewed it in detail, commenting on the methodology. After having highlighted the absence of actuarial risk instruments or structured risk instruments to determine risk and having noted the absence of psychometric methods to determine the presence or absence of offence-related variables, he came to the following conclusions: the assessment conducted by the risk assessor was methodologically unsound, and any decisions informed by the report of the risk assessment should be reviewed given the unreliability of the methods utilised. The salient point of his analysis was that the assessor breached the remit of risk assessment by determining, or attempting to determine, who was telling the truth, and attempting to assert whether one version of events was more or less believable than another version of events. The assessors were guilty of these assumptions with the very limited information and data at their disposal. Dr Randall was prepared to give a more detailed analysis and critique, if required. I then consulted Dr Patricia Casey, one of the foremost psychiatrists on the subject of false memory syndrome, as all three appellants claimed to have blocked the alleged sexual abuse out of their memories, which caused the long delay in reporting it. She kindly gave me the written views of Dr Elizabeth Loftus, another foremost psychiatrist in this area. Mgr Dooley knew that, according to canon 1645, I could apply for restitutio in integrum in regard to my case with the new material supplied by the above consultants to challenge the first instance of the Cloyne tribunal and the second instance of the CDF, and again I would be presumed innocent until the findings of this application were published. We collated the evidence and sent the application to the CDF.

My bishop did not believe that I could reopen my case until Mgr Dooley explained the canon law to him on my challenge under canon 1645. There is only one appeal to a verdict, and when that appeal is rejected, it becomes a res judicata (an adjudged matter), to which there is no further appeal. However, this is not an appeal as such. Rather it is a challenge under canon 1645 of the original verdict. My bishop reluctantly accepted the explanation, but he was adamant that I was not presumed innocent while the appeal was being processed. Mgr Dooley sent numerous letters to him outlining the clear law on the presumption of innocence, but he still refused to presume me innocent. The child liaison delegates organised a meeting in my house about implementing the covenant which was agreed upon when the appeal of the second instance found me guilty and sentenced me to laicisation, which was suspended until the time when the result of the challenge is finalised. We had tea and refreshments, and the meeting proceeded. I told them that I was presumed innocent and was saying Mass in my house. They immediately shouted their disapproval and left in haste to report back to the bishop. He wrote to me, expressing 'dismay' at my behaviour and saying that he would not accept that I was presumed innocent and that I had no right to say Mass. It would be no surprise to me and Mgr Dooley if my alleged insubordination was reported to the CDF. My faith in the hierarchical church is rapidly diminishing, and indeed, their manipulation rather than interpretation of canon law is deeply worrying. The law is very clear on the subject of the right to presumption of innocence, and now the church, the alleged bastion of Christian rights, is vacillating. It ignored the basic principle of natural, civil, and canon law not once, but multiple times during my trials. Mgr Dooley will recount the exact number of times canon law was seemingly flouted by the tribunals. I will refer to one glaring factual error in the verdict of the second instance: I went to extreme lengths to demonstrate that all the claimants came to me voluntarily and without solicitation, corroborating my evidence. Regarding age, the one who asserts has the burden of proof. Naveen gave four different ages to various agencies. Surely there must be doubt about the correct age she was when she claimed to be abused. The tribunal found her consistent. Her evidence was so inconsistent that the DPP took only one instance of alleged abuse in the book of evidence. She criticised the DPP for not taking all her statements. The tribunal had all those discrepancies at their disposal and chose to ignore them, citing a consistency in her evidence and claiming that all the claimants were young vulnerable girls who had been invited to visit me in my house. I challenge the tribunal to produce the evidence for this assertion. In her first Garda statement Naveen said that I invited her and the others to my house. Then she contradicted it in a later statement, saying she didn't know how it came about that she started calling on me. 'Which one are you, the jury, going to believe?' she asked. The tribunal made its choice. The confusion arose from the claimants' assertion that they were calling on me, when in fact they were calling on another priest. Donelle insisted that she was a young 'Mother Teresa' because of the number of times she was compelled to call on my house to look after my mother, and she said that I invited her, when in actual fact, I was discouraging her from calling. The tribunal accepted that nobody is expected to incriminate themselves. Canon 1728 states that the right to silence is not to be questioned. I had to invoke that canon three times; I replied 'not guilty', and that was interpreted as a lie by the tribunal.

The first instance placed so much emphasis and dependence on the risk assessment that it would be difficult for them to extract the content from the previous verdict. Alas, I was disillusioned with the optimism and good faith in the CDF and the Vatican when the verdict arrived. They ignored the findings of Dr Randall, and they accepted the risk assessment in its entirety, claiming that it was official. It had been commissioned by the bishop. The principal judge commented in a letter to my advocate that, because of that, my 'best interests would not be foremost in the risk assessor's mind'. It's up to the jury to interpret that comment. They ignored the salient point that it is beyond the scope of a risk assessment to determine which party has told the 'truth' or whether a version of events is more or less believable than another version of events. The assessor made judgements on the truth of one set of events over another in a very biased and patent manner. The CDF didn't even mention false memory syndrome and the findings of modern psychiatry. At this stage I began scratching my head in disbelief. To summarise, I remember an old saying from an incorrigible debater of the past: 'My mind is made up. Don't confuse me with the facts.' I'm now thinking that it's a waste of my very sparse energy pursuing my quest for justice, and I would be sinking lower and lower, slowly but surely, into the fathomless abyss of despair were it not for my God, the G factor, my family and many friends, golf, and my animal and bird mates. I am still a priest, and the recitation of the Divine Office, the breviary, was and is great consolation. The psalms bear new meaning since the allegations were launched against me: they were refreshing springs in the bitter valley of mental anguish and desolation.

Hymn from Matins, Saturday 3

How great a tale, that there should be,
In God's Son's heart, a place for me!
That on a sinner's lips like mine,
The cross of Jesus Christ should shine!
Christ Jesus, bend me to thy will,
My feet to urge, my griefs to still;
That e'en my flesh and blood may be
A temple sanctified to thee.
No rest, no calm my soul may win,
Because my body craves to sin;
Till thou, dear Lord, thyself impart,
Peace on my head, light in my heart.
May consecration come from far,
Soft shining like the evening star.
My toilsome path make plain to me,
Until I come to rest in thee.

The daily recitation of the rosary was very important to me too in the dark days of my trials. The rosary is sometimes called the ordinary punter's prayer. Simple: ten fingers to count a decade, and five decades for one rosary. Because of the repetition, it is easy to fall asleep. My father was always on the watch for culprits during our family rosary in my youth, with walking stick at the ready. Should he spot a defaulter and gently prod him or her to awaken, it would be very embarrassing for such a person to have fallen asleep and missed the turn to recite a decade. If one of us missed the call, which would signalled with a deafening silence, everyone would join in disapproving sounds and mock coughing. The custom of daily recital of the rosary was good, but if we had a better understanding of its meaning and efficacy, there would be no need for the stick. It was only when I got involved with the Legion of Mary and started preaching homilies on the rosary that I really understood it as the most powerful prayer, next to the Eucharist. The Lord's Prayer is the ultimate of all prayers; it begins with 'Our Father', not 'My Father' as in a single plea. Jesus said: 'You must call no one on earth your father, since you have only one father, and he is in heaven' (Matthew 23). God is the father of us all, and we come to him in unison as a family. He is in heaven, and therefore he can, and will, help us if we ask. We praise him: 'Hallowed be thy name, thy kingdom come.' His kingdom isn't territorial like those of the kings of the world; the kingdom of God is within us: righteousness, truth, peace, love, mercy, and all Christ's teachings. 'Thy will be done on earth as it is in heaven': perfect harmony here on earth as there is in heaven. The animal world and the human race have a lot in common when they embrace their own kind. Dogs size each other up by sometimes fawning respect and by scenting each other before acceptance or rejection; the human communicates by body language and words. When a person wants something, he or she will praise the other before making a request. I recall, as a youngster, the travelling people calling on my mother for food and clothes, and they would begin with praise: 'God bless you, ma'am. You have a fine son there. God bless him.' Then came the request: 'Any bit of food for a poor starving woman and child?' The child was the banker. It works everywhere. I was standing outside the church in Assisi, and an Italian woman, selling souvenirs, came over and greeted me and the young man who was with me with 'Bello bambino'(lovely boy). She said this assuming he was my son, and then she asked me to buy her merchandise.

The Our Father starts with praise before the request: 'Give us this day our daily bread' (give us all our needs for today),'and forgive us our trespasses as we forgive those who trespass against us.' God will forgive us if we forgive those who hurt us, a fair trade not easily practised. Don't ask God to forgive you if you won't forgive others. That is plenty of food for thought. 'And lead us not into temptation, but deliver us from evil.'

The Hail Mary. Satan used Eve, the first woman, to tempt Adam, the first man, to take the forbidden apple. Women were seen by succeeding generations as 'the weaker sex' until Mary was chosen as the mother of God and by saying, 'Be it done unto me according to your word.' The loss of Eden is about to be restored. 'I will put enmity between you and the woman, and she will crush your head.' Mary is the new Eve and mother of the new Adam, and women are no longer seen as the weaker sex. Christ, the new Adam, has bestowed great honour on Mary. The Lord is with her, and she is the most graceful of all women because she carries the Son of God in her womb. The first part of the Hail Mary is attributing praise and honour to Mary, mother of God, who is with the Lord at all times in a very influential position, the most blessed of all women, yet a woman who adopted us as her children and is always willing to help. We pay her our profoundest respect and honour her as the most blessed of all women and mother of God. We now ask for her prayers for the most important times of our lives, now and at the hour of our death, and one day those twin times will coincide. It's comforting to know that Mary will be with us when we breathe our last. I learned during my ministry that those who said the rosary regularly were always so calm and peaceful on their deathbed. The soldier of two world wars, referred to earlier, was aware of its power when watching his Irish comrade soldiers fearless in battle with their rosary beads around their necks. The concluding prayer is the doxology of praise for the Trinity. The repetition gives the rosary its strength; it's easy to break single threads singly, but twist all the single threads into a rope and it's not easily broken. Present a single flower and it's barely acceptable; present a bouquet and it's very welcome. The rosary is one of our most authentic prayers, having the words of Christ in the Lord's Prayer, the archangel Gabriel's words in the first half of the Hail Mary, and the church supplying the remainder.

My family ties are very strong, and all the members know my situation and are very supportive. Only four of us are alive. Pat and Lil are in America, and Tess is in Dublin. We were and are a very united family. Tom, Jim, Ger, and Mary are deceased. Tom and Jim and Mary were like third parents to me. Ger was, and Pat, Tess, and Lil are, like my twins. I regard my nephews and nieces as my children. They are scattered around the world, but we still keep in contact. The family members in Cork are near me, and they see me quite often. There are four houses I visit. The dogs, cats, and hens, and even a pet pig every now and then, belong to my nephew Dan and his mother, Lilly. Dan has an organic garden for fruit and vegetables. There is no shortage of game birds as he runs a pheasant shoot every year. Like his late father, he is keen in marksmanship and gaming. He also has four brood sows and rears a pig for organic bacon for the house. Lilly is a great cook, and there is nothing to compare with her baking. Her recipes for apple tart and rhubarb tart, scones, queen cakes, ice cream, soups, jams, crab juice, brown bread, and corned beef and cabbage are better than any others I have tried. One little secret ingredient is the quality of the organic free-range eggs she uses. Mary, her daughter and my niece, comes home from Dublin at weekends, and she is an excellent cook like her mother. She teaches special needs children in Dublin. I love taking out the three dogs, Sally, Molly, and Cocobama, for a golf run in the fields; I hit a wedge into the high grass, and they strive with each other to find it and bring it back. They would spend all day at it if I had the time and energy. They usually end up with equal plaudits, and I treat them all to a 'prize' at the end, a dog biscuit. My DNA bids me to be close to the grass and earth, and there is nothing more relaxing than a stroll in the fields with the dogs. Watching the hens exercise their pecking order is amusing and entertaining, as is seeing the roosters battling for their attention. There is something fascinating about cluckers (brooding hens) sitting for three weeks on a nest of eggs with very little food and drink. It seems but little time compared to the gestation of most mammals, but it is so intense and boring for a hen who is normally on the move all day long, scratching out her food, to be sitting on eggs all day and all night for three weeks. Three weeks is a long time in the life of a hen (in human terms, it is about three months). When the chickens emerge, she is busy scratching for them and calling them to every bit of food she finds, and then she will sit on them for hours to keep them warm. It's no wonder that Christ made the comparison of God's love for the Jews of Jerusalem to a mother hen and her chickens. Animals and birds when given trust will return it with interest. It's sad that when people lose trust in others, they entrust themselves completely to animals for friendship. I have had plenty of betrayal in my life, but I still trust my many human friends. Not everyone can be trusted, and yet there are many who can be. Humans need human friends to stretch out a hand of friendship rather than a dog to offer its paw.

Michael, my nephew, and his wife, Jackie, and their family live in Ballintlea, about a mile from Ballyshera, my original home. He runs a dairy farm with over a hundred cows, along with calves, yearlings, pedigree Hereford bulls, two brood mares, one racehorse, and two foals. Ballintlea was the first farm, *c.* 180 acres, owned by my great-grandfather Michael Duane. They have five in the family. They are the third generation, but I regard them as more like my siblings because of the frequency of my visits and interaction since I retired. It's like a home away from home with the effervescence of youthful energy and familial love. It's like Ballyshera with the number of mouths to be fed, but Jackie is well capable of dealing with crowds and is another great cook. The whole family are capable of looking after themselves. When I go there for Christmas it's like Ballyshera in the old days. I made myself useful by helping them at their homework insofar as I could, but the education system has changed so much that my help was limited. Despite all the cattle, they have no sheepdog, so I use the old jeep or quad to bring the cows in for milking on the odd summer evening. And again it was interesting to study the pecking order. The same cow would lead the way, and the weakest cow would be last. It was the same in the milking parlour; they usually lined up in order of seniority to be milked. I used to milk the cows by hand when I was young in Ballyshera and later with the milking machine, which was slow. The modern milking parlour can do the milking in a quarter of the time and with less labour.

The original house in Ballyshera is a ruin now except the northern annex. It was replaced by a bungalow in 1974. Bernadette, my niece, lives there, and that's another house on my visiting itinerary. She doesn't farm anymore and lets the land. She is happy and content with the quiet and peace of the countryside and wouldn't trade it for the urban. She has a beautiful view from her sitting room of the lawn with its ancient oaks and rich pasture. It revives happy memories when I visit the yard that once buzzed with life; the yard is cobbled with sandstone and dates back to the early nineteenth century. There is a trough running parallel to the north wall, which I helped to build in 1949 to accommodate the yearling calves. The old dairy from where we ambushed unsuspecting grain buyers is dilapidated now, but the yard gate, the target, is still there. Ophelia, the great storm of October 2017, whipped the hay barn in its path, but happily my favourite oak tree and its comrades survived. It was struck by lightning in 1991 and survived. Unfortunately, thirteen of Tom's cows were killed beneath it. A flock of jackdaws were hit as well and were strewn for yards around, completely singed and oven ready, such was the power of the lightning strike. The sight of the huge truck carrying the bodies of the dead cows, with their legs pointing to the sky, winding its way down the avenue is forever imprinted in my memory, as is Tom's sad countenance as a huge part of his livestock and work dissipated from his view. He never recovered fully from that trauma and died within a few years.

The garden wall still stands high, the wall I tumbled off while searching for shamrock. The old house is just a shell, but the steps outside the hall door are still there, as are the cracks which would devour a precious half-crown if it fell from a young hand, never to be retrieved. The steps were limestone slabs with a natural white streaks running through them, forming a Freemason sign, so we were told. The kitchen is still there with its flagstone floor; it was a sign of wealth and affluence in the early nineteenth century. It was very dangerous because it was so smooth and slippery. I remember on one summer Sunday I was demonstrating with a dance to Mike Morrissey the pros and cons of a new pair of slip-on shoes which were just becoming fashionable, when one of them flew off and hit the window behind him as he was eating his dinner. It didn't break the window by hitting the timber frame, but it made a mighty racket. Before the mob could express disapproval, Mike casually responded, 'Ha ha then, but they wouldn't be much good for ploughing!' There was relief all round, but for me, it was an embarrassing moment that would be recalled as fuel for future reference.

The hall door is gone, but the fan light peculiar to Georgian architecture still exists. It's sad to see a once proud building decline into ruins, but the cost of restoration is prohibitive and reality rules. When I drive up the avenue, I get a great sense of joy of times spent in a happy childhood, and as I leave, I get a sense of sadness like that which I experienced each time I left for St Colman's and Maynooth, bidding farewell to those happy times.

Christmas was always special when all my siblings would come home for a week and the house would be filled with noise and banter. The provision of holly, preparing the goose and the ham and plum pudding, the gradual crescendo of excitement leading up to midnight Mass, listening to Hughie and Wally Birmingham render 'Silent Night' and 'Adeste Fideles', and then Christmas Day, getting up at daybreak, eating a huge fried breakfast, bedding and foddering the animals, giving them their Christmas dinner, and then going off with the dogs shooting for the day. The women were delighted with the men out of the way. The men were delighted with fresh air to develop an appetite. The men returned with huge appetites in early evening, the table extended to accommodate everybody and the dinner, the goose stuffed with mashed and spiced potato with its unique flavour, the plum pudding doused with punch, and Sullivan's lemonade to flush it down. After dinner we would go to the parlour or drawing room and enjoy a smoke and have a game of cards and generally laze about. The important thing was that we were all together for a few days. On the pre-Christmas nights Mary used to play the piano, and those of us who could sing gave the Christmas carols an airing. Mary was a good singer. I have tape recordings of those happy nights. My father would get presents of cigarettes, usually a box containing 100, and he had the misfortune of leaving them on the mantelpiece. Each of us would help ourselves, unbeknown to each other, to a few fags until the box was nearly empty, and of course he would half-heartedly give out, but they were free anyway.

St Stephen's Day was another exciting day. The wren boys, all camouflaged, called, and we tried to identify them. There was the choice to go racing or shooting or follow the hounds and then get ready for the big dance that night. I went to my first dance in 1955 in the Mayflower in Mitchelstown and danced (or walked) to Mick Delahunty's band. I didn't have a step in me, but Mary and Tess helped me to 'walk' for the first few dances. The place was so packed that it was impossible to dance, which suited me fine. I stood on a few feet, but I was only returning the compliments being paid to me. That was Christmas in Ballyshera! As everyone got married, the numbers dwindled. There was more goose but less fun.

The fourth house of my itinerary is in Shanagarry, where my nephew Tommy and his fiancée, Brigid, live with their eleven dogs. They say the apple doesn't fall very far from the tree, and it's certainly true in Tommy's case. His father, and my brother, Ger, was an out-and-out marksman and totally dedicated to shooting. Tommy is even more dedicated to shooting, hence the eleven gun dogs. They have a lovely house in Bernabeau, just up the road from Ballymaloe, where I now have my Christmas dinner sometimes. Brigid is an excellent cook, and Tommy is an excellent host. That combination works well in the entertainment of visitors. I don't drink regularly, but I might have a glass of wine at Christmas. And they have overnight accommodation, if I so wish to stay. I know all the dogs by name, and they respond by a wag of the tail. Tommy and Brigid live near Ballycotton, and they gave me an open invitation to go deep-sea fishing in the summer whenever I like. I'm not short of places to go and things to do.

My sister Tess lives in Dublin. I visit her every Christmas and Easter and a few times during the rest of the year. She is two years older than I, and Lil is a year and a half younger than I, so we are close in age and familial love. Tess is confined to her house. Her health is worse than mine, but she still likes company and news from her relations and the native village. She has four daughters, Deirdre, Maura, Sinead, and Patsy, and one son, Shay, all married. Three are living near her, one lives in Australia, and one lives in Holland. She reached her 80th birthday last year, and they were all there for the celebrations.

Jim and Mary lived in Dublin, and their respective families live in Dublin. I visited Jim and Theresa a lot when I was in Maynooth. They had four daughters, Mary, Fiona, Eimear, and Maeve. We still keep in touch. Joe and Mary had five in their family, Micheal, Paul, Marguerite, John, and Eamonn, and they come down south quite often.

Lil and Rolf live in Ridgefield, Connecticut, USA. Their two daughters, Monica and Ursula, are married and living in the United States. I visit all of them as often as I can, and we are in constant contact. They come here on visits and stay with me for vacation. I love going to the US on vacation; I have good friends as well as relations there. Two years ago I visited Ursula and her two boys, Victor and Conor, in Maryland. It's not far from Gettysburg, Pennsylvania, the site of the Civil War between North and South. My visit there was inspiring and educational. The battlefield is very well maintained and documented with the names of the slain etched on stone, many of whom were Irish, on both sides of the Civil War. There is so much to see in the US, and I love the Americans. I visit Monica and Thomas and their children, Niamh and Declan, in upstate Connecticut.

Monica is a music teacher and loves the Irish music. A consummate Irish step dancer and teacher, she is keen to pass the skills to the kids. Thomas doesn't shoot, but he is a firearms engineer and has designed his own shotgun. He is also an accomplished Irish step dancer, so the DNA of Irish dancing is pretty strong in their kids.

Pat and Mary live in the Bronx, New York, and if you were to walk down the street, you would think you were in Ireland. They have one son, Michael, a retired NYPD officer, who lives in Yonkers. Pat spends a lot of time there cultivating his tomatoes, and like me, he likes to be close to the soil. He retired twice and enjoys his retirement. He used to come to Ireland in November every year for the pheasant shooting, but the flight is too demanding on his health now, so he hasn't been for the last few years. We keep in touch by phone. He loves to hear all the news from home. Recently he was admitted to a nursing home because of his deteriorating health. We were great buddies in former years when he came home for the shooting season, and prior to that when he taught me to use the long tom, a single-barrel shotgun.

I play golf two or three times a week, and I grow tomatoes, strawberries, and flowers. I take 'my' dogs for exercise every day, and they express their gratitude in their canine language, as do 'my' hens, chickens, and ducks. They all belong to my nephew and sister-in-law Lilly, but I have adopted them as extended family. I shop in Kanturk and Mallow and meet my many friends, who stop to talk and offer their support and prayers. I'm so grateful for these pillars of support. I would never have survived mentally if not for them. I felt like a scapegoat being thrashed and beaten, going from one tribunal to another, never again to practise ministry. As Psalm 69:11–12 puts it, 'They make me a byword, the gossip of men at the gates, the subject of drunkards' songs.' I didn't indulge in gossip, and it never bothered me what people thought, but my family took the brunt.

I didn't wallow for long in self-pity, because life is short when you reach the late seventies. I decided, with the help of Mgr Maurice Dooley, my Rock of Cashel, to appeal to the Pope, under canon 1417, for a review of my case. Maurice is a brilliant canon and civil lawyer, and a great friend to boot, helping me even financially. He has been at my beck and call since 2009 without any remuneration; I could only offer him benefit in kind by prayerful gratitude. Knowing the impasse between His Holiness and the Curia, and the CDF in particular, I wasn't even cautiously confident of a positive outcome. I put my case before His Holiness, the Pope, accompanied by a personal entreaty. It was the Holy Year of Mercy and I read where he said that too much emphasis was placed on justice rather than on mercy in the past. I didn't plead mercy, only justice.

The Result of the Papal Appeal

I received a letter from the bishop with the result of the papal appeal. In it the Pope referred my concerns, regarding injustice, back to the CDF, its place of origin, for judgement, and the CDF pronounced judgement on their own judgement, thereby violating natural justice. *Nemo judex in causa sua (nobody is judge of their own case)*. The verdict is couched in complex language making it difficult for somebody not fluent in English to understand. On finding no fault with their original judgement, the letter stated that the Pontiff 'did not express any disapproval' with their verdict.

CHAPTER 13

IS PREXIT LOOMING?

There is no more I can do now to clear my name in canon law. Abandoned by Rome, but not by Caesar, I'm pinning my hope on his law, the State. Irish law is paramount to all other legal systems in Ireland, including canon law. The crux of the problem is, did the Cloyne tribunal adhere to the law of the land and all other laws that the land has pledged to uphold? There will be a huge burden of proof to reach, and the acquisition of adequate evidence to reach the threshold of 'beyond reasonable doubt' will be difficult, but my advocate seems to think that there is considerable evidence to convince a court that the tribunal did breach my human rights. I'm still a priest and will remain so forever. The second instance gibed at my advocate's reference to the Court of Human Rights as a course of appeal to their verdict, obviously unaware of a successful appeal by a Swiss priest against the Swiss State and Church for wrongful conviction two years ago, and also unaware of my advocate's work for the Vatican at said court. It also illustrates the arrogance and lack of accountability of the CDF. This is not my opinion; it's the opinion of many canon lawyers I have heard and read. I have read also that the Pope is in an unenviable position with regard to restructuring the Curia, and progress is described as slow.

I have made a statement to the Gardai with regard to Donelle, citing her allegation against me as mendacious and malicious, and I will be submitting a review of that case when I have garnered more evidence. I will be making similar statements on Naveen and Edana regarding their claiming to have been children and giving false ages. I will pursue the other claimants when I have collated the relevant evidence. If the criminal appeal for false allegation fails, I will still have recourse to the civil courts. The wait continues. The elusive Godot has yet to appear. Sadly, my brother Pat passed away since I began to write these memoirs, and another part of me has died with him (RIP).

I visited Ballyshera one fine September and searched for acorns from the beloved oak. Then I sat down in the warm autumn sunshine and, pondering on past decisions and my present plight, decided to pen these memoirs and state my case for posterity's analysis, outlining my exoneration by Caesar (the Irish justice system) and condemnation by Rome (the CDF), and still protected from the executioner's hand by the Most High in whose shelter I dwell.

The old principle that 'the end never justifies the means' gets little attention these days, but it still prevails. My present situation, and that of other priests in the same situation, is closely affected by this. We all have civil rights, and these rights are being violated unnecessarily to justify the cause. The end never justifies the means. It is not fitting that any innocent person should be condemned to atone for the good name of the church.

The church, through its manipulation of canon law, has denied me these basic natural rights: the right to a good reputation and the right to be presumed innocent. These rights are clearly defined in canon law. I'm a member of the ACP (Association of Catholic Priests of Ireland), an organisation that has been very supportive of me and understands my predicament. In a desperate attempt to atone for its past failings, the Hierarchy is willing to railroad civil and church rights of priests to appease the cries of their critics, unaware of the statistics: 6 per cent of all sexual allegations are false, and this does not include unsubstantiated allegations, which run at 45 per cent, where the main contributing factors are personal gain and revenge. Exact statistics are not available because of so many variables. Sir Mathew Hale stated in 1847: 'It is true rape is a most detestable crime—that it is an accusation easily to be made and hard to be proved, and harder to be defended by the party accused' (Schafran, 1993, p. 634). That is still true today. In the twenty-first century, forensic science has made it easier in cases of rape, but sexual assault is still difficult to prove and more difficult to deny. In order to prove an allegation of sexual abuse false, it must be clearly established that a crime did not occur. Nevertheless, the Gardai have treated my claim of false allegation against Donelle seriously. While I'm content to live as I am now, I will never cease to try to clear my name.

When one scans the Cloyne report, one finds that my name leaps off of every page as guilty. The allegations are clearly stated in their entirety, while my defence is condensed to mere denial in a single sentence. This is the chief reason why I am encouraged by my legal team to write this autobiography and redress the justice that I was denied by the Cloyne report and the Cloyne Church Tribunal. I am stating the allegations and my defence in full, so that the readers can make their own judgements. I will still strive to seek justice until I die, and I'm comforted by sharing my plight with you, my reader.

Resume

THE LIES THAT ROCKED CHURCH AND STATE

It began in 1985 with an allegation of 'kissing' in the house. It developed into 'sexual assault' in 1995, and by 2008 it became 'child rape over a three-year period' (with the claimants being 14–17years of age). In April 2008 the father of this woman claimed 'his daughter and her friend of fourteen years were plied with alcohol, hypnotised, and raped by a priest in his house over a three-year period'(*Sunday Tribune*, 20 Apr. 2008). The fact is, the priest during this three-year period was living 25 kilometres away (date of birth of daughter, 28 May 1970) (the priest arrived in their parish September 1986). When she eventually came to his house in 1988–9 for counselling, she was 18.

This lie gathered momentum when the father was joined by another woman who claimed to have been raped at 14by the same priest in the 1970s. She was on friendly terms (up to three months before she made the allegation in 2005) with him, calling to his house for advice, although secretly, because of her 'controlling' partner, discussing family and financial problems with him. She was under pressure to pay a debt incurred before she met her partner (and that he was unaware of) and was desperate for financial help. The priest gave her a loan of £1,000 in 2001. She got more familiar, and he suspected another motive for her visits, which were of short duration for fear of her partner finding out. She wrote to him explaining her difficulties and finally her desire to have an affair. 'I want to make love …' The rest is unprintable. He still has these letters. She also brought tapes of her favourite music and songs, mostly Jerry Fish hits, and also a video of *Quills*, in which a priest and a young female artist are lovers, reminding him of the alleged resemblance to both herself and the priest. This put the priest on his guard.

During all these visits she was edging towards closer intimacy and insisted that all the doors be locked. On her last visit in April 2005 she intimated her sexual desires, which he rejected, and insisted that these secret visits cease. A few months later she made the allegation (2005). Her allegation to the DPP was found to have 'no evidence'. The priest had clear alibis; he was in the USA and had spent two years in further education in Dublin. She had included in her allegation the geography of his house and the detailed description of his bedroom, omitting to mention that while he was in Dublin, she had befriended his mother and had full access to his house. The priest enlightened the DPP of these facts and said that she had confided in him re her first sexual encounter with a man at 19 because she needed medical attention afterwards and needed a loan to go to a strange doctor in Cork rather than her family GP.

All this behaviour is in stark contrast to what she wrote after her allegation was rejected by the DPP. In an article penned in the *Irish Examiner*, 2008, under the pseudonym Sinead, she claimed, 'Every time I am out for a walk or driving around town and a certain model car whizzes past I freeze—unable to lift an arm or breathe—and am rendered speechless. It doesn't have to be him. All it takes is the possibility that it could be that car.' Years earlier she had written in her diary that when she saw the priest's car, she would abandon her friend Francis and run towards it to get a glimpse of the priest. Francis, she said, hated the priest because of this.

Sinead and the father of the 14-year-old alleged rape victim went to the HSE and CEO with these allegations which eventually led to the Elliot report and then on to the Cloyne report, costing the state millions of euros, the Diocese of Cloyne its reputation, and a bishop his tenure of office. It caused a minister of state to refer to 'those evil men in Cloyne' (on the publication of the Cloyne report), and led to the former Taoiseach's infamous speech on the Cloyne report on 'the torture and rape of children', resulting in the greatest split between Church and State since its foundation. (There was no reference to rape or torture in the Cloyne report. All their actions are recorded in the report's Chapter 9.)The priest is tarred with being one of the 'evil men of Cloyne' and is still fighting to clear his name. 'When elephants fight, only the humble grass is trampled' (Kipling's idiom is apt).

Meanwhile, the claimants were rewarded by the church with hefty compensation, hefty sums for their mendacious malice. They bragged about it in the media and with friends. They both initiated a vicious campaign against the priest in the media (*Irish Examiner, Sunday Times,* the *Corkman, Morning Ireland, The Marianne Finucane Show,* RTÉ News, and social media). The father of the alleged victim claimed to be 'the voice for all the victims' and claimed there were 'ten more victims' waiting to come forward. 'I want justice for all the victims. I am their voice.' They picketed the DPP's office and the Dáil (Irish Parliament) and met with Pat Rabbitte and Sean Sherlock, who thought they had a strong case (*Sunday Times,*19 Dec. 10). 'The case they made was very compelling and the facts are very disturbing. I would have thought the letter [of apology] has to raise a presumption of sustainability of the case in the DPP's office.' Three weeks previously the DPP had warned against members of the public pushing for a prosecution of the Cloyne curate. Weeks later the DPP changed his mind and retrieved all files with a view to prosecute, but these two cases each again received a nolle prosequi.

The priest, knowing his innocence, was upset and shocked at the decision to prosecute, having to face all the stress and distasteful nightmare of the trials, but in hindsight he is grateful that the bubble of lies was shattered. He witnessed an altercation between the social media protagonists and the North Cork Ten outside the courthouse after the book of evidence was issued in the first trial—no mention of child rape, which the two claimed for all the allegations. The social media, using the RAT website, were not seen again, and their use of the website ceased.

The priest is Dan Duane. Why is he breaking silence now? Simple! Having spent forty-two years in active ministry with the Diocese of Cloyne, he now faces penury and homelessness. His Ordinary has docked almost one-third of his diocesan pension and ordered him to leave his residence. The former is not entitled to do this according to canon law, but Dan Duane insists that his experience of canon law over the last six years is comical and goes on to explain, 'It's not the law itself; it's the way it can be manipulated because of the secrecy and non-transparency. Unlike with civil law, justice cannot be seen to be done or not done. The lack of real cross-examination of witnesses, complainants, and defendants is a serious obstacle when seeking the truth and achieving moral certitude. It lacks the legal process to direct a mistrial and instead uses "sanation". The CDF can rectify mistakes, and in my trial it did this—and seemingly overlooked my right to "presumption of innocence". The trial of Susanna in the Old Testament is clear testimony to the deficiency of canon law; Daniel accused the Jews of negligence in non-cross-examining the witnesses and found Susanna innocent in the process.

'I was found guilty of the sexual assault of two female (alleged) minors by a church tribunal in 2011 and threatened with dismissal from the clerical state. I appealed to the CDF in Rome and was again found guilty. I applied for reinstatement with new evidence, and again it was rejected. Finally I applied to the Pope in November 2015, and he informed my bishop in January 2017 that he referred my case to the CDF. The wait continues. It started in 2009.

'During all of this time I, according to canon law and natural law, am presumed innocent. My Ordinary does not agree and will not disclose his source of advice. "Innocent until proven guilty" is quite topical at present. The ex-Taoiseach had emphasised in the Dáil the horror of an allegation of sexual abuse. If the allegation has no substance, it's devastating with all its consequences: removal from public ministry, and the HSE (health board) contacting and informing your family. That is the case of Donelle against me. The DPP directed a nolle prosequi, citing the reason that there was no evidence of criminal sexual behaviour. In the case of Naveen, I was tried and acquitted in the Circuit Criminal Court in Cork (November2011). It took the jury a mere fifty minutes to reach a unanimous verdict of not guilty. While the State has declared me innocent, the church has found me guilty.'

There are always two sides to an allegation: its substance or lack of it. The following is a list of queries and observations Mgr Maurice Dooley and I sent to the Pope on the CDF's rejection of my plea for reinstatement:

Denial of the presumption of innocence

Donelle, despite the failure of her legal quest for money, was rewarded and received a letter of apology for Fr Duane's alleged abuse from the archbishop before the tribunal the latter had established commenced.

The votum (recommendation) sent to the CDF by the bishop with the allegation was summary dismissal from the priesthood without even a preliminary trial. He claimed 'it was a clear case of sexual assault of a minor, because she had a diary'. It transpired that Donelle's entries in the diary had ceased before the alleged abuse began.

The archbishop set up the tribunal, selecting his child advocate as principal judge, who would be privy to the compensation and apology issued to the complainants.

The presumption of innocence was compromised on the resumption of the tribunal after the civil trial of Naveen. She was compensated shortly after the trial. In announcing the resumption of the trial on *Morning Ireland*, the archbishop invited Fr Duane's 'victims' to participate, repeating that it would be all about Fr Duane's 'victims'. This was blatant prejudice, and Fr Duane's lawyers objected strongly in a letter to the archbishop and advised Fr Duane not to participate.

After the publication of the Cloyne report, the archbishop again stated: 'They [the claimants] were denied the justice they deserved. Justice delayed is justice denied.' Had we known about the compensation and letters of apology, we would not have participated. All these violations of natural and canon law could have a serious impact on the mental disposition of the judges of the tribunal the bishop established and seriously affect the outcome.

Risk assessment as corroboration

The promoter of justice (the DPP) agreed in his pleadings (book of evidence) that there was no contemporaneous corroboration of the complainants' allegations, but he advised the inclusion of a risk assessment delivered on Fr Duane, privately commissioned by the bishop, as possible circumstantial evidence. We objected to this because of its manifest prejudice and paucity of evidence. I commissioned a well-known forensic psychologist with a proven track record in this subject, and he found the risk assessment 'completely unreliable, lacking any methodology, and unscientific', adding that 'it is beyond the scope of a risk assessment to [make judgements] to determine which party has told the truth or whether a version of events is more or less believable than another version of events'. We alerted the judges to where the risk assessment made these unsound judgements. We were ignored. We also alerted them to the unreliability of 'false memory evidence', having consulted Dr Patricia Casey, who kindly furnished all her expertise on this and forwarded this evidence, and were ignored.

Neglect of the law

It is expected of judges of all codes of law to be competent in identifying and summarising all the evidence presented to them for adjudication in a manner which is equitable to all parties.
We identified the following omissions:
the vacillation in the claimant's evidence;
twenty-four discrepancies in Donelle's testimony;
the ignoring of the infringements of due process; and
Naveen's variation on her age when the alleged abuse occurred.

Robert Dore & Co.
2, City Gate Bridge
Dublin 8

4 May 2017

Bishop of Cloyne
Bishop's Palace
Spy Hill
Cobh
Co. Cork, P24 RK54

Dear Bishop:

I represent Daniel Duane of Cecilstown, Mallow, County Cork, in regard to the sentence of the Cloyne Diocesan Tribunal dated 12 March 2013 condemning him to dismissal from the clerical state, a sentence against which he unsuccessfully appealed within the church.

Fr Duane still protests his innocence and is deeply disappointed at his experience at the hands of his church, some of whose officials persistently denied him the presumption of innocence and assumed his guilt in regard to the allegations made against him, to his very great disadvantage. In contrast to their attitude towards Fr Duane, the church officials believed his accusers, favoured them, and apparently paid large sums of money to them.

In spite of two separate acquittals of Fr Duane in the Cork Circuit Criminal Court, the apostolic administrator of Cloyne, the archbishop, with the authorisation of the Congregation for the Doctrine of the Faith (CDF), promoted an ecclesiastical trial to dismiss Fr Duane from the priesthood, resulting in the above-mentioned sentence. Fr Duane found this trial, and his subsequent appeals, deeply disillusioning and highly prejudicial in the literal sense of that word, in that the archbishop and his chosen principal judge prejudged Fr Duane as guilty and deserving of the maximum penalty of defrocking.

To briefly summarise the ecclesiastical proceedings, the Diocese of Cloyne with the authorisation of the Roman Congregation for the Doctrine of the Faith promoted a penal or criminal trial in which the prosecutor (called in canon law the 'promoter of justice') lodged a petition or charge sheet charging Fr Duane with violations of canon 1389 §2 (concerning child sexual abuse) against seven specified persons, and of canon 1387 (concerning solicitation in confession to sexual sin) with one specified person, and asking for the penalty of dismissal from the clerical state in regard to each of the eight charges. The Cloyne Diocesan Tribunal in 2013 returned guilty verdicts in regard to four of the charges of child sexual abuse (violation of canon 1389), dismissed with negative verdicts two of the charges of child sexual abuse where the named accusers did not appear in court and no evidence was presented, and did not deal with one of the charges of child sexual abuse where the complainant was deceased and no evidence was presented. The Cloyne tribunal returned a guilty verdict also in regard to the one charge of solicitation in confession (violation of canon 1387). The Cloyne tribunal imposed the penalty of dismissal from the clerical state in regard to each of the five guilty verdicts.

On appeal to the second instance tribunal, which is the Apostolic Tribunal of the Congregation for the Doctrine of the Faith (CDF) in Rome, three of the guilty verdicts of the Cloyne tribunal were confirmed and two were not. The penalty of dismissal from the clerical state was confirmed.

On further appeal for what in canon law is called restitutio in integrum (essentially a plea to go back to the beginning because of a miscarriage of justice), this plea was rejected by the CDF and the decision of the same CDF in the second instance was confirmed. A final appeal, addressed to the Pope personally in accordance with canon 1417 §1, was referred to the CDF and 'on the 10th November 2016 was presented [by the CDF (!)] to the Holy Father for his consideration. During the aforementioned audience, the Holy Father did not express any disapproval regarding the canonical procedures followed or the final judicial resolution of the matter' (letter from the adjunct secretary of the CDF to the bishop, dated 2 February 2017).

I am not directly concerned with these ecclesiastical proceedings but, rather, with the legal consequences in Irish civil law arising from the Cloyne sentence which you are enforcing or seeking to enforce. Daniel Duane joins me in addressing this letter to you, and his advocate has provided me with canonical and other information, for which he takes responsibility.

Having without success exhausted the appeal procedures available to him in the ecclesiastical forum under canon law, Daniel Duane now wishes to investigate what possibilities lie open to him to vindicate his rights under the laws of the Irish State, to which you are subject on the same basis as any other person in Ireland, without any special privilege deriving from your ecclesiastical dignity. This involves considering the possibility of 'going public' and taking a case against you in the Irish and/or European courts, and this in turn necessitates demanding from you all the material you have on file in regard to Fr Duane which would be pertinent to a case he may take against you in the Irish Civil or Criminal Courts or in the Court of Human Rights in Strasbourg. The principal purpose of this letter is to demand from you the information which Fr Duane needs, and is entitled to, for the purpose of taking such a case against you in order to vindicate his rights.

Request for documentation. As a courtesy to you, I set out hereunder some information which will explain this request to you for information and documentation. This would commonly be referred to as a need for transparency. The jargon in human rights circles refers to this availability of information and documentation to *both* sides as a basic right to 'equality of arms' and regards concealment of relevant information and documentation as a gross infringement of human rights, in particular of the right to defence.

The rights Fr Duane wishes to vindicate include the right to a fair trial, the right to the presumption of innocence, and the rights of maintenance and accommodation resulting from his contract of service with the Diocese of Cloyne. To vindicate his rights, Fr Duane, and I as his advisor, will need various documents and information from you pertinent to his case. These you are obliged to supply, either in accordance with the Data Protection Acts of 1988 and 2003 (as interpreted and adjudicated, not by you, but by the Data Protection Commissioner, and subject to a fine of up to €100,000 in case of noncompliance) and/or, if the case goes to court, in accordance with requests through the court for discovery of documents and information in your possession which in the view of the application for discovery are relevant to his case and, in case of dispute, are adjudged by the judge to be discoverable in accordance with the Circuit Court Rules (Discovery) 2011. [12]

There are two principal aims in the present effort to achieve justice:

> to establish that the ecclesiastical trials were not in conformity with the justice guaranteed in Irish State law, and

> to establish that your actions in reducing Fr Duane's emoluments are an unjust violation of his contractual entitlements.

Right to a fair trial. It may seem strange to you that someone sentenced as a criminal by his church should have the gall to attack the church's centuries-old legal system as unfair, but I draw your attention to the following statements by the promoter of justice in his doctoral thesis *The Presumption of Innocence in Canonical Trials of Clerics Accused of Child Sexual Abuse*,[13] in which the promoter frankly admits the impossibility of getting a fair trial under canon law as implemented by the Catholic Church in Ireland at present. Ironically, he was the prosecutor (in canon law terminology, the 'promoter of justice') in the Cloyne trial of Fr Duane. After 300 pages of learned, documented discussion in his thesis, the promoter concludes as follows (emphasis in boldface added):

> Faced with a direct question from a cleric accused of the sexual abuse of minors— 'Do I have a right to a fair trial? Am I not presumed innocent until proven guilty?'—there can be only one answer. **At the beginning of the 21st century, a cleric accused of child sexual abuse does not**

---

[12] Statutory Instrument No. 122 of 2011: Circuit Court Rules (Discovery), 2011.

[13] Leuven Peeters, *The Presumption of Innocence in Canonical Trials of Clerics Accused of Child Sexual Abuse*, 2011.

have the right to a trial, let alone a fair trial. … More troubling still, the arbitrary procedures endorsed by the bishop's conference in Ireland presume allegations of sexual abuse against clerics to be true. No court of law, secular or canonical, is allowed to have the last word, unless a trial results in conviction. (p. 304)

In Ireland an arbitrary procedure without any legal basis has been established. It is founded on the false premise of the *paramount principle*[14]and the illegal assertion that the regulation of the rights of clerics includes the power to remove rights by administrative procedure. Courts of law, state or canonical, are not accepted as having the ultimate power to determine the innocence or guilt of the accused. **Accused clerics are deemed guilty until they have proved themselves innocent.** (p. 303)

Suing the church for unfair trials and for denial of presumption of innocence. The church, either in its institutions or in its individual members, can of course be sued in Irish law[15] for violation of any citizen's rights to a fair trial and for denial of the presumption of innocence until proven guilty, which is guaranteed in Irish State law and in international law, incorporated into Irish law by acceptance of the United Nations

---

[14] The 'paramount principle' in this context is that 'the welfare of the child is first and paramount consideration', a phrase taken from the Guardian of Infants Act, 1964, but used out of context in the Irish Episcopal Conference document *Our Children Our Church*, 7.

[15] The statute of *præmunire* was repealed in the Statute Revision Act, 1983, but an Irish citizen can still take an action against the attempt to enforce in Ireland any decisions by those outside the Irish jurisdiction which conflict with Irish law.

Universal Declaration on Human Rights[16] and ratification of the European Convention of Human Rights. [17]

---

[16] UN Universal Declaration of Human Rights, Article 11. (1) *Everyone charged with a penal offence has the right to be presumed innocent until proved guilty according to law in a public trial at which he has had all the guarantees necessary for his defence.* (2) No one shall be held guilty of any penal offence on account of any act or omission which did not constitute a penal offence, under national or international law, at the time when it was committed. Nor shall a heavier penalty be imposed than the one that was applicable at the time the penal offence was committed.

[17] European Convention on Human Rights, Article 6, Right to a fair trial. 1. *In the determination of his civil rights and obligations or of any criminal charge against him, everyone is entitled to a fair and public hearing within a reasonable time by an independent and impartial tribunal established by law.* Judgment shall be pronounced publicly, but the press and public may be excluded from all or part of the trial in the interests of morals, public order, or national security in a democratic society, where the interests of juveniles or the protection of the private life of the parties so require, or to the extent strictly necessary in the opinion of the court in special circumstances where publicity would prejudice the interests of justice. 2. *Everyone charged with a criminal offence shall be presumed innocent until proved guilty according to law.* 3. Everyone charged with a criminal offence has the following minimum rights:(a) to be informed promptly, in a language which he understands and in detail, of the nature and cause of the accusation against him; (b) to have adequate time and facilities for the preparation of his defence; (c) *to defend himself in person or through legal assistance of his own choosing* or, if he has not sufficient means to pay for legal assistance, to be given it free when the interests of justice so require; (d) *to examine or have examined witnesses against him and to obtain the attendance and examination of witnesses on his behalf under the same conditions as witnesses against him*; (e) to have the free assistance of an interpreter if he cannot understand or speak the language used in court. European Court of Human Rights, *Heaney and McGuinness v. Ireland* (2000), Decision, §40: 'The Court recalls its established case-law to the effect that, although not specifically mentioned in Article 6 of the Convention, the rights relied on by the applicants, *the right to silence and the right not to incriminate oneself, are generally recognised international standards which lie at the heart of the notion of a fair procedure under Article 6.* Their rationale lies, inter alia, in the protection of the accused against improper compulsion by the authorities, thereby contributing to the avoidance of miscarriages of justice and to the fulfilment of the aims of Article 6. *The right not to incriminate oneself, in particular, presupposes that the prosecution in a criminal case seek to prove their case against the accused without resort to evidence obtained through methods of coercion or oppression in defiance of the will of the accused.* ... The right not to incriminate oneself is primarily concerned, however, with respecting the will of an accused person to remain silent.

United Nations and Council of Europe Convention rights. Ireland has accepted the United Nations Universal Declaration on Human Rights and has ratified the Council of Europe's Convention on Human Rights, but the church (either the supranational Holy See or the Vatican City State) has ratified neither. The Holy See participates in meetings at the United Nations at New York and Geneva, and at the Council of Europe in Strasbourg, mostly with observer status but with full membership status in a few meetings. The Holy See is generally welcomed and appreciated at these international meetings, but in the last couple of years it has met a very hostile reaction in Geneva at meetings because of allegations in regard to the church's dealings with child sexual abuse.

The Holy See has signed and ratified some international instruments, often with reservations, but not the European Convention on Human Rights. Also, not being a member of the Council of Europe, the Holy See cannot be brought directly before the European Court of Human Rights in Strasbourg, but there have been two fairly recent cases where the church's legal system came tangentially into question, the Pellegrini case against Italy, in which Italy was found to have failed to verify that the church's matrimonial trial system was up to the standard required for the Italian court to be able to give legal effect to the church's decisions, and the Peltereau-Villeneuve case against Switzerland, where Switzerland was fined €20,000 with €25,000 in costs for denial of a priest's presumption of innocence in an abuse case, and where the church consequentially had to reverse its ecclesiastical verdict of guilty in the same case.

Fr Duane's ecclesiastical trial was a violation of the European Convention. Fr Duane's ecclesiastical trial and conviction in the Cloyne Diocesan Tribunal violated his right to fair trial as guaranteed by the United Nations and European Human Rights conventions. This is obvious from the contradictions between the canon law on church criminal trials and what these Conventions guarantee (see emphasised phrases in footnotes 5 and 6 *supra*). For example, the European Convention says that 'in the determination of his civil rights and obligations or of any criminal charge against him, everyone is entitled to a fair and public hearing' and, *as a minimum*, 'has the right to examine or have examined witnesses against him and to obtain the attendance and examination of witnesses on his behalf'.

Contrary to this, canon law trials are not public but conducted in secret behind closed doors; the accused is not allowed to confront his accusers; he is not allowed to be present at the examination of his accusers or witnesses (even his own witnesses); and no cross-examination of accusers or witnesses is allowed. All proceedings in the appeal stage to the Congregation for the Doctrine of the Faith (CDF) are subject to pontifical secrecy (the highest grade of secrecy). Fr Duane was expressly warned of this before being allowed even to see the verdict of the CDF.

Apart from these conflicts in the general structure applicable to all ecclesiastical trials, Fr Duane's actual trials themselves violated many legal requirements of both canon and civil law, such as the need for corroboration of evidence before it has any probative value, the need to address the legal arguments actually made instead of answering points not made at all by the accused, and the right to record the evidence given (one of the judges demanded that the advocate's recording device be left outside the courtroom). There were multiple violations of technical requirements of law too, which in a proper legal system would have warranted a declaration of a mistrial, but which the CDF blandly 'sanated' or remedied by decree, without even considering which requirements were not just technicalities but went to the substance of the arguments of Fr Duane's case.

All this is easily understood if you remember that the CDF is just a rebranded version of the Roman Inquisition,[18] and even its recent activities have much in common with the old Star Chamber in Westminster which changed or made up the laws to suit the prosecution, and the royal *lettres*

---

[18] The Roman Inquisition was rebranded as the 'Supreme Sacred Congregation of the Holy Office' in 1908 and rebranded again as the 'Sacred Congregation for the Doctrine of the Faith' in 1965 at the end of Vatican II. Shortly thereafter the Pope gave up being prefect of the congregation, and the word *sacred* was dropped from all the congregations in the new code in 1983, though it took until 1985 before this took full effect. More importantly, for as long as the Pope was nominally prefect, the Inquisition and the Holy Office acted as being in practice above the law since the Pope/Prefect could overrule the law. I suspect the CDF still does.

de cachet en blanc (blank warrants under the royal seal for arrests where the names of those to be arrested could be filled in later) which were one of the grievances which brought about the French Revolution.

Fr Duane's presumption of innocence was denied to him not only in media statements, but also in diocesan official statements and actions such as the payment of money, whether as hush money, compensation, or redress, to those described as the 'victims' of Fr Duane and to whom the archbishop, the apostolic administrator, or the bishop made apologies for Fr Duane's alleged actions, which were accepted implicitly to have been crimes against the complainants. This violation of the right to the presumption of innocence and persistent assumption of guilt of Fr Duane was verified even after Fr Duane's acquittal, twice, in the Cork Circuit Criminal Court and prior to any of the ecclesiastical verdicts of guilt. Fr Duane has compiled a list of examples of such violations of his right to the presumption of his innocence.

Although it may not be possible to sue the church directly in Strasbourg for these violations, as the Holy See has not signed or ratified the European Convention on Human Rights, the precedents established in the Pellegrini and Peltereau-Villeneuve cases may make you, as current bishop of Cloyne, liable to be sued under Irish State law for using the ecclesiastical trials of Fr Duane (which so clearly violate the rights guaranteed in the European Convention) to penalise him by instructing the Cloyne Sick Priests Committee to cut his emoluments and by trying to drive him from the house he now occupies.

Suing the church for denial of entitlement to support and accommodation. In regard to Fr Duane's entitlement to support and accommodation, I draw to your attention the fact that when Daniel Duane applied in 1962–3 for promotion to holy orders, he was required[19] to supply documents, written in his own handwriting and signed by him, which inter alia promised that he would devote himself *permanently* to the ecclesiastical ministry. Matching this, canon law required the bishop of Cloyne for

---

[19] By the instruction *Quam ingens* issued by the Congregation for the Sacraments in 1930.

himself and his successors to undertake to provide Fr Daniel Duane with a *canonical title* to support, which had to be 'both truly secure *for the whole of the ordained's life* and truly sufficient for his worthy support in accordance with norms to be given by the bishops in accordance with the differing needs and circumstances of places and times'.[20] Thus ordination to the priesthood established a legitimate expectation that in return for a priest's work for the diocese, the bishop clearly had an obligation to provide the priest with 'worthy support', which would involve lifelong housing and adequate financial support. This would be analogous to the legitimate expectation of a married couple's mutual support 'for better or worse, for richer or poorer, in sickness and in health, till death do us part'.

Even if the worst should come to the worst and the priest is sentenced by a five-priest tribunal (or a bishop by a thirteen-bishop tribunal) to reduction to the lay state and to canonical deposition and degradation,[21] he still has a right that 'if he is truly in need, the Ordinary in proportion to his charity, and in the best way it can be done, is to take care to provide for him, lest with disgrace to the clerical state he be forced to go begging'[22]

Without going into the complex history of the benefice system of clerical support, which was effectively abandoned by the Second Vatican Council, I will say that the traditional 'canonical title' for the support of secular clergy in Ireland was the title of 'service of the diocese', funded by the voluntary offerings of the faithful (collections, parish houses and farms, stole fees, endowments, etc., regulated by diocesan laws and customs) and used to provide 'suitable sustenance' (housing, finance, and produce) for the support of the clergy.

---

[20] Canons 974, §1,7°, and 979 of the 1917 Code of Canon Law then in force.

[21] Old code, canon 1576, and *Pontificale Romanum*.

[22] Old code, canon 2303. In the current Code of Canon Law, in the equivalent canon, 'reduction to the lay state' is toned down to 'dismissal from the clerical state' to avoid the slur on the laity implied in the older phrase, and the disgrace to the clerical state by forcing the priest into beggary is passed over in silence. The revised canon just states, 'If a person is truly in need because he has been dismissed from the clerical state, the Ordinary is to provide in the best way possible' (canon 1350 §2).

In the absence of social security in the past, sometimes this was supplemented by special funds, called Retirement Funds, Sick Priests Funds, Clergy Benevolent Funds, and so on, to provide for sick, elderly, retired, or other priests in need, including those silenced, on the seachrán for drink, or otherwise in trouble.

These special funds were owned by those who set them up and contributed to them. Sometimes the bishop had control of these funds; generally he did not. The basic criteria of ownership and control of property in canon law are that property is owned by whoever lawfully acquires it and that property is 'ecclesiastical property', subject to canon law property rules, if, and only if it is owned by a church 'moral' or 'juridical' person such as a diocese or a parish. Otherwise it is just private property of an individual or group of individuals and is not subject to the canon law property rules. It is not owned, controlled, or supervised by the bishop or other diocesan authorities, but is controlled by the person or group of persons who is or are the owner or owners.

In the aftermath of the Second Vatican Council (1962–5), the old benefice system was scrapped. The obligation of the bishop to provide for the remuneration of his clergy is now laid down in canons 281 and 1274 of the 1983 Code of Canon Law, which speak not only of remuneration during the priest's working life but also of such social welfare as priests may need in infirmity, sickness, or old age. But effectively the legitimate expectation of the priest to lifelong support is maintained and indeed reinforced. Even in the case of a priest dismissed from the clerical state, condemning him to homelessness and penury is not likely to be seen by an Irish court as provision 'in the best way possible', as canon 1350 §2 requires of his bishop.

I understand that Fr Duane, in accordance with his 1963 written engagement to work permanently for the Diocese of Cloyne mentioned above, began such work after his ordination in 1963 and worked at the tasks assigned to him faithfully until he was forced to 'step aside' by decree of the bishop in 2005, said decree being renewed by the archbishop and by you as the bishop. Fr Duane in 2005 was aged 67 and beyond the normal age of lay retirement but had not yet reached the 75-year retirement age suggested in canon 538 for priests. He was, however, still available for service in the diocese were it not blocked by the bishop's decree. During his working career he was paid, the same as other priests, either by the parish or diocese, or by the state (while working in St Colman's as a careers guidance counsellor). He paid the usual diocesan levy of 2. 5 per cent of his income into the Sick Priests Fund, the same as other priests, until his forced retirement. So he should have the *same* entitlements as other priests to support and social security as specified in canon 1274 based on his canonical title of 'service of the diocese' (for over forty-two years, and more if it had been left to his willingness) and the *same* entitlement as other priests to subvention from the Sick Priests Committee. His State Old Age Pension is based on his PRSI payments and is no business of the church, any more than is any other private or family income or earnings or property or investments he might or might not have.

Demand for files and other documentation. In the light of this preliminary, which I provide so that you can verify the legitimacy of Daniel Duane's and my demand for the following information, Daniel Duane hereby requests you to forward to him in accordance with the Data Protection Acts 1988 and 2003, in particular Section 4, within the statutory period of forty days therein specified, copies of all the data you have on him in files, either computerised or manual, including paper files and transcripts. You will be aware that there is a fine of up to €100,000 for noncompliance with that request, and if his legal entitlement is not honoured, he will have no alternative but to involve the data protection officer to enforce compliance.

You need not supply Fr Duane with the material in his files under your control which was previously supplied by Archbishop in response to Fr Duane's request dated 5 January 2012, nor need you supply him with the documentation of his trials which was already supplied to him by the Cloyne Diocesan Tribunal.

However, I am informed by Fr Duane that much of what the archbishop supplied was heavily 'redacted', the usual euphemism for blacked out to conceal information that he or his legal advisors (Mason Hayes &Curran,

incorporating Arthur O'Hagan) did not want revealed. (This corresponds with what I have myself experienced in other cases in regard to requests for files under the Data Protection or Freedom of Information acts and seems to be part of a deliberate church policy to conceal relevant information to which my clients are legally entitled.)

The usual specious excuse offered in an attempt to justify refusal to give the applicant *all* documents and information on file against him, contrary to the clear purpose of the Data Protection Acts, is the claim that applicants have a right of access only to information about themselves, but not about others, necessitating heavy redaction of documents. Apart from the fact that this is essentially a claim that the redactor is entitled to be judge in his own case in interpreting Section 4 of the Data Protection Acts so as to evade giving the applicant the information he requires to defend himself, it cannot be denied that the Data Protection Acts do oblige the data controller, in this case you, the bishop, under threat of heavy penalties, to give the applicant *all* the material referring to him, even if in 'redacted' form, or to accurately quote the Data Protection Acts, 'where the circumstances are such that it would be reasonable for the data controller to conclude that, if any particulars identifying some other individual were omitted, the data could then be disclosed as aforesaid without his being thereby identified to the data subject [applicant], the data controller [bishop] shall be obliged to disclose the data to the data subject with the omission of those particulars'. He is entitled to 'redact' only as much of the particulars as would identify 'some other individual'. In this particular case, Fr Duane is well acquainted with practically everyone involved in the case, and I would imagine that redactions would be hard to justify except in very special instances.

I make this clarification in the light of information given to me by Fr Duane that the archbishop or his agents 'redacted' vitally important information relevant specifically to Fr Duane alone in the archbishop's initial application to the CDF, a redaction which was entirely unjustified on the criterion quoted above from the Data Protection Act. The beginning of all Fr Duane's troubles was his being reported by his bishop to the Congregation for the Doctrine of the Faith, one of the first steps required by the law[23] to canonically prosecute a priest for alleged child sexual abuse. Knowledge of the details of the allegation and the punishment sought are obviously vitally important for the accused priest, and Fr Duane rightly expected that this information would be honestly disclosed to him in response to his lawful request in January 2012 under the Data Protection Acts.

But the fact is that what was disclosed to Fr Duane by the archbishop was essentially different from what was actually sent to the CDF in January 2009. When requesting authorisation to prosecute a priest for child sexual abuse, the bishop had to send the request on a standardised form, which included a summary of the alleged abuse and the bishop's recommendation for the appropriate penalty to be applied. In the document sent to Fr Duane in response to his request under the Data Protection Acts, after giving an account of some of the incidents of child sexual abuse alleged against Fr Duane, the bishop's recommendation was 'that this priest be encouraged to seek a dispensation from the obligations arising from Sacred Orders'. According to the Cloyne report[24], however, this actual request to Rome in January 2009 was altogether different, namely that 'The bishop asked that "a derogation from prescription be granted so that a penal judicial process may be initiated, or that he be dismissed from the clerical state ex officio et in poenam"'. In other words, Fr Duane was being fooled into thinking that the bishop had sought only that he be invited to voluntarily seek laicisation, whereas in fact the bishop had asked that he be kicked out of the priesthood involuntarily and possibly without any of the inconvenient

---

[23] In the document *Sacramentorum sanctitatis tutela*, issued in 2001 and revised in 2010.

[24] Cloyne report, §9. 126, p. 166.

formalities of a trial. [25](As it happened, this duplicity was in vain as the unredacted document had been supplied to the Murphy Inquiry and the relevant part published by them in December 2010, over a year before Fr Duane requisitioned his file from the archbishop.)

Judge Yvonne Murphy discovered similar duplicity in the case of the other Cloyne priest (Fr Caden). These cases triggered the Cloyne Inquiry, in that the bishop produced two different and incompatible accounts of one and the same meeting, a true account sent to the CDF, and a false account sent to his own advisory committee to conceal the truth from them. Judge Murphy in the Cloyne report §§21. 14ff. is scathing in her comments on this duplicity. [26]

In the light of these facts, Fr Duane is justifiably suspicious that what was supplied to him in response to his 2012 request may not have been all that should have been supplied, and therefore Fr Duane's current request extends to his entire files, without any redactions other than those strictly justified under the terms of the Data Protection Act quoted previously.

Fr Duane and I would regard your correspondence with the Holy See as vitally important material which you should release to Fr Duane under the Data Protection Acts. For example, in the archbishop's letter of 25 February 2017, he refers to the content of letters from you to the CDF in which 'Your Lordship has noted in the past Mr Duane's refusal to engage with the

---

[25] The document supplied is not a copy of the standardised request form prescribed by the CDF, but a typescript headed 'Bishop's Votum', with some redactions or blacked-out lines, and purported to be signed by the bishop of Cloyne, and dated 30 January 2009. Some six weeks later, on 7 March 2009, the bishop stepped down from active administration of the Diocese of Cloyne and was replaced by the archbishop as apostolic administrator and actually running the Diocese of Cloyne (as well as his own dioceses). A year later, on 24 March 2010, the bishop formally resigned. The archbishop continued to run the diocese until a new bishop was appointed on 24 November 2012. This meant that the bishop played no further part in the trial of Fr Duane after he sent his request to the CDF, and it was the archbishop who controlled everything until November 2012, by which time the Cloyne trial of Fr Duane was nearing completion.

[26] Incidentally, compiling or uttering false documents or using them in an ecclesiastical matter is a crime in canon law, canon 1391.

safeguarding personnel in the Diocese of Cloyne'. Naturally, Fr Duane is interested in, and entitled to know, what other adverse comments against him you or your predecessors have expressed in your correspondence with the CDF. Refusal to release such material to him, or 'redaction' which effectively conceals such material, would clearly contravene the rights given in the Data Protection Acts to receive *all* relevant material.

Fr Duane and I would also regard the monies paid by the diocese to the complainants as relevant material which Fr Duane is entitled to know, both because this would provide an explanation of their motivation in making their allegations and because it would provide a measure of the quantum of damages he might seek from the Diocese of Cloyne for violating his rights. In preparing his case to defend himself in the church courts, he sought this information but was told by the principal judge that the latter did not know how much was paid. The relevance of this information can be gauged from the fact that when it was submitted to the CDF court in the second instance, 'it was credibly reported that several hundred thousands of euros had been paid to the complainants'. [27] The second instance made no effort to refute this but dismissed it out of hand as just 'a tall claim'. [28]

Fr Duane and I would be interested too in the threat in the last line of archbishop's letter: 'Were you to deem it prudent and warranted, you are free to issue a penal precept (CIC can. 1319) to Mr Duane, threatening the imposition of further penalties in the case of disobedience or contumacy.' If Fr Duane is dismissed from the clerical state—and cannot therefore be penalised any more than the local postman or greengrocer or any other

---

[27] The advocate for Fr Duane submitted in his brief to the Cloyne tribunal, 'The prospect of financial compensation was a relevant factor in making the allegations in some cases. The complainants have admitted being paid off by the diocese, but the amounts have not been made public, though it is credibly reported to have been several hundred thousand euros in all.'

[28] The CDF sentence in the second instance dismissed this as just a tall claim: 'A desire for a financial compensation had also been raised. The description of the incidents is invasive and emotionally distressing. To claim that such acts materialized as recounted in the evidence of the accusers for financial gain or vindictiveness is a tall claim.' What should matter is whether the claim is true.

layperson—what penalties are you being invited to impose? And if you do impose any penalty, need Mr Duane pay any heed to you?

Fr Duane and I realise that this request for information is likely to be burdensome for you to comply with, but his life has been blighted and perhaps endangered, and his reputation has been tarnished by the actions of the diocese and its agents as well of by the hostility of the anti-Catholic media and the persisting vendetta of the complainants. One of the complainants, according to the Cloyne first instance judgement §126, 'in her meetings with the judges always came across as someone who was credible'. Since she expressed in court her highly colourful but murderous desires that Fr Duane be castrated, crucified, dissolved in a bath of acid, or hatcheted, we hope that the court was mistaken on her credibility in this regard at least and that she will not fulfil her fantasies.

We look forward to your reply in due course to this statutory request for a full disclosure of all the material you have on file in regard to Daniel Duane.

Yours sincerely,

Robert Dore, Solicitor,
on behalf of Daniel Duane

> Psalm 91
>
> He who dwells in the shelter of the Most High,
> and abides in the shade of the Almighty,
> says to the Lord, 'My refuge,
> my stronghold, my God in whom I trust!'
> He will free you from the snare of the fowler,
> from the destructive plague;
> he will conceal you with his pinions,
> and under his wings you will find refuge.
> His faithfulness is buckler and shield.
> You will not fear the terror of the night,
> nor the arrow that flies by day,

nor the plague that prowls in the darkness,
nor the scourge that lays waste at noon.
A thousand may fall at your side,
ten thousand fall at your right:
you it will never approach.
Your eyes have only to look
to see how the wicked are repaid.
For you, O Lord, are my refuge.
You have made the Most High your dwelling.
Upon you no evil shall fall,
no plague approach your tent.
For you has he commanded his angels
to keep you in all your ways.
They shall bear you upon their hands,
lest you strike your foot against a stone.
On the lion and the viper you will tread,
and trample the young lion and the serpent.
Since he clings to me in love, I will free him,
protect him, for he knows my name.
When he calls on me, I will answer him;
I will be with him in distress;
I will deliver him, and give him glory.
With length of days I will content him;
I will show him my saving power.

By: GIA Publications Inc.

1 :The author kissing the Blarney Stone. 2: atop Blarney Castle with Lil and Rolf. 3. In serious mood.

3. Author leaving for St. Colman's. 4. Author extreme left in two family pics. at 9 and 15 sitting on the butt of the twin oak.

Photo 1. Author's ordination pic. 2. Ordination group. 3. Author with his family outside Ballyshera.

Photo: Author giving his first blessing to Aunt Madge.

Lightning Source UK Ltd.
Milton Keynes UK
UKHW01f0026180918
329061UK00001B/28/P

9 781546 291350